SSAT

词汇
一本通

郑思韬◎编著

SSAT基础词汇　SSAT强化词汇　SSAT冲刺词汇

上海交通大学出版社
SHANGHAI JIAO TONG UNIVERSITY PRESS

内容提要

本书根据 SSAT 真题考试中单词出现的频率进行筛选,精选出 SSAT 基础词汇、SSAT 强化词汇和 SSAT 冲刺词汇。每个词条都搭配了中英双语解释和权威例句,方便学生理解单词的准确意思和单词用法,突破 SSAT 考试的词汇难关。本书适合 SSAT 备考学生和教师使用。

图书在版编目(C I P)数据

SSAT 词汇一本通 / 郑思韬编. —上海:上海交通大学出版社,2018

ISBN 978 - 7 - 313 - 20683 - 1

Ⅰ.①S… Ⅱ.①郑… Ⅲ.①英语-词汇-高中-入学考试-美国-自学参考资料 Ⅳ.①G643.413

中国版本图书馆 CIP 数据核字(2018)第 289061 号

SSAT 词汇一本通

编　　者:	郑思韬		
出版发行:	上海交通大学出版社	地　　址:	上海市番禺路 951 号
邮政编码:	200030	电　　话:	021 - 64071208
印　　刷:	上海新华印刷有限公司	经　　销:	全国新华书店
开　　本:	787mm×1092mm　1/16	印　　张:	20.5
字　　数:	556 千字		
版　　次:	2018 年 12 月第 1 版	印　　次:	2018 年 12 月第 1 次印刷
书　　号:	ISBN 978 - 7 - 313 - 20683 - 1/G		
定　　价:	78.00 元		

波士顿私立中学行记

多年前的那个春天,我到美国波士顿出差兼顾旅游观光,住在哈佛大学校内一个叫Harvard Square Hotel 的酒店里。公事办完忙里偷闲和当地朋友租了个车到波士顿郊外踏春。一路交通畅通阳光明媚,我们从哈佛广场出发,驱车一个半小时便来到了康科德(Concord)小镇附近的一个野湖。那时天空蓝得纯粹,树木已经泛绿。野湖不大非常原生态,沿湖一周被树林包围,一条小路可以直接向下延展到湖边。初春上午的波士顿郊外春寒料峭水寒风冷,湖面仍被厚厚的冰层和薄薄的白雪覆盖,只有接近湖边才有点融化的水痕,岸边则是还未融化的皑皑积雪。湖边不远处有一个小木屋,木屋低矮小巧,一门一窗一烟筒,隔小玻璃窗往里窥视,屋里的全部家俱好像只有一张单人床。小木屋感觉像个著名景点知名度极高,因为前来瞻仰合影的各色游人络绎不绝。它由一个当地美国人在 18 世纪 50 年代左右亲手搭建,据说他在这个小木屋里与世隔绝,苦行僧般居住了两年零两个月,他叫梭罗(Thoreau),本科毕业于哈佛大学,是美国著名作家和哲学家。在小木屋里梭罗写出了代表作《瓦尔登湖》(Walden),也就是小木屋边上的这个美丽野湖。

告别梭罗的小木屋和瓦尔登湖,我们决定驱车导航去参观一所知名的私立中学。中学是创建于 1865 年的 Cushing Academy。汽车沿着导航 Waze 指引路线,七绕八拐驶出大路后拐入一条有点坡度的小道,小道旁边一块长方形的大石碑,上面镌刻着这所中学的校名和创建时间。美国中学基本都是没有校门没有围墙,任何人均可随便出入。沿着小路往里即是中学校园,校园显得很是空旷,几栋雄伟的教学楼错落有至,教学楼红砖黑顶白窗,在四周白雪的映衬下格外壮观。偏隅一角是一个诺大的橄榄球场,四周被树木和白雪包围,人造的绿绒赛场在蓝天下白雪中非常醒目,让人有种运动的冲动。推开笨重合开的金属门进入教学楼,楼道两边墙上橱窗里张挂着各种宣传海报,和学校曾经获得过的一些荣誉证明。教室里老师和学生正在课堂进行时,各色着装不同肤色的学生聚在一起,米色课桌面和浅灰色的地面干净整洁。看到有陌生人拿手机拍照张望也浑然不知,当然也有偶然注意到的学生会注视你两眼。于是立刻被浓郁的学习气息包裹,不由得让人回忆起曾经学生时代的那段芳华时光……

美国中学和大学性质一样区分为公立和私立。公立中学由国家或州政府出资设立,私立中学则由当地土豪大款名人出资建成。公立中学用人民的纳税钱办学,虽然允许招收国际学生,但法律规定最多只能允许一年以内的交换交流。私立中学全自费且学费昂贵,因此招生外国学生可以不受时间限制。私立中学又分为走读和住宿,能住宿的私立中学数量不多,如果要走读就要在学校附近寻找美国的寄宿家庭。寄宿家庭虽然可以解决住宿,但由于中美文化的差异会劳心伤神。因此除非万不得已，一般美高留学不推荐住宿家庭。从地理分布上来看，美国知名私立中学分布和美国大学也基本一致，名校以东西海岸居多。西海岸以加州洛杉矶为中心，东海岸以纽约和波士顿为中心。波士顿市区及周边中学质量都比较高，比如 Phillips Academy（俗称安多福，Andover），Concord Academy、the Cambridge School of Weston 等。那天下午及以后的几天，我还分别参访了 Woodstock Middle School、Hyde School、the Winchenton School 等私立中学。以后还曾到访过位于新罕布什州埃克塞特（Exeter）小镇上的菲利普斯埃克塞特学院（Phillips Exeter Academy），Facebook 创始人扎克伯格曾在这里就读。

美国普通私立中学申请相对简单，只需要提交小托福即 TOEFL Junior 成绩即可，分数高低与申请的知名程度成正比。美国顶尖私立中学申请的竞争就会十分惨烈，甚至超过美国常春藤大学的申请，因为拿到顶尖私立中学的录取，就相当于一只脚已经踏入常春藤大学。美国人申请著名私立中学，除了要提供一系列复杂的材料手续和正式的面试外，还需要提供"美国中考"SSAT 或 ISEE 成绩。我曾咨询位于莱克星顿镇知名 SSAT 培训机构 Chyten，当地华人俗称柴藤，以一对一和小班教学为主。接待者是西装革履英俊潇洒的白人顾问，培训价格也比较高，SSAT 一对一培训每小时收费好像要 375 美元。对中国申请者而言，除了提供良好的 SSAT 或 ISEE 成绩，还要提供小托福、托福等语言成绩。即使这样，获得美国顶尖私立中学的录取也很艰难，以位于安多福的菲利普斯学院和位于埃克塞特的菲利普斯埃克塞特学院两所牛校为例，每年从中国大陆录取的学生都是个位数，申请这两所中学单从标化成绩来说，托福低于 110 分，SSAT 成绩低于 90% 几乎没有希望。

当然，申请美国私立中学只是一个桥梁，最终目标还是进入美国大学。很多中国父母历尽千辛万苦把孩子送到美国私立中学就读，除了追求知识外，更重要的可能就是培训孩子一种独立人格，追求自由和真理的精神，亦如哈佛的校训：与亚里士多德为友，与柏位图为友，更与真理为友。又亦如梭罗在《瓦尔登湖》所言：我不要爱，不要金钱，也不要名誉，我只要真理。

王文山

（沃邦教育创始人）

前　言

  SSAT 单词成千上万,对于大多初中学生来说短时间内消化的确并非易事,而帮助同学们如何在短时间内把这些单词背好,同时又能最大化背词效率、规避背词误区,这是本书的根本目的。

  本书把单词分为如下几个等级,同学们可以根据备考时间,以及书中的词汇测试进行自我调节:

  1. SSAT 基础词汇

  如同学有备考托福的话会发现这个等级的单词属于高难度托福词汇。在托福考试中同学往往会觉得这类单词不经常在文中出现而忽视,而在授课过程中也发现即使母语是英语的同学,对于这个等级的单词的掌握其实也并不牢固。如想取得考试高分,这类单词不仅在阅读和词汇部分经常涉及,在写作部分同样需要掌握它们的拼写。另外,还需注意熟词僻义现象,比如"exploit",在托福中只考过"利用"的意思,而这个单词还有"英雄事迹"的意思。备考时间充裕的同学对此等级的单词应既要掌握单词的多个意思,又要掌握拼写及用法。

  2. SSAT 强化词汇

  根据对往年考试真题的总结和未来的考试预测,我们整理出了强化词汇。这类单词是重复频率最高、最常考的单词。在背诵这类单词时,除了要掌握单词的准确意思之外,还需要掌握单词的同义词以方便同学攻破词汇同义难关。书中也为单词配上了最常考的同义词和例句,帮助同学深层理解单词。备考时间有限,需要短时间内快速入门,且基础不错的同学可从此等级单词开始着手准备。

  3. SSAT 冲刺词汇

  这类单词和强化单词难度接近,这部分更侧重于词汇的广度,用来补充前几类单词的词汇缺口。本书中收录了大量近几次实考中反复出现的单词,临考的同学一定要把这个等级的单词背熟。

• 背词误区

  笔者根据近年学生课堂反馈,总结出了以下常见的背词误区:

  1. 不及时复习

  很多同学有时心血来潮背几十上百个单词,但是之后又不复习,过段时间再检查,发现单词已经完全忘光了。那之前花的精力也白费了,长此以往也就慢慢失去了背单词的兴趣。记住一句话:单词是复习出来的,除非你记忆力超群,过目不忘。SSAT 单词的难度其实不小,这些单词通常需要你至少四到五遍的复习。

  2. 不看英文释义

  很多同学背过托福单词,不少中学生觉得 SSAT 等级中的单词词义比较简单,不过很少有人会特意关注英文解释。其实,在 SSAT 等级单词中,所有单词都需要同学对单词英文解释精确理解,甚至在同义题选项中就出现了英文释义中的单词,如 null,它的英文释义为"having or associated with the value zero,"而选择的答案就是"zero value"。其次,SSAT 有很多容易让人望文生义词的词,比如 porcupine,中文叫"豪猪",有同学就以为这是一种猪了,其实看完英文释义"a large rodent with defensive spines or quills on the body and tail",你就了解了首先它是一种啮齿动物(rodent),而且它还有防御性的刺(defensive spines and quills),这是在类比题中都出现过的题目。

3. 不区分单词

一本词汇手册拿来,有些单词已经认识,而有些单词都没见过,那首先应该把这两个等级的单词区分开来,着重背新词,而已经会的单词只需要复习一下,看一下有没有新的词义就行了。在背诵过程中,对不好掌握的单词可以加上难词记号,多背几遍,有的放矢。建议每个同学准备一个可以随身携带的小本子,把背到的难词或者书里看到的生词摘录下来,随时随地扩充自己的词汇量。

4. 没有掌握背词方法

大多数同学都是死记硬背单词,这样做不仅自己觉得枯燥,背得慢,同时记忆效果也差,甚至有同学已经死记硬背到能想起来一个单词是在哪本书的哪一页出现,上面下面各是什么单词,但就是想不起单词的意思来,这很明显就是死记硬背出来的。这里给大家推荐几个背词方法:

第一,词根词缀法。这也是最正统的记忆方法。英文单词的词根词缀在我看来就像是中文的偏旁部首,比如,在中文里,只要是有含"氵"的,就和水有关,比如海、河;在英文里,只要单词中出现了"pre",那往往这个单词就和"前"有关,比如 previous(之前的)、predict(预言)。掌握基本的词根词缀除了能帮助我们更好记住单词之外,还能在考试解题中帮助我们识别单词的大概意向,判断一个单词到底是褒义词还是贬义词。本书附录中已经收录了基础的前缀,大家也可参照 *Merriam-Webster's Vocabulary Builder*,里面有完整的词根词缀和词源的讲解。

第二,比较记忆法。比较记忆法分为两种,一种是形近词比较,比如在 SSAT 单词中大量以 ab 开头的单词,如:abdicate, abyss, abysmal, abhor 等等,而很多同学在背诵过程中不注意区分,一到使用的时候就想起哪个是哪个来。英语有句谚语"Use this word three times, and it's yours",平时可以把自己觉得易混的词写在一起。考前分清,考试时就不会那么茫然了。第二种是意近词,单词千千万,特别是在 SSAT 单词中,比如"激怒",我们需要掌握的单词有:anger, infuriate, incense, madden, inflame; antagonize, provoke, exasperate。大家可以自己总结一下这样的意群,一来单词组合起来方便记忆,二来同义题也就在这些同义词中考。这样的意群,我们在附录中也已经帮大家整理了一些。

• 如何备考 SSAT 词汇部分

能否成功的背好单词的关键,其实就在于同学们是否能做好一个周密的背词计划,并且严格地执行下去。切勿"三天打鱼,两天晒网",而是要周而复始,不断重复。在这里,就以此书为例推荐一个比较合理的背词计划给大家:

请大家注意在第一遍背诵单词的时候,只需要掌握单词基本释义和其特征部分,比如常用词根词缀,双写字母等,有模糊记忆即可,大可不必执着于第一遍就一定要把单词的所有意思都准确地背诵出来。

本书一共 108 个 List,除了冲刺词汇中的类比部分之外,每个 List 为 20 个单词。一般来说,同学们每天能抽出来集中背词的时间也就一个小时,其他碎片时间用于复习单词。大多数同学们一小时能背 100 个新词,但注意这 100 个新词背完之后,请从头到尾重新复习一遍,打破记忆曲线,保证背诵效率。

根据个人经验来说,推荐的背词时间是早上,同学们可以利用早上通勤或者早自习时间来背,此时背词效率也最高。而在晚上睡觉之前,同学可以拿出一点时间复习一天的新词和自己的难词。

除了每天的新词背诵之外,请至少把前一天的单词和自己的标记出来的难词复习好,时间有富余的同学可以顺便把前 2、4、7 天的单词拿出来复习,根据艾宾浩斯遗忘曲线,这几个时间节点是遗忘的高峰。

学生也可以按照自己的时间和进度安排背词时间表。单词一天不背就会忘记,一个月不背就前功尽弃,同学即使没有时间复习,都请一定要坚持每天抽时间出来复习,直到考试结束。

词 汇 测 试

Level 1 TOEFL Low

sufficient	abandon	foundation	successor	adapt
prospect	apparent	contain	investigate	thrive
vast	curious	innovate	domestic	visible
predict	confirm	epoch	dwell	insulate
potential	proceed	passive	accessible	hesitate
concentrate	positive	option	select	persist
exploit	rare	elevate	principle	immense
eliminate	flee	function	goal	instinct

Level 2 TOEFL High

compatible	conceal	sumptuous	facilitate	perspective
perilous	overlap	hinder	demonstrate	simultaneous
fluctuate	prevalent	copious	permanent	versatile
immerse	dissipate	arid	vulnerable	anonymous
ubiquitous	textile	contaminate	arduous	moderate
ambiguous	consensus	institute	demise	descendant
simulate	prominent	reluctant	superficial	corporate
contemplate	vacuous	fastidious	camouflage	meticulous

Level 3 SSAT

divert	cantankerous	philanthropist	belligerent	cursory
straightforward	euphonious	posthumous	soporific	deride
proliferate	mercurial	predilection	pretentious	extemporaneous
disparity	equivocal	fecund	itinerant	cacophonous
predicament	languid	glutton	docile	fabricate
impugn	mundane	pertinacious	sanctimonious	tangible
cordial	canine	appease	esoteric	impasse
loquacious	trunk	repugnant	profound	pernicious

　　本测试将单词分为三个等级,每级根据上表只有 40 个单词;第一级为托福基础词;第二级为托福高阶词,即 SSAT 基础词汇;第三个等级为 SSAT 单词。一个等级掌握 90％～95％ 即可算作掌握。

　　如第一个等级单词没有掌握,说明学生基础词汇缺乏,学习 SSAT 各科会比较吃力,可从托福单词着手准备;如第一级单词基本掌握,而第二级单词大量不会,那可从本书开始入门 SSAT 词汇;如第三级单词也基本掌握,那说明你已经准备好 SSAT 考试的词汇部分了,可以进入冲刺阶段。

目　录

SSAT 冲刺词汇

SSAT

基础词汇

resort [rɪˈzɔːt]

❶ *n*. a place where people go for vacations（度假）胜地

例 a ski **resort**

❷ *n*. something that you choose for help 求助的人（或物）；凭借的手段（或方法）

例 The company will only declare bankruptcy as a last **resort**.

单词助记

resurgence [rɪˈsɜːdʒəns]

n. a growth or increase that occurs after a period without growth or increase 复苏

例 There has been some **resurgence** in economic activity recently.

fringe [frɪndʒ]

❶ *n*. an ornamental border of threads left loose or formed into tassels or twists，used to edge clothing or material 流苏

例 The jacket had leather **fringes**.

❷ *n*. the outer，marginal，or extreme part of an area，group，or sphere of activity 边缘

例 They lived together in a mixed household on the **fringe** of a campus.

glare [gleə(r)]

❶ *vi*. to look directly at someone in an angry way 怒目而视

例 The teacher **glared** at him as he walked in late.

❷ *vi*. to shine with a harsh，bright light 发出刺眼的光

例 The white snow **glared** in the morning sunlight.

❸ *n*. 怒视；刺眼的光

例 I shielded my eyes from the **glare** of the sun.

compatible [kəmˈpætəbl]

❶ *adj*. able to exist together without trouble or conflict：going together well 相容的，协调的

例 My roommate and I are very **compatible**.

❷ *adj*. of devices and especially computers：able to be used together 兼容的

例 This printer is **compatible** with most PCs.

devote [dɪˈvəʊt]

vt. to decide that (something) will be used for (a special purpose)：to use (time，money，energy，attention，etc.) for (something) 把(时间、精力等)致力于

例 He **devoted** his life to helping the poor.

Part of the class was **devoted** to questions from last week's reading.

pessimistic [ˌpesɪˈmɪstɪk]

adj. having or showing a lack of hope for the future；expecting bad things to happen 悲观的

例 The film gives a very **pessimistic** view of human nature.

单词助记 【反义词】optimistic

interrupt [ˌʌnˌɪntəˈrʌpt]

❶ *vt*./ *vi*. to ask questions or say things while another person is speaking；to do or say something that causes someone to stop speaking 打断

例 It's not polite to **interrupt**.

❷ *vt*. to cause（something）to stop happening for a time 中断

例 We **interrupt** this program to bring you a special announcement.

preclude [prɪˈkluːd]

❶ *vt*. to make（something）impossible；to prevent（something）from happening 使（某事）不可能

例 Bad weather **precluded** any further attempts to reach the summit.

❷ *vt*. to prevent（someone）from doing something 阻止（某人做某事）

例 The injury **precluded** her from having an athletic career.

reconcile [ˈrekənsaɪl]

❶ *vt*./ *vi*. to cause people or groups to become friendly again after an argument or disagreement（使）和解

例 His attempt to **reconcile** his friends was unsuccessful.

After many years，they finally **reconciled** with each other.

❷ *vt*. to find a way of making（two different ideas，facts，etc.）exist or be true at the same time 使一致，调和

例 It can be difficult to **reconcile** your ideals with reality.

moderate [ˈmɒdərət]

❶ *adj*. neither large nor small in amount or degree 适度的，适中的

例 These extreme shifts would have put a lot of stress on the bodies of animals that were used to a more **moderate** range of temperatures.

❷ *adj*. avoiding behavior that goes beyond what is normal，healthy，or acceptable 有节制的

例 He believes that **moderate** drinking is healthy.

❸ *vt*./ *vi*. to make（something）less harsh，strong，or severe or to become less harsh，strong，or severe（使）缓和

例 The wind **moderated** after the storm.

tempt [tempt]

vt. to cause（someone）to do or want to do something even though it may be wrong，bad，or unwise 引诱，诱惑

例 Students may be **tempted** to cheat on the test.

infinite [ˈɪnfɪnɪt]

❶ *adj*. having no limits；endless 无穷的，无限的

例 Obviously，no company has **infinite** resources.

❷ *adj*. extremely large or great 极大的

例 There seemed to be an **infinite** number of possibilities.

engrave [ɪnˈɡreɪv]

vt. to cut or carve lines，letters，designs，etc.，onto or into a hard surface 雕刻

例 The image was **engraved** on the plaque.

conceal [kən'siːl]

❶ *vt.* to hide (something or someone) from sight 掩盖，隐藏

例 The controls are **concealed** behind a panel.

❷ *vt.* to keep (something) secret 隐瞒（信息），掩饰（情感）

例 The editorial accused the government of **concealing** the truth.

animate ['ænɪmeɪt]

❶ *vt.* to give life to 赋予……以生命

例 The soul **animates** the body.

❷ *vt.* to make (someone or something) lively or excited 使有生气

例 The writer's humor **animates** the novel.

agitate ['ædʒɪteɪt]

❶ *vt.* to move or stir up (a liquid) 搅动

例 gently **agitate** the water with a finger or paintbrush

❷ *vt.* to disturb，excite，or anger (someone) 使焦虑不安

例 If I talk about the problem with him it just **agitates** him even more.

拓展 *n.* **agitation** /ˌædʒə'teɪʃən/

例 He spoke with increasing **agitation** about the situation.

dwindle ['dwɪndl]

vi. to gradually become smaller 缩小，减少

例 The factory's workforce has **dwindled** from over 4,000 to a few hundred.

staunch [stɔːntʃ]

adj. very devoted or loyal to a person，belief，or cause 坚定的

例 She is a **staunch** advocate of women's rights.

crucial ['kruːʃəl]

adj. extremely important 至关重要的，关键的

例 Vitamins are **crucial** for maintaining good health.

prohibit [prə'hɪbɪt]

vt. to order (someone) not to use or do something 禁止

例 The town **prohibited** teenagers from being in the streets after 10 p.m..

launch [lɔːntʃ]

❶ *vt.* to send or shoot (something，such as a rocket) into the air or water or into outer space 发射

例 NASA plans to **launch** a satellite to study cosmic rays.

❷ *vt.* to throw (something) forward in a forceful way 投掷

例 I was terrified when the ferocious animal suddenly **launched** itself at me.

❸ *vt.* to begin (something that requires much effort) 发起

例 The enemy **launched** an attack at sunrise.

n.

例 The company's spending has also risen following the **launch** of a new Sunday magazine.

ambivalent [æm'bɪvələnt]

adj. having or showing very different feelings (such as love and hate) about someone or something at the same time (情绪、心理、态度)矛盾的

例 She has a deeply **ambivalent** attitude about religion.

bud [bʌd]

n. a small part that grows on a plant and develops into a flower，leaf，or new branch 芽；花蕾

例 The bush has plenty of **buds** but no flowers yet.

wary ['weərɪ]

adj. not having or showing complete trust in someone or something that could be dangerous or cause trouble 谨慎的，小心的

例 Dogs that have been mistreated often remain **wary** of strangers.

segregate ['segrɪgeɪt]

vt. to separate groups of people because of their particular race，religion，etc. 隔离，分开

例 He grew up at a time when blacks were **segregated** from whites.

单词助记

stagnate [stæg'neɪt]

vi. to stop developing，progressing，moving，etc. 停滞不前

例 Industrial production is **stagnating**.

单词助记【同义词】 still，motionless，static，stationary，standing

havoc [ˈhævək]

n. a situation in which there is much destruction or confusion 大破坏，毁灭

例 Rioters caused **havoc** in the centre of the town.

gist [dʒɪst]

n. the general or basic meaning of something said or written 主旨，要点

例 The **gist** of her argument was that the law was unfair.

refinement [rɪˈfaɪnmənt]

❶ *n.* a small change that improves something 改进，完善

例 Several engine **refinements** have resulted in increased efficiency.

❷ *n.* the quality of a person who has the good education，polite manners，etc., that are expected in people who belong to a high social class 文雅，教养

例 a person of great **refinement**

deter [dɪˈtɜː(r)]

vt. to cause (someone) to decide not to do something 阻止

例 They hoped that the new law would **deter** advertisers from making false claims.

frigid [ˈfrɪdʒɪd]

adj. very cold 极冷的

例 The **frigid** gusts of wind stung their faces.

shiver [ˈʃɪvə(r)]

❶ *vi.* to shake slightly because you are cold，afraid，etc. 颤抖

例 She was **shivering** with fear.

❷ *n.* a small shaking movement caused by cold or strong emotion 颤抖

例 She felt a **shiver** of delight when she opened the gift.

shuttle [ˈʃʌtl]

n. a spacecraft that can be used more than once and that carries people into outer space and back to Earth：space shuttle 航天飞机

例 A **shuttle** takes people from the parking lot to the airport.

haphazard [ˌhæpˈhæzəd]

adj. having no plan，order，or direction 随意的，任意的，无计划的

例 We were given a **haphazard** tour of the city.

might [maɪt]

n. power to do something：force or strength 力量

例 He swung the bat with all his **might**.

absolute [ˈæbsəluːt]

❶ *adj.* always used before a noun：complete and total — often used informally to make a statement more forceful 完全的，绝对的

例 You can't predict the future with **absolute** certainty.

❷ *adj.* not allowing any doubt 确凿的

例 He says that he has **absolute** proof that his client is innocent.

bombard [bɒmˈbɑːd]

❶ *vt.* to attack (a place) with bombs，large guns，etc. 炮轰，炮击

例 The navy **bombarded** the shore.

❷ *vt.* to hit or attack (something or someone) constantly or repeatedly 不断击打，激烈攻击

例 Fine particles of sand **bombard** exposed rock surfaces.

单词助记

sumptuous [ˈsʌmptjʊəs]

adj. very expensive, rich, or impressive 奢华的

例 She produces elegant wedding gowns in a variety of **sumptuous** fabrics.

ignite [ɪgˈnaɪt]

❶ *vt.* to set (something) on fire: to cause (something) to burn: light 点燃；着火
  to begin burning: to catch fire

例 The fire was **ignited** by sparks.

❷ *vt.* to give life or energy to (someone or something) 使激动,激起

例 Three wins in a row **ignited** the team.

单词助记 "nite"表示"夜晚","ignite"谐音"一个晚上",需要点亮夜晚

adorn [əˈdɔːn]

vt. to make（someone or something）more attractive by adding something beautiful；decorate 装饰

例 The walls are **adorned** with her paintings.

单词助记 区分："adore"，意为："喜欢"。

elapse [ɪˈlæps]

vi. of time：to pass by（时间）流逝

例 Weeks **elapsed** before he returned home.

congenital [kənˈdʒenɪtəl]

adj. existing since birth 先天性的

例 When John was 17，he died of **congenital** heart disease.

单词助记 区分："congenial"，表示"令人愉悦的；意气相投的"。

perilous [ˈperɪləs]

adj. full of danger 危险的

例 The road grew even steeper and more **perilous**.

单词助记 【同义词】dangerous, hazardous, risky, unsafe, precarious

irritate [ˈɪrɪteɪt]

❶ *vt*. to make（someone）impatient，angry，or annoyed 激怒

例 The child's rudeness was very **irritating** to us.

❷ *vt*. to make（part of your body）sore or painful 刺激

例 Harsh soaps can **irritate** the skin.

拓展 *n*. irritation [ˌɪrɪˈteɪʃən]

例 These oils may cause **irritation** to sensitive skins.

vigor [ˈvɪgə(r)]

n. strength，energy，or determination 力量；活力

例 She defended her beliefs with great **vigor**.

jolt [dʒəʊlt]

vt. to surprise or shock（someone）震惊

例 She **jolted** the medical world with her announcement.

thrive [θraɪv]

vi. to grow or develop successfully：to flourish or succeed 茁壮成长；兴旺发达

例 The region **thrived** under his rule.

单词助记 【同义词】flourish, prosper, burgeon

拓展 *adj*. thriving [θraɪvɪŋ]

例 His business is **thriving**.

squat [skwɒt]

vi. to bend your knees and lower your body so that you are close to your heels or sitting on your heels 蹲下

例 He **squatted** behind the bush to avoid being seen.

单词助记

cease [siːs]

❶ *vi.* to stop happening：to end 停止

例 The fighting along the border has temporarily **ceased**.

❷ *vt.* to stop doing（something）停止，不再（做某事）

例 A small number of firms have **ceased** trading.

impending [ɪmˈpendɪŋ]

adj. happening or likely to happen soon 即将发生的

例 We need to prepare for their **impending** arrival.

单词助记 【同义词】imminent

insulate [ˈɪnsjʊleɪt]

vt./vi. to add a material or substance to（something）in order to stop heat，electricity，or sound from going into or out of it 使隔离（如绝缘、隔热、隔音）

例 Our heating bills are high because our house is poorly **insulated**.

threshold [ˈθreʃhəʊld]

❶ *n.* a piece of wood，metal，or stone that forms the bottom of a door and that you walk over as you enter a room or building 门槛

例 He stepped across the **threshold**.

❷ *n.* the point or level at which something begins or changes 开端；界限，临界点

例 He has a high pain **threshold**.

单词助记

tortuous [ˈtɔːtjʊəs]

adj. having many twists and turns 弯弯曲曲的，曲折的

例 The only road access is a **tortuous** mountain route.

spark [spɑːk]

❶ *n.* a small piece of burning material that comes from a fire or is produced by rubbing or hitting two hard objects together 火花

例 A **spark** from the fireplace set the rug on fire.

❷ *vt.* to cause（something）to start or happen 引发

例 The question **sparked** a debate.

exterminate [ɪksˈtɜːmɪneɪt]

vt. to destroy or kill（a group of animals，people，etc.）completely 消灭，灭绝

例 The invaders nearly **exterminated** the native people.

ridiculous [rɪ'dɪkjʊləs]

adj. extremely silly or unreasonable 荒谬的, 可笑的

例 That's an absolutely **ridiculous** price for that sweater.

单词助记 【同义词】absurd, preposterous, ludicrous, ridiculous

stance [stæns]

n. a publicly stated opinion 态度, 立场

例 She has maintained a neutral **stance** during the negotiations.

hamper ['hæmpə(r)]

vt. to slow the movement, progress, or action of (someone or something) 妨碍, 束缚

例 Bad weather could **hamper** our search efforts.

单词助记 【同义词】hinder, obstruct, impede, inhibit, retard, balk, thwart, foil, curb

refuge ['refjuːdʒ]

n. a place that provides shelter or protection 避难所

例 He was forced to take **refuge** in the Chinese embassy.

dwarf [dwɔːf]

❶ *n*. in stories: a creature that looks like a small man and that often lives underground and has magical powers 小矮人

例 *Snow White and the Seven Dwarfs*

❷ *vt*. to make (something) look very small or unimportant when compared with something else 使显得矮小，使相形见绌

例 The bike was **dwarfed** by the truck next to it.

单词助记

fictitious [fɪkˈtɪʃəs]

adj. not true or real 虚构的

例 The characters in the book are all **fictitious**.

单词助记 【同义词】fictional

disaster [dɪˈzɑːstə(r)]

n. something (such as a flood, tornado, fire, plane crash, etc.) that happens suddenly and causes much suffering or loss to many people 灾难

例 The earthquake was one of the worst natural **disasters** of this century.

单词助记 【同义词】catastrophe, calamity, cataclysm

strive [straɪv]

vi. to try very hard to do or achieve something 努力

例 We must all **strive** to do better.

obsolete [ˈɒbsəliːt]

adj. no longer used because something newer exists 过时的，被淘汰的

例 The system was made **obsolete** by their invention.

单词助记 【同义词】outdated, out of date, outmoded, old-fashioned, out of fashion; no longer in use, disused, fallen into disuse, behind the times, superannuated, outworn, antiquated, antediluvian

legislation [ˌledʒɪsˈleɪʃən]

n. a law or set of laws made by a government 立法

例 She proposed **legislation** for protecting the environment.

discord [ˈdɪskɔːd]

n. lack of agreement between people, ideas, etc. 不和

例 The city has long been known as a scene of racial intolerance and **discord**.

单词助记 【反义词】concord，accord

oversee [ˌəʊvəˈsiː]

vt. to watch and direct（an activity，a group of workers，etc.）in order to be sure that a job is done correctly 监督

例 He was hired to **oversee** design and construction of the new facility.

patent [ˈpeɪtənt]

❶ *n.* a government authority or license conferring a right or title for a set period 专利

例 The company holds a **patent** on the product.

❷ *adj.* easily recognizable；obvious 明显的

例 His explanation turned out to be a **patent** lie.

conform [kənˈfɔːm]

vi. to obey or agree with something 遵从；符合

例 Employees have to **conform** with company rules.

hostile [ˈhɒstaɪl]

❶ *adj.* not friendly：having or showing unfriendly feelings 怀有敌意的，敌对的

例 Her suggestions were given a **hostile** reception.

❷ *adj.* unpleasant or harsh（环境和条件等）不利的

例 The camel is specially adapted to its **hostile** desert habitat.

pesticide [ˈpestɪsaɪd]

n. a chemical that is used to kill animals or insects that damage plants or crops 杀虫剂，农药

例 A plant attacked by a pest evolves a **pesticide** in its leaves.

单词助记

optimal [ˈɒptɪməl]

adj. best or most effective 最佳的

例 Under **optimal** conditions，these plants grow quite tall.

incursion [ɪnˈkɜːʃən]

n. a sudden invasion or attack：an act of entering a place or area that is controlled by an enemy 侵入

例 Traditional crafts remain remarkably unchanged by the slow **incursion** of modern ways.

residue [ˈrezɪdjuː]

n. a usually small amount of something that remains after a process has been completed or a thing has been removed 残留物

例 The grill was covered in a greasy **residue** from the hamburgers.

trend [trend]

❶ *n.* a general direction of change：a way of behaving，proceeding，etc.，that is developing and becoming more common 趋势

例 There is a disturbing **trend** toward obesity in children.

❷ *n.* something that is currently popular or fashionable 时尚

例 The latest **trend** is gardening.

intermediate [ˌɪntəˈmiːdɪət]

❶ *adj.* occurring in the middle of a process or series 中间的

例 an **intermediate** stage of growth

❷ *adj.* relating to or having the knowledge or skill of someone who is more advanced than a beginner but not yet an expert 中级的

例 I'm taking **intermediate** French this year.

intact [ɪnˈtækt]

adj. not damaged or impaired in any way；complete 完好无损的

例 The vase remained **intact** despite rough handling.

spell [spel]

❶ *vt.* to say，write，or print the letters of (a word or name) 拼写

例 Please **spell** out your full name.

❷ *n.* a short period of time usually marked by a particular activity or condition（某种天气或活动的）短暂发生期

例 The flowers died during a cold **spell**.

mortal [ˈmɔːtl]

adj. certain to die 终有一死的

例 Every living creature is **mortal**.

List 5

soar [sɔː(r)]

❶ *vi.* to rise quickly upward to a great height 向上飞，升空

例 The rocket **soared** into the sky.

❷ *vi.* to increase very quickly in amount or price 急剧增加

例 The nation's divorce rate has **soared**.

(单词助记)

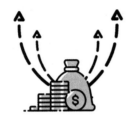

premise [ˈpremɪs]

❶ *n.* a statement or idea that is accepted as being true and that is used as the basis of an argument 前提

例 If the **premise** is true，then the conclusion must be true.

❷ *vt.* to take as true or as a fact without actual proof 假定

例 Let us **premise** certain things，such as every person's need for love，before beginning our line of reasoning.

blossom [ˈblɒsəm]

❶ *n.* a flower especially of a fruit tree（果树的）花

例 delicate pink **blossoms**

❷ *vi.* to produce flowers（树）开花

例 The trees have finished **blossoming**.

❸ *vi.* to change，grow，and develop fully 成功发展

例 Their business seemed to **blossom** overnight.

hollow [ˈhɒləʊ]

❶ *adj.* having nothing inside：not solid 空心的

例 a **hollow** tree

❷ *adj.* curved inward or down 凹陷的

例 He looked young，dark and sharp-featured，with **hollow** cheeks.

❸ *n.* an empty space inside of something 空心

例 The owls nested in the **hollow** of a tree.

❹ *n.* a place or area（especially on the ground）that is lower than the area around it 凹陷处

例 Below him the town lay warm in the **hollow** of the hill.

(单词助记) 注意与"hallow"区分，意为"神圣的"

tact [tækt]

n. adroitness and sensitivity in dealing with others or with difficult issues 圆通

例 The peace talks required great **tact** on the part of both leaders.

symphony [ˈsɪmfənɪ]

n. an elaborate musical composition for full orchestra 交响乐

例 She's a member of the Chicago **Symphony** Orchestra.

desolate [ˈdesələt]

adj. lacking the people，plants，animals，etc.，that make people feel welcome in a place 荒凉的

例 We drove for hours along a **desolate** stretch of road.

单词助记 【同义词】desert

boast [bəʊst]

❶ *vt./vi.* to express too much pride in yourself or in something you have，have done，or are connected to in some way 吹嘘

例 The novelist **boasted** about his new work.

❷ *vt.* to have (something that is impressive) 拥有

例 The museum **boasts** some of the rarest gems in the world.

allude [əˈluːd]

vi. to speak of or mention (something or someone) in an indirect way 暗指，间接提及

例 I'm interested in hearing more about the technology you **alluded** to a minute ago.

adept [əˈdept]

adj. very good at doing something that is not easy 擅长的，娴熟的

例 She's **adept** at fixing flaws in the system.

replenish [rɪˈplenɪʃ]

vt. to fill or build up (something) again 重新填满，补充

例 He **replenished** his supply of wood in preparation for the winter.

amplify [ˈæmplɪfaɪ]

❶ *vt.* to make (something，such as a musical instrument) louder by increasing the strength of electric signals 扩大（声音）

例 The music was **amplified** with microphones.

❷ *vt.* to make (something) stronger 增强

例 Her anxiety about the world was **amplifying** her personal fears about her future.

拓展 *n.* amplification [ˌæmplɪfɪˈkeɪʃən] 扩大；详述

例 The new rules require some **amplification**.

infect [ɪnˈfekt]

vt. to cause (someone or something) to become sick or affected by disease 传染

例 They were unable to prevent bacteria from **infecting** the wound.

mandatory [ˈmændətərɪ]

adj. required by a law or rule 强制性的；法定的

例 This meeting is **mandatory** for all employees.

单词助记 【同义词】obligatory，compulsory，binding，required，requisite，imperative

perish [ˈperɪʃ]

❶ *vi.* to die or be killed （因恶劣条件或事故）死亡

例 Most of the butterflies **perish** in the first frosts of autumn.

❷ *vi.* to slowly break apart by a natural process （食物等）腐烂

例 The rubber will **perish** with age.

sacred [ˈseɪkrɪd]

❶ *adj*. worthy of religious worship：very holy 神圣的

例 The burial site is **sacred** ground.

❷ *adj*. relating to religion 宗教的

例 **sacred** songs/texts

dual [ˈdjuːəl]

adj. having two different parts，uses，etc. 双重的

例 The song's lyrics have a **dual** meaning.

crawl [krɔːl]

❶ *vi*. to move with the body close to or on the ground 爬行

例 The soldiers **crawled** forward on their bellies.

❷ *vi*. to move slowly 缓慢行进

例 They're doing construction on the road，so traffic is **crawling**.

discrepancy [dɪsˈkrepənsɪ]

n. a difference especially between things that should be the same 差异

例 There were **discrepancies** between their accounts of the accident.

irreparable [ɪˈrepərəbl]

adj. too bad to be corrected or repaired 不可补救的

例 The oil spill did **irreparable** harm to the bay.

List 6

approximate [əˈprɒksɪmət]

❶ *adj.* close in value or amount but not precise 大概的

例 Can you give me the **approximate** cost of the repair?

❷ *vt.* to calculate the almost exact value or position of（something）估算,估计

例 Students learned to **approximate** the distance between the Earth and the planets.

❸ *vt.* [əˈprɑːksɪˌmeɪt] to be very similar to but not exactly like（something）近似于

例 I've finally found a vegetarian burger that **approximates** the taste of real beef.

inception [ɪnˈsepʃən]

n. the time at which something begins 开始,开端

例 Since its **inception**，the business has expanded to become a national retail chain.

indigenous [ɪnˈdɪdʒɪnəs]

adj. produced，living，or existing naturally in a particular region or environment 本土的,当地的

例 He grows a wide variety of both **indigenous** and exotic plants.

单词助记 "in"表示"里面"，"di"谐音成中文"地"；"gen"是词根,表示生。连起来就是本地生的,本土的。

flee [fliː]

vt. / *vi.* to run away from（a place）逃离

例 Many people **fled** the city to escape the fighting.

单词助记 谐音成"飞离"

ostentatious [ˌɒstenˈteɪʃəs]

adj. displaying wealth，knowledge，etc.，in a way that is meant to attract attention，admiration，or envy 炫耀的；铺张的

例 She's got a lovely way with language without ever sounding **ostentatious**.

单词助记 【同义词】showy, pretentious, conspicuous, flamboyant, gaudy, extravagant

单词助记

confident [ˈkɒnfɪdənt]

adj. having a feeling or belief that you can do something well or succeed at something：having confidence 自信的,有信心的

例 I am **confident** about my ability to do the job.

humid [ˈhjuːmɪd]

adj. having a lot of moisture in the air 潮湿的

例 It's very hot and **humid** today.

wander ['wɒndə(r)]

vt./vi. to move around or go to different places usually without having a particular purpose or direction 闲逛,漫游

例 I was just **wandering** around the house.

单词助记 【同义词】 stroll，amble，saunter，dawdle，ramble，meander

carve [kɑːv]

vt. to make (something, such as a sculpture or design) by cutting off pieces of the material it is made of 雕刻

例 He **carved** the sculpture out of marble.

canal [kə'næl]

❶ n. a long narrow place that is filled with water and was created by people so that boats could pass through it or to supply fields，crops，etc.，with water 运河;水渠

例 irrigation **canals**

❷ n. a tube or passageway in the body（体内的）管道

例 alimentary **canal**

cardinal ['kɑːdɪnəl]

adj. basic or most important 基本的,首要的

例 My **cardinal** rule is to always be honest.

rehearse [rɪ'hɜːs]

vt./vi. to prepare for a public performance of a play, a piece of music, etc., by practicing the performance 排练

例 The band stayed up late **rehearsing** for the big show.

【同义词】 fundamental，primary，crucial

precipitous [prɪ'sɪpɪtəs]

❶ adj. very steep 陡峭的

例 a **precipitous** slope

❷ adj. happening in a very quick and sudden way（变化）突然的,急剧的

例 There has been a **precipitous** decline in home sales recently.

单词助记

squander ['skwɒndə(r)]

vt. to use (something) in a foolish or wasteful way 挥霍,浪费

例 The government **squandered** the money on failed programs.

manufacture [ˌmænjʊ'fæktʃə(r)]

❶ vt. to make (something) usually in large amounts by using machines（大规模）制造,生产

例 We import foreign **manufactured** goods.

❷ *n*. the process of making products especially with machines in factories（大规模）制造，生产

例 We're developing new methods of paper **manufacture**.

submissive [səbˈmɪsɪv]

adj. willing to obey someone else 顺从的

例 Most doctors want their patients to be **submissive**.

单词助记【同义词】compliant，yielding，obedient，docile，pliant

unanimous [juːˈnænɪməs]

adj. having the same opinion 一致同意的

例 The councilors were **unanimous** in their approval of the report.

faction [ˈfækʃən]

n. a small，organized，dissenting group within a larger one，especially in politics 派别

例 The committee soon split into **factions**.

epitomize [ɪˈpɪtəmaɪz]

vt. to be the epitome of（something）是……的典型，体现

例 He **epitomizes** laziness.

sniff [snɪf]

vt./ *vi*. to smell（something or someone）by putting your nose close to it and taking air in through your nose in short breaths（吸着气）闻，嗅

例 The dog **sniffed** the carpet.

List 7

scale [skeɪl]

❶ *n*. an arrangement of the notes in any system of music in ascending or descending order of pitch 全音阶

例 a major **scale**

❷ *n*. an instrument for weighing. 天平, 秤

例 He stepped onto the bathroom **scales**.

❸ *n*. a graduated range of values forming a standard system for measuring or grading something 规模, 范围

例 On a **scale** of 1 to 10, I give the movie a 9.

fastidious [fæsˈtɪdɪəs]

adj. liking few things：hard to please 非常讲究的, 挑剔的

例 He was **fastidious** about his appearance.

单词助记 【同义词】 scrupulous, punctilious, painstaking, meticulous

inquire [ɪnˈkwaɪə(r)]

v. ask for information from someone 询问, 打听

例 We **inquired** the way to the station.

kindle [ˈkɪndl]

❶ *vt*. to cause (a fire) to start burning 点燃

例 I came in and **kindled** a fire in the stove.

❷ *vt*. to cause the start of (something) 激起, 引发

例 The incident **kindled** a new national debate.

euphoric [juːˈfɒrɪk]

adj. having a feeling of great happiness and excitement 狂喜的

例 The war had received **euphoric** support from the public.

单词助记 【同义词】 elated, exhilarated, jubilant, exultant；ecstatic, blissful

单词助记

retard [rɪˈtɑːd]

vt. to slow down the development or progress of (something) 减缓, 阻碍

例 The problems have **retarded** the progress of the program.

suspect [səˈspekt]

❶ *vt*. to have feelings of doubt about (something)：to be suspicious about (something) 怀疑

例 I **suspected** his motives in giving me the money.

❷ *n*. [səˈspekt] a person who is believed to be possibly guilty of committing a crime 嫌疑犯

例 She is a possible **suspect** in connection with the kidnapping.

status [ˈsteɪtəs]

❶ *n*. the position or rank of someone or something when compared to others in a society, organization, group, etc. 地位

例 She married a man of **status** and wealth.

❷ *n*. the current state of someone or something 状况

例 What is the **status** of the project?

proponent [prəˈpəʊnənt]

n. a person who argues for or supports something: advocate 支持者

例 He is a leading **proponent** of gun control.

gulf [ɡʌlf]

n. a large area of ocean that is partly surrounded by land — often used in proper names 海湾

例 Hurricane Andrew was last night heading into the **Gulf** of Mexico.

preordain [ˌpriːɔːˈdeɪn]

vt. to determine the fate of (something) in advance 预先注定

例 Some people believe that fate has been **preordained** whether they will be happy or not.

accessory [əkˈsesərɪ]

❶ *n*. something added to something else to make it more useful, attractive, or effective 附件, 配饰

例 computer **accessories**

❷ *adj*. present in a minor amount and not essential as a constituent 非主要的, 次要的

例 She was charged as an **accessory** before/after the fact.

hitherto [ˌhɪðəˈtuː]

adv. until now: before this time 到目前为止, 迄今

例 The biography reveals some **hitherto** unknown facts about his early life.

steer [stɪə(r)]

❶ *vt*. to control the direction in which something (such as a ship, car, or airplane) moves 驾驶, 操纵

例 She **steered** the ship through the strait.

❷ *n*. a male domestic bovine animal that has been castrated and is raised for beef 小公牛

vein [veɪn]

❶ *n*. any one of the tubes that carry blood from parts of the body back to the heart 静脉

例 Many **veins** are found just under the skin.

❷ *n*. any one of the thin lines that can be seen on the surface of a leaf or on the wing of an insect (植物的)叶脉; (昆虫的)翅脉

例 the serrated edges and **veins** of the feathery leaves.

mandate [ˈmænˈdeɪt]

vt. to officially demand or require（something）要求，强制执行

例 The law **mandates** that every car have seat belts.

swell [swel]

❶ *vi.* to become larger than normal 肿胀

例 Her broken ankle **swelled** badly.

❷ both *vt./vi.* to increase in size or number（使）增大

例 Immigrants have **swelled** the population.

❸ *n.* an increase in size or number 增大

例 a **swell** in the population

extant [eksˈtænt]

adj. in existence：still existing 现存的

例 There are few **extant** records from that period.

【反义词】decrease，dip

skim [skɪm]

vt./vi. to look over or read（something）quickly especially to find the main ideas 略读

例 She only **skimmed** the reading assignment.

spray [spreɪ]

vt. to put a stream of small drops of liquid on（someone or something）喷，喷射

例 We were **sprayed** by water from the crashing waves.

mute [mjuːt]

❶ *adj.* not able or willing to speak 无声的，缄默的

例 She knew the answer, but she decided to remain **mute**.

❷ *vt.* to make (a sound) softer or quieter 降低(声音)

例 We **muted** our voices.

❸ *vt.* to make (something) softer or less harsh 使变温和

例 The loud colors in this room need to be **muted**.

❹ *n.* a deaf person who is unable to speak 哑巴

concur [kənˈkɜː(r)]

❶ *vi.* to agree with someone or something 同意，意见一致

例 We **concur** that more money should be spent on education.

单词助记 【同义词】agree

❷ *vi.* happen at the same time 同时发生

例 The events of his life **concurred** to make him what he was.

exert [ɪgˈzɜːt]

❶ *vt.* to use (strength, ability, etc.) 运用

例 He had to **exert** all of his strength to move the stone.

❷ *vt.* to cause (force, effort, etc.) to have an effect or to be felt 施加

例 He **exerts** a lot of influence on the other members of the committee.

vanish [ˈvænɪʃ]

vi. to stop existing 消失，消亡

例 Dinosaurs **vanished** from the face of the earth millions of years ago.

obsession [əbˈseʃən]

n. the state of being obsessed with someone or something 沉迷

例 He's concerned about money to the point of **obsession**.

单词助记

rudimentary [ˌruːdɪˈmentərɪ]

adj. involving or limited to basic principles 基础的，最初的

例 This class requires a **rudimentary** knowledge of human anatomy.

triumph [ˈtraɪəmf]

❶ *n.* a great or important victory 胜利

例 They earned a magnificent **triumph** over the invading army.

❷ *v.* achieve a victory; be successful 战胜

例 Spectacle has once again **triumphed** over content.

ingenuity [ˌɪndʒɪˈnjuːɪtɪ]

n. skill or cleverness that allows someone to solve problems, invent things, etc. 足智多谋,创造力

例 She showed amazing **ingenuity** in finding ways to cut costs.

emperor [ˈempərə(r)]

n. a man who rules an empire 皇帝,君主

例 Roman **emperors**

staple [ˈsteɪpl]

adj. used, needed, or enjoyed constantly by many people 主要的,基本的

例 Rice is the **staple** food of more than half the world's population.

tenuous [ˈtenjʊəs]

adj. not certain, definite, or strong: flimsy, weak, or uncertain 脆弱的

例 The local theater has had a **tenuous** existence in recent years.

antecedent [ˌæntɪˈsiːdənt]

❶ *n*. ⟨antecedents⟩ the people in a family who lived in past times 祖先

例 He is proud of his Scottish **antecedents**.

单词助记 【同义词】ancestor, forefather, forebear, progenitor, primogenitor

❷ *n*. something that came before something else and may have influenced or caused it 前例,先例

例 We shall first look briefly at the historical **antecedents** of this theory.

discern [dɪˈsɜːn]

vt. to come to know, recognize, or understand (something) 识别,理解

例 The purpose of the study is to **discern** patterns of criminal behavior.

disguise [dɪsˈgaɪz]

❶ *vt*. to change the usual appearance, sound, taste, etc., of (someone or something) so that people will not recognize that person or thing 伪装

例 She **disguised** herself in a wig and glasses.

❷ *vt*. to hide (something) so that it will not be seen or noticed 掩饰

例 I could not **disguise** my surprise.

 单词助记

discriminate [dɪˈskrɪmɪneɪt]

❶ *vt./vi*. to notice and understand that one thing is different from another thing: to recognize a difference between things 辨别,区分

例 He is incapable of **discriminating** between a good idea and a terrible one.

❷ *vi*. to unfairly treat a person or group of people differently from other people or groups 区分对待,歧视

例 It is illegal to **discriminate** on the grounds of sex.

reign [reɪn]

　　n. the period of time during which a king, queen, emperor, etc., is ruler of a country 统治时期,在位期

　　例 the **reign** of Queen Elizabeth

sustain [səˈsteɪn]

　　vt. to provide what is needed for (something or someone) to exist, continue, etc. 保持,维持,使持续不断

　　例 There is not enough oxygen to **sustain** life at very high altitudes.

malleable [ˈmælɪəbl]

　　❶ *adj*. capable of being stretched or bent into different shapes 有延展性的

　　例 Silver is the most **malleable** of all metals.

　　单词助记 【同义词】pliable, ductile, plastic, pliant

　　❷ *adj*. capable of being easily changed or influenced 易受外界影响的,可变的

　　例 She was young enough to be **malleable**.

　　单词助记 【同义词】susceptible, pliable, amenable, compliant, tractable

prevalent [ˈprevələnt]

　　adj. widespread in a particular area at a particular time 流行的

　　例 The social ills **prevalent** in society today.

disturb [dɪˈstɜːb]

　　❶ *vt*. to stop (someone) from working, sleeping, etc.; to interrupt or bother (someone or something) 打扰

　　例 She doesn't want to be **disturbed** while she's working.

　　❷ *vt*. to worry or upset (someone) 使不安

　　例 The news **disturbed** him.

firm [fɜ:m]

❶ *n*. a business organization 公司

例 The **firm**'s employees were expecting large bonuses.

❷ *adj*. fairly hard or solid；not soft 结实的

例 **firm** muscles

absurd [əbˈsɜːd]

adj. wildly unreasonable，illogical，or inappropriate 荒唐的

例 The allegations are patently **absurd**.

单词助记【同义词】absurd, preposterous, ludicrous, ridiculous

anomaly [əˈnɒməlɪ]

n. something that deviates from what is standard，normal，or expected 反常的事物或人

例 We couldn't explain the **anomalies** in the test results.

contrive [kənˈtraɪv]

❶ *vt*. to form or make（something）in a skillful or clever way 精巧设计，发明

例 They **contrived** a mask against poison gas.

❷ *vt*. to form or think of（a plan，method，etc.）策划，图谋

例 The prisoners **contrived** a way to escape.

revere [rɪˈvɪə(r)]

vt. to have great respect for（someone or something）：to show devotion and honor to（someone or something）尊敬，尊崇

例 He is **revered** as a hero.

vehicle [ˈviːɪkl]

❶ *n*. a machine that is used to carry people or goods from one place to another 运输工具

例 The **vehicle**'s driver was severely injured in the crash.

❷ *n*. the thing that allows something to be passed along，expressed，achieved，or shown 媒介，工具

例 Water and insects can be **vehicles** of infection.

prodigious [prəˈdɪdʒəs]

❶ *adj*. very big 巨大的

例 This business generates cash in **prodigious** amounts.

❷ *adj*. amazing or wonderful：very impressive 令人印象深刻的

例 He impressed all who met him with his **prodigious** memory.

【同义词】enormous, tremendous, colossal, monumental

inequality [ˌɪnɪˈkwɒlɪtɪ]

n. an unfair situation in which some people have more rights or better opportunities than other people 不平等，不公平

例 They discussed the problem of **inequality** between students.

sporadic [spəˈrædɪk]

adj. happening often but not regularly: not constant or steady 不时发生的,零星的

例 **Sporadic** cases of the disease were reported.

单词助记【同义词】occasional, infrequent, irregular, periodic

拓展 *adv.* sporadically [spəˈrædɪklɪ]

例 Occurrences of the disease were **sporadically** reported.

recap [ˈriːkæp]

vt./vi. to give a brief summary of what has been done or said before 概括

例 Before we continue, let's **recap** what we have done so far.

overlap [ˌəʊvəˈlæp]

❶ *vt./vi.* to lie over the edge of (something): to cover part of the edge of (something) 重叠,交搭

例 The petals of the flower **overlap** with each other.

❷ both *vt./vi.* to have parts that are the same as parts of something else 重合,部分相同

例 Some of the material in the course **overlaps** with what I was taught in another course.

❸ *n.* a part or amount which overlaps 重叠部分

例 There is some **overlap** between the two courses.

lumen [ˈluːmen]

n. the SI unit of luminous flux 流明(光的单位)

例 The light perceived by the human eye is measured in units called **lumen**-hours.

arduous [ˈɑːdjʊəs]

adj. very difficult 艰难的

例 He went through a long and **arduous** training program.

单词助记【同义词】onerous, taxing, difficult, laborious, burdensome, strenuous

peel [piːl]

❶ *vt.* to remove (a covering, shell, etc.) from something 剥掉

例 They **peeled** off the old wallpaper.

❷ *n.* the outer covering or rind of a fruit or vegetable 皮

例 banana **peel**

posture [ˈpɒstʃə(r)]

❶ *n.* the way in which your body is positioned when you are sitting or standing 姿势

例 Human beings have an upright **posture**.

❷ *n.* a particular way of dealing with or considering something 立场,态度

例 a militant **posture** towards negotiation.

surveillance [sɜːˈveɪləns]

n. the act of carefully watching someone or something especially in order to prevent or detect a crime 监视

例 He was arrested after being kept under constant **surveillance**.

rebellion [rɪˈbelɪən]

❶ *n.* an effort by many people to change the government or leader of a country by the use of protest or violence 叛乱

例 The king's army suppressed the **rebellion**.

❷ *n*. refusal to obey rules or accept normal standards of behavior，dress，etc. 反抗

例 Women are waging a quiet **rebellion** against the traditional roles their mothers have played.

单词助记

glimpse [glɪmps]

　　n. a brief or quick view or look 一瞥；初步的感受

　　例 We caught a **glimpse** of him through the window as his car sped past.

tenacious [tɪˈneɪʃəs]

　　❶ *adj*. not easily stopped or pulled apart：firm or strong 紧握的；黏着力强的

　　例 The company has a **tenacious** hold on the market.

单词助记 【同义词】persevering，tenacious，persistent，indefatigable，staunch，steadfast

　　❷ *adj*. very determined to do something 执着的

　　例 He is a **tenacious** negotiator.

　　拓展 *n*. **tenacity** [təˈnæsətɪ] the quality or state of being tenacious 韧性；不屈不挠

　　例 She fought with great **tenacity**.

comply [kəmˈplaɪ]

　　v. force or oblige（someone）to do something 强迫

　　例 There will be penalties against individuals who fail to **comply**.

suspicious [sə'spɪʃəs]

adj. causing a feeling that something is wrong or that someone is behaving wrongly 可疑的

例 The **suspicious** vehicle was reported to police.

patriotic [ˌpætrɪ'ɒtɪk]

adj. having or showing great love and support for your country 爱国的

例 A **patriotic** fervor swept the country.

toss [tɒs]

vt. to throw (something) with a quick, light motion 扔，抛

例 He **tossed** his dirty socks onto the floor.

resume [rɪ'zjuːm]

❶ both *vt*./*vi*. to begin again after stopping 重新开始

例 She sat down and **resumed** her work.

❷ *n*. [rɪ'zjuːm]（or résumé also resumé）a short document describing your education, work history, etc., that you give an employer when you are applying for a job 简历

例 If you would like to be considered for the job, please submit your **résumé**.

judicial [dʒuː'dɪʃəl]

adj. of or relating to courts of law or judges 司法的，审判的

例 the **judicial** system

invoke [ɪn'vəʊk]

❶ *vt*. to refer to (something) in support of your ideas 援引，求助于

例 She **invoked** history to prove her point.

❷ *vt*. to mention (someone or something) in an attempt to make people feel a certain way or have a certain idea in their mind 唤起

例 He **invoked** the memory of his predecessor.

supersede [ˌsjuːpə'siːd]

vt. to take the place of (someone or something that is old, no longer useful, etc.) 取代

例 Hand tools are relics of the past that have now been **superseded** by the machine.

expedient [ɪks'piːdɪənt]

❶ *adj*. providing an easy and quick way to solve a problem or do something, even though it may not be morally right 权宜的，便利的

例 They found it **expedient** to negotiate with the terrorists.

❷ *n*. an easy and quick way to solve a problem or do something: an expedient solution 权宜之计，应急手段

例 The government chose short-term/temporary **expedients** instead of a real economic policy.

greedy ['griːdɪ]

adj. having or showing a selfish desire to have more of something（such as money or food）贪婪的

例 He blames all his problems on **greedy** lawyers.

单词助记【同义词】avaricious，acquisitive，covetous

adore [əˈdɔː(r)]

vt. to love or admire（someone）very much 爱慕

例 He's a good doctor. All his patients **adore** him.

单词助记 注意与"adorn"区分开，adorn 意为"装饰"。

realm [relm]

❶ *n*. a country that is ruled by a king or queen 王国

例 Defence of the **realm** is crucial.

❷ *n*. an area of activity, interest, or knowledge 领域

例 Students' interests are mostly limited to the academic **realm**.

crew [kruː]

❶ *n*. the people who work on a ship except the officers and captain 全体船员

例 The surviving **crew** members were ferried ashore.

❷ *n*. a group of people who do a specified kind of work together 工作人员

例 A construction **crew** will begin work on the house next week.

copious [ˈkəʊpɪəs]

adj. very large in amount or number 丰富的，大量的

例 The storm produced a **copious** amount of rain.

单词助记【同义词】abundant，plentiful，ample，profuse，copious

clog [klɒg]

❶ *vt*./*vi*. to slowly form a block in（something，such as a pipe or street）so that things cannot move through quickly or easily 堵塞

例 The sink was **clogged** with dirt and grease.

❷ *n*. a shoe with a thick wooden sole. 木屐

例 a pair of **clogs**

void [vɔɪd]

❶ *adj*. not containing anything：empty 空的

例 a **void** space

❷ *n*. a large empty space 空白，空虚

例 After she left，there was a **void** in my life.

stamina [ˈstæmɪnə]

n. great physical or mental strength that allows you to continue doing something for a long time 毅力

例 You have to have a lot of **stamina** to be a top-class dancer.

relentless [rɪˈlentləs]

adj. oppressively constant；incessant 持续的，不懈的

例 The hunter was **relentless** in pursuit of his prey.

单词助记【同义词】persistent，continuing，constant，continual，continuous，nonstop

例 The sun is beating down **relentlessly**.

单词助记【同义词】harsh，grim，cruel，severe，strict，remorseless，relentless，ruthless

precedent [ˈpresɪdənt]

n. a similar action or event that happened at an earlier time 先例，前例

例 There are no **precedents** for these events.

hail [heɪl]

❶ *n.* pellets of frozen rain that fall in showers from cumulonimbus clouds 冰雹

例 Many cars were damaged by **hail** during the storm.

❷ *v.* acclaim enthusiastically as being a specified thing 赞美

例 The new drug has been widely **hailed** as a great breakthrough.

【同义词】eulogize，compliment，lionize，exalt，admire，hail

detached [dɪˈtætʃt]

adj. not emotional：not influenced by emotions or personal interest 超然的，不带感情的，客观的

例 The article takes a **detached** view of the issue.

List 11

prevail [prɪˈveɪl]

❶ *v.* prove more powerful than opposing forces 战胜

例 Our soccer team **prevailed** despite the bad weather.

❷ *v.* be widespread in a particular area at a particular time 流行

例 The house was built in the style that **prevailed** in the 1980s.

单词助记【同义词】triumph

hazard [ˈhæzəd]

n. a source of danger 危险

例 Young people should be educated about the **hazards** of excessive drinking.

【同义词】menace，peril，danger，risk

solicit [səˈlɪsɪt]

vt./vi. to ask for（something, such as money or help）from people，companies，etc. 请求给予

例 The center is **soliciting** donations to help victims of the earthquake.

covert [ˈkʌvət]

adj. made，shown，or done in a way that is not easily seen or noticed：secret or hidden 秘密的,隐秘的

例 He has taken part in a number of **covert** military operations.

【反义词】overt

sigh [saɪ]

vi. to take in and let out a long, loud breath in a way that shows you are bored，disappointed，relieved，etc. 叹气

例 He **sighed** with/in relief when he saw that he passed the test.

blemish [ˈblemɪʃ]

❶ *n.* a mark that makes something imperfect or less beautiful：an unwanted mark on the surface of something 瑕疵

例 The table had a few scratches and minor **blemishes**.

❷ *n.* a fact or event that causes people to respect someone or something less 小缺点

例 The book fails to mention any of the organization's many **blemishes**.

acclaim [əˈkleɪm]

adj. to praise（someone or something）in a very strong and enthusiastic way 称赞，

赞扬

例 Her performance was **acclaimed** by the critics.

单词助记 【同义词】eulogize，compliment，lionize，exalt，admire，hail

mundane [ˌmʌnˈdeɪn]

❶ *adj.* relating to ordinary life on earth rather than to spiritual things 世俗的，非宗教的

例 prayer and meditation helped her put her **mundane** worries aside

❷ *adj.* dull and ordinary 平凡的，单调的

例 They lead a pretty **mundane** life.

zenith [ˈzenɪθ]

n. the strongest or most successful period of time 天顶，顶峰，鼎盛时期

例 That was the **zenith** of her career.

单词助记 【同义词】acme，peak，pinnacle，apex，apogee，crown

单词助记
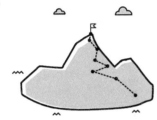

milestone [ˈmaɪlstəʊn]

n. an important point in the progress or development of something：a very important event or advance 里程碑

例 The birth of their first child was a **milestone** in their marriage.

hasten [ˈheɪsn]

vt. to cause (something) to happen more quickly 加速

例 A factory was built，**hastening** the town's growth.

stalk [stɔːk]

❶ *n.* a thick or tall stem of a plant (植物的)茎，杆

例 A single pale blue flower grows up from each joint on a long **stalk**.

❷ *vt.* to follow (an animal or person that you are hunting or trying to capture) by moving slowly and quietly 悄悄跟踪

例 The lions **stalked** the herd.

strip [strɪp]

❶ *n.* a long，narrow piece of something 条，条状地带

例 The simplest rag-rugs are made with **strips** of plaited fabric.

❷ *vt.* to remove an outer covering or surface from something 剥落

例 The prisoners were **stripped** naked.

engulf [ɪnˈgʌlf]

vt. to flow over and cover (someone or something) 吞没

例 Flames **engulfed** the building.

vivid [ˈvɪvɪd]

❶ *adj.* of a picture，memory，etc.：seeming like real life because it is very clear，bright，or detailed (图画、记忆)栩栩如生的

例 The book includes many **vivid** illustrations.

❷ *adj*. very bright in color 鲜艳的

例 The fabric was dyed a **vivid** red.

posterity [pɒˈsterətɪ]

n. people in the future 后代，后世

例 **Posterity** will remember her as a woman of courage and integrity.

fuse [fjuːz]

❶ *vt*./*vi*. to join or become joined because of heat or a chemical reaction 熔化，熔合

例 Particles are **fused** to form a new compound.

❷ both *vt*./*vi*. to join or combine (different things) together 融合

例 His compositions **fuse** jazz and rhythm and blues elements.

deprive [dɪˈpraɪv]

vt. to take something away from someone or something：to not allow (someone or something) to have or keep (something) 剥夺

例 They're **depriving** him of a chance to succeed.

stride [straɪd]

❶ *vt*. to walk with very long steps 大步走

例 She **strode** across the room towards me.

❷ *n*. a long step 大步

例 She crossed the room in only a few **strides**.

oscillate [ˈɒsɪleɪt]

vi. to move in one direction and then back again many times 浮动，波动

例 Stock prices have continued to **oscillate**.

单词助记 【同义词】fluctuate

单词助记

socket [ˈsɒkɪt]

❶ *n*. an electrical device receiving a plug or light bulb to make a connection 插口，插座

例 She plugged the lamp into the **socket**.

❷ *n*. You can refer to any hollow part or opening in a structure which another part fits into as a socket 承槽；窝

weird [wɪəd]

adj. unusual or strange 奇怪的

例 My little brother acts **weird** sometimes.

potent [ˈpəʊtənt]

❶ *adj*. very effective or strong 强效的

例 The drug is extremely **potent**，but causes unpleasant side effects.

❷ *adj*. having a very powerful effect or influence on someone 强有力的；有说服力的

例 He had **potent** arguments for going to war.

calculating [ˈkælkjʊleɪtɪŋ]

adj. carefully thinking about and planning actions for selfish or improper reasons 精明的，会算计的

例 Northbridge is a cool，**calculating** and clever criminal who could strike again.

【同义词】cunning，wily，crafty，sly

exude [ɪgˈzjuːd]

vt./ *vi*. If something **exudes** a liquid or smell or if a liquid or smell exudes from it，the liquid or smell comes out of it slowly and steadily. 渗出，散发出

例 The flowers **exuded** a sweet fragrance.

neglect [nɪˈglekt]

vt. to fail to do (something) or pay no attention to 忽视，忽略不计

例 We often **neglect** to make proper use of our bodies.

inert [ɪˈnɜːt]

❶ *adj*. unable to move 不动的

例 He covered the **inert** body with a blanket.

❷ *adj*. moving or acting very slowly 迟缓的，无生气的

例 How does he propose to stimulate the **inert** economy and create jobs?

prolong [prəˈlɒŋ]

vt. to make (something) last or continue for a longer time 延长

例 High interest rates were **prolonging** the recession.

tactile [ˈtæktaɪl]

adj. of or connected with the sense of touch 触觉的

例 Heat，cold，**tactile** and other sensations contribute to flavour.

shrink [ʃrɪŋk]

vt. / vi. to become or cause（something）become smaller in amount，size，or value（使）缩小

例 Meat **shrinks** as it cooks.

integrity ［ɪnˈtegrɪtɪ］

❶ *n.* the quality of being honest and having strong moral principles 正直

例 He has a reputation for **integrity** in his business dealings.

❷ *n.* the state of being whole and undivided 完整

例 Without music，the film loses its **integrity**.

camouflage ［ˈkæmʊflɑːʒ］

❶ *n.* something（such as color or shape）that protects an animal from attack by making the animal difficult to see in the area around it 伪装手段，保护色

例 The rabbit's white fur acts as a **camouflage** in the snow.

❷ *vt.* to hide（something）by covering it up or making it harder to see 伪装，掩饰

例 The entrance was **camouflaged** with bricks and dirt.

immerse ［ɪˈmɜːs］

vt. to put（something）in a liquid so that all parts are completely covered 把……浸入

例 The electrodes are **immersed** in liquid.

legible ［ˈledʒəbl］

adj.（of handwriting or print）clear enough to read 清晰可读的

例 My handwriting isn't very **legible**.

impose ［ɪmˈpəʊz］

❶ *vt.* to cause（something，such as a tax，fine，rule，or punishment）to affect someone or something by using your authority 强制实行

例 The judge **imposed** a life sentence.

❷ *vt.* to force someone to accept（something or yourself）把（观点、信仰等）强加于

例 He **imposes** his personal beliefs on his employees.

❸ *vt.* to establish or create（something unwanted）in a forceful or harmful way 使承受（令人不快之事物）

例 The filming **imposed** an additional strain on her.

scrupulous ［ˈskruːpjʊləs］

adj. very careful about doing something correctly 谨小慎微的

例 The work requires **scrupulous** attention to detail.

illuminate ［ɪˈljuːmɪneɪt］

vt. to supply（something）with light：to shine light on（something）照亮

例 Candles **illuminate** the church.

notorious ［nəʊˈtɔːrɪəs］

adj. well-known or famous especially for something bad 臭名昭著的

例 The coach is **notorious** for his violent outbursts.

brittle ［ˈbrɪtl］

❶ *adj.* easily broken or cracked 易碎的

例 **brittle** glass

单词助记【同义词】breakable，fragile，delicate

❷ *adj.* not strong：easily damaged 脆弱的

例 The countries formed a **brittle** alliance.

astonish [əsˈtɒnɪʃ]

vt. to cause a feeling of great wonder or surprise in（someone）使惊讶

例 The garden **astonishes** anyone who sees it.

edible [ˈedɪbl]

adj. suitable or safe to eat 可食用的

例 All of the decorations on the gingerbread house were **edible**.

refractory [rɪˈfræktərɪ]

❶ *adj.* difficult to control or deal with 难驾驭的

例 a **refractory** child

单词助记【同义词】obstinate, stubborn, mulish, obdurate, headstrong, self-willed

❷ *adj.* capable of enduring high temperature（矿物或金属）耐高温的

例 **refractory** material

toil [tɔɪl]

❶ *n.* work that is difficult and unpleasant and that lasts for a long time: long, hard labor 苦活

例 days of **toil** and sweat

❷ *vi.* to work very hard for a long time 辛苦工作

例 Workers **toiled** long hours.

lease [liːs]

❶ *vt.* to use (something) for a period of time in return for payment 租进

例 I have **leased** this house for the last four years.

❷ *vt.* to allow someone to use (something) for a period of time in return for payment 租出

例 We **leased** the house to a young married couple.

quiver [ˈkwɪvə(r)]

❶ *v.* tremble or shake with a slight rapid motion 颤抖

例 He was **quivering** with excitement.

❷ *n.* an archer's portable case for holding arrows 箭筒

例 A **quiver** is a container for carrying arrows in.

exploit [ɪksˈplɔɪt]

❶ *n.* a bold or daring feat 英雄事迹

例 He enjoys talking about his youthful **exploits**.

单词助记【同义词】feat, adventure, achievement, accomplishment

❷ *adj.* make full use of and derive benefit from (a resource) 充分利用；开发

例 He has never fully **exploited** his talents.

scorching [ˈskɔːtʃɪŋ]

adj. very hot 酷热的

例 The day was **scorching** hot.

单词助记【同义词】blazing, flaming, blistering, searing, sweltering, torrid

stealthy [ˈstelθɪ]

adj. quiet and secret in order to avoid being noticed 鬼鬼祟祟的

例 I would creep in and with **stealthy** footsteps explore the second-floor.

【同义词】furtive，secretive，secret，surreptitious，sneaking，sly

拓展 *adv*. stealthily [ˈstelθəlɪ]

例 She moved **stealthily** from room to room.

单词助记

eccentric [ɪkˈsentrɪk]

❶ *adj*. tending to act in strange or unusual ways 古怪的

例 He was a kind but **eccentric** man.

❷ *adj*. not following a perfectly circular path（天体轨道）不正圆的，椭圆的

例 an **eccentric** orbit

empire [ˈempaɪə(r)]

n. a group of countries or regions that are controlled by one ruler or one government 帝国

例 the Roman **Empire**

pigment [ˈpɪgmənt]

n. a substance that gives color to something else 颜料；色素

例 Red **pigment** is mixed into the ink.

odor [ˈəʊdər]

n. a particular smell 气味

例 The cheese has a strong **odor**.

单词助记 【同义词】scent

stunt [stʌnt]

vt. to stop (someone or something) from growing or developing 阻碍

例 Poor soil can **stunt** a plant's growth.

单词助记 【同义词】inhibit，impede，hamper，hinder，restrict，retard

fiction [ˈfɪkʃən]

❶ *n*. written stories about people and events that are not real：literature that tells stories which are imagined by the writer 小说

例 She mainly writes **fiction**.

❷ *n*. something that is not true 虚构

例 His explanation of what happened was pure **fiction**.

astute [əˈstjuːt]

adj. having or showing an ability to notice and understand things clearly：mentally sharp or clever 机敏的，敏锐的

例 She made some **astute** observations about the movie industry.

scarlet [ˈskɑːlət]

adj. bright red 猩红的，鲜红的

例 a bird with **scarlet** feathers

cessation [seˈseɪʃən]

n. a stopping of some action：a pause or stop 停止

例 With news of the treaty came a **cessation** of hostilities.

boulder [ˈbəʊldə(r)]

n. a very large stone or rounded piece of rock 大卵石，巨砾

例 It is thought that the train hit a **boulder** that had fallen down a cliff on to the track.

maneuver [məˈnuːvə(r)]

❶ *vt*./*vi*. to move (something or someone) in a careful and usually skillful way (熟练地) 移动，演习

例 She **maneuvered** her car into the tiny garage.

❷ *n*. a clever or skillful action or movement 移动；策略，花招

例 Through a series of legal **maneuvers**，the defense lawyer kept her client out of jail.

provoke [prəˈvəʊk]

vt. to cause the occurrence of (a feeling or action)：to make (something) happen 引起

例 The results of the election have **provoked** a lot of discussion.

List 14

maximum ['mæksɪməm]

n. the highest number or amount that is possible or allowed 最大值，最大量

例 It helps the leaves expose an **maximum** of surface

devotee [ˌdevə'tiː]

n. a person who is very interested in and enthusiastic about someone or something 爱好者，崇拜者

例 Mr Carpenter is obviously a **devotee** of Britten's music.

safari [sə'fɑːrɪ]

n. an expedition to observe or hunt animals in their natural habitat 游猎

例 He went on a **safari** in Africa last year.

单词助记【同义词】expedition

dissipate ['dɪsɪpeɪt]

❶ *vt*. to cause (something) to spread out and disappear 驱散

例 The morning sun **dissipated** the fog.

❷ *vi*. to separate into parts and disappear or go away 消散，散去

例 By noon the crowd had **dissipated**.

amnesia [æm'niːzjə]

n. a condition in which a person is unable to remember things because of brain injury, shock, or illness 记忆缺失，失忆症

例 People suffering from **amnesia** don't forget their general knowledge of objects.

sturdy ['stɜːdɪ]

❶ *adj*. strongly made 结实的

例 The camera was mounted on a **sturdy** tripod.

❷ *adj*. strong and healthy 强壮的

例 She was a short, **sturdy** woman in her early sixties.

单词助记【反义词】frail, flimsy

单词助记

negotiate [nɪ'ɡəʊʃɪeɪt]

❶ *vt./vi*. to discuss something formally in order to make an agreement 谈判

例 Teachers are **negotiating** for higher salaries.

❷ *vt*. to get over, through, or around (something) successfully 成功越过

例 The driver carefully **negotiated** the winding road.

ubiquitous [juː'bɪkwɪtəs]

adj. being present everywhere at once 无所不在的

例 Sugar is **ubiquitous** in the diet.

plausible [ˈplɔːzəbl]

adj. possibly true：believable or realistic 似乎合理的

例 It's a **plausible** explanation for the demise of that prehistoric species.

单词助记【同义词】credible，feasible，tenable，possible，conceivable

pragmatic [præɡˈmætɪk]

adj. dealing with the problems that exist in a specific situation in a reasonable and logical way instead of depending on ideas and theories 务实的,实际的

例 His **pragmatic** view of public education comes from years of working in city schools.

单词助记【同义词】practical

strife [straɪf]

n. very angry or violent disagreement between two or more people or groups 冲突

例 Money is a major cause of **strife** in many marriages.

单词助记

terminate [ˈtɜːmɪneɪt]

vi. When you terminate something or when it terminates，it ends completely. 终止,结束

例 The rail line **terminates** in Boston.

detrimental [ˌdetrɪˈmentəl]

adj. causing damage or injury 有害的

例 The **detrimental** effects of overeating are well known.

单词助记【同义词】injurious，hurtful，inimical，deleterious，destructive，ruinous

convict [kənˈvɪkt]

❶ *vt*./ *vi*. to prove that someone is guilty of a crime in a court of law 证明……有罪

例 He was **convicted** in federal court. / There is sufficient evidence to **convict**.

❷ *n*. a person who has been found guilty of a crime and sent to prison 囚犯

例 an escaped **convict**

integral [ˈɪntɪɡrəl]

adj. very important and necessary 构成整体所必需的,必不可少的

例 Industry is an **integral** part of modern society.

momentous [məʊˈmentəs]

adj. very important：having great or lasting importance 重大的

例 My college graduation was a **momentous** day in my life.

单词助记【同义词】important，significant，historic，portentous，critical，crucial

straightforward [streɪtˈfɔːwəd]

adj. honest and open 坦率的

例 He was very **straightforward** with us.

单词助记 【同义词】 honest，frank，candid，forthright，plain-speaking，direct

ingenious [ɪnˈdʒiːnjəs]

adj. very smart or clever：having or showing ingenuity 巧妙的，有独创性的

例 The book has an **ingenious** plot.

单词助记 【同义词】 inventive，creative，imaginative，innovative，pioneering，resourceful

单词助记 区分："ingenuous"：天真的

optimistic [ˌɒptɪˈmɪstɪk]

adj. having or showing hope for the future：expecting good things to happen 乐观的

例 People are increasingly **optimistic** that the problem can be corrected.

单词助记 【反义词】 pessimistic

creep [kriːp]

❶ vi. to move slowly with the body close to the ground 爬行，匍匐

例 A spider was **creeping** along the bathroom floor.

❷ vi. to move slowly and quietly especially in order to not be noticed 缓慢移动，蠕动

例 She **crept** into bed next to her sleeping husband.

List 15

praise [preɪz]

vt. to say or write good things about (someone or something): to express approval of (someone or something) 称赞

例 The American president **praised** Turkey for its courage.

单词助记【同义词】eulogize, compliment, lionize, exalt, admire, hail

burgeon ['bɜːdʒən]

vi. to grow or develop quickly 迅速成长,迅速发展

例 The market for collectibles has **burgeoned** in recent years.

trial ['traɪəl]

n. a test of the quality, value, or usefulness of something 试验

例 Early **trials** have shown that the treatment has some serious side effects.

surmise [sə'maɪz]

❶ *vt.* to form an opinion about something without definitely knowing the truth 猜测

例 We can only **surmise** what happened.

❷ *n.* 猜测

例 This is no more than a **surmise**.

singular ['sɪŋɡjʊlə(r)]

❶ *adj.* better or greater than what is usual or normal 突出的,非凡的

例 Her father noticed her **singular** talent for music.

❷ *adj.* strange or odd 奇怪的,奇特的

例 He had a **singular** appearance.

textile ['tekstaɪl]

n. fabric, cloth especially: a fabric that is woven or knit 纺织品

例 They import fine silk **textiles** from China.

expedition [ˌekspɪ'dɪʃən]

❶ *n.* a journey especially by a group of people for a specific purpose (such as to explore a distant place or to do research) 远征,探险,考察

例 a scientific **expedition** to Antarctica

单词助记【同义词】safari

❷ *n.* a group of people who travel together to a distant place: a group of people who go on an expedition 远征队,探险队,考察队

例 The **expedition** discovered an ancient burial site.

单词助记

contaminate [kən'tæmɪneɪt]

vt. to make (something) dangerous, dirty, or impure by adding something harmful or undesirable to it 污染

例 The water was **contaminated** with chemicals.

interval ['ɪntəvəl]

n. a period of time between events; pause（时间上的）间隔

例 There might be long **intervals** during/in which nothing happens.

intersect [ˌɪntə'sekt]

vt./vi. to divide (something) by passing through or across it; cross 相交

例 A dry stream bed **intersects** the trail in several places.

viable ['vaɪəbl]

❶ *adj.* capable of living or of developing into a living thing 能存活的

例 **viable** seeds/eggs

❷ *adj.* capable of being done or used; workable 可行的

例 He could not suggest a **viable** alternative/option.

utter ['ʌtə(r)]

❶ *vt.* to make (a particular sound) or say (something) 发出（声音）；说

例 She **uttered** a cry of pleasure.

❷ *adj.* complete and total 完全的，彻底的

例 The children displayed an **utter** lack of interest in the performance.

flattery ['flætərɪ]

n. praise that is not sincere 奉承

例 He is ambitious and susceptible to **flattery**.

defend [dɪ'fend]

❶ *vt.* to fight in order to keep (someone or something) safe; to not allow a person or thing to hurt, damage, or destroy (someone or something) 保护

例 They have every right to **defend** themselves from those who would hurt them.

❷ *vt.* to speak or write in support of (someone or something that is being challenged or criticized) 为……辩护

例 He **defended** his claim successfully.

tenet ['tiːnet]

n. a belief or idea that is very important to a group 信条，宗旨

例 Non-violence and patience are the central **tenets** of their faith.

单词助记【同义词】principle, belief, doctrine, precept, creed, credo

auditorium [ˌɔːdɪ'tɔːrɪəm]

n. a large room or building where people gather to watch a performance, hear a speech, etc. 礼堂，会堂

例 a high school **auditorium**

tackle ['tækl]

vt. to deal with (something difficult) 处理，应付

例 We found new ways to **tackle** the problem.

polish ['pɒlɪʃ]

vt. to make (something) smooth and shiny by rubbing it 抛光，磨光，擦亮

例 He **polished** his shoes.

单词助记【同义词】burnish

freight [freɪt]

　　n. goods that are carried by ships，trains，trucks，or airplanes 货物

　例 trains that carry both passengers and **freight**

　单词助记【同义词】cargo

precious [ˌpreʃəs]

　❶ *adj*. rare and worth a lot of money（物品、材料等）珍贵的

　例 Water is becoming an increasingly **precious** resource.

　❷ *adj*. very valuable or important：too valuable or important to be wasted or used carelessly 珍贵的

　例 We can save **precious** time by taking this shortcut.

List 16

plug [plʌg]

❶ *n.* a part at the end of an electric cord that has two or three metal pins that connect the cord to a source of electricity 插头

例 The only way to turn the machine off is to pull the **plug**.

❷ *vt.* to fill or cover (a hole，space，etc.) with something 堵上,塞上

例 We were able to **plug** (up) the hole with cement.

单词助记 socket：插座

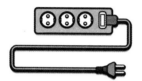

fragile [ˈfrædʒaɪl]

adj. easily broken or damaged 易碎的,脆弱的

例 He leaned back in his **fragile** chair.

tribute [ˈtrɪbjuːt]

n. something that you say，give，or do to show respect or affection for someone 敬意,称赞

例 The concert was a **tribute** to the musician.

heir [eə(r)]

n. a person who has the legal right to receive the property of someone who dies 继承人

例 She is the sole **heir** to her family's fortune.

diligent [ˈdɪlɪdʒənt]

adj. working hard in a careful and thorough way 勤奋的

例 Many hours of **diligent** research were required.

单词助记

ponder [ˈpɒndə(r)]

both *vt./vi.* to think about or consider (something) carefully 仔细思考

例 The team **pondered** their chances of success.

单词助记 【同义词】 contemplate，meditate on，muse on，ruminate on

submit [səbˈmɪt]

❶ *vt*. to give（a document, proposal, piece of writing, etc.）to someone so that it can be considered or approved 提交

例 **Submit** your application no later than January 31st.

❷ *vi*. to stop trying to fight or resist something：to agree to do or accept something that you have been resisting or opposing 屈从

例 He refused to **submit** to their demands.

transitory [ˈtrænsɪtərɪ]

adj. lasting only for a short time：temporary 短暂的

例 Most teenage romances are **transitory**.

单词助记【同义词】transient, temporary, ephemeral, momentary, fleeting

salutary [ˈsæljʊtərɪ]

adj. having a good or helpful result especially after something unpleasant has happened 有利的, 有益的

例 The accident should be a **salutary** lesson to be more careful.

extraneous [eksˈtreɪnɪəs]

❶ *adj*. existing on or coming from the outside 外来的；外部的

例 **extraneous** light

❷ *adj*. not forming a necessary part of something 不重要的, 非必要的

例 She speeded up the process by eliminating all **extraneous** steps.

divest [daɪˈvest]

vt. to take（something）away from（someone or something else）剥夺

例 He was **divested** of his power.

cripple [ˈkrɪpl]

❶ *vt*. to cause（a person or animal）to be unable to move or walk normally 使跛, 使伤残

例 Thousands of people have been **crippled** by the disease.

❷ *vt*. to make（something）unable to work normally：to cause great damage to（something）严重损害

例 The disease **cripples** the body's immune system.

yearn [jɜːn]

vi. to feel a strong desire or wish for something or to do something 渴望

例 I **yearned** to be a movie actor.

neutral [ˈnjuːtrəl]

❶ *adj*. not supporting either side of an argument, fight, war, etc. 中立的

例 He remained **neutral** while his brothers argued.

❷ *adj*. not having an electrical charge 中性的, 不带电的

例 a **neutral** molecule

saturate [ˈsætʃəreɪt]

❶ *vt*. to make（something）very wet 使湿透

例 That last rain really **saturated** the ground.

❷ *vt*. to fill（something）completely with something 使充满

例 The room was **saturated** with perfume.

complement [ˈkɒmplɪmənt]

❶ *vt*. to complete something else or make it better 补充

例 There will be a written examination to **complement** the practical test.

❷ *n*. [ˈkɑːmpləmənt] something that completes something else or makes it better 补充物

例 The scarf is a perfect **complement** to her outfit.

retract [rɪˈtrækt]

❶ *vt.*/*vi*. to pull（something）back into something larger that usually covers it （使）缩回

例 The pilot **retracted** the plane's landing gear.

❷ *vt*. to say that something you said or wrote is not true or correct 收回，撤销

例 She was forced to **retract** her statement.

trivial [ˈtrɪvɪəl]

adj. not important 不重要的，微不足道的

例 Compared to her problems，our problems seem **trivial**.

subsidiary [səbˈsɪdɪərɪ]

adj. not as important as something else 次要的

例 The economics ministry has increasingly played a **subsidiary** role to the finance ministry.

单词助记【同义词】subordinate，secondary，ancillary，auxiliary

catastrophe [kəˈtæstrəfɪ]

n. a terrible disaster 灾难

例 The oil spill was an environmental **catastrophe**.

ornament [ˈɔːnəmənt]

❶ *n*. a way to make something look more attractive and less plain 装饰

例 The columns are there purely as **ornament**—they have no structural function.

单词助记【同义词】decoration，adornment，embellishment，ornamentation，trimming，accessories

❷ *vt*. to make (something) more attractive by adding small objects to it 装饰

例 A satin bow was used for **ornament**.

cushion [ˈkʊʃən]

❶ *n*. soft object or part that is used to make something (such as a seat) more comfortable or to protect a surface from damage: a soft pillow，pad，etc.垫子，坐垫

例 There is a **cushion** under the rug to protect the floor.

❷ *vt*. to make (something，such as a fall or collision) less severe or painful: to soften or reduce the bad effect of (something) 缓冲，缓解

例 The helmet **cushions** the head against violent collisions.

underpin [ˌʌndəˈpɪn]

vt. to strengthen or support (something) from below 支撑，加固

例 a report **underpinned** by ample research

institute [ˈɪnstɪtjuːt]

❶ *n*. an organization created for a particular purpose (such as research or education) 协会，研究所，学院

例 They founded an **institute** for research into the causes of mental illness.

❷ *vt*. to begin or create (something，such as a new law，rule，or system) 制定，创立

例 The organization was **instituted** in 1910.

meager [ˈmiːgə(r)]

adj. very small or too small in amount 很少的，不足的

例 He took another job to supplement **meager** family income.

consensus [kənˈsensəs]

n. a general agreement about something: an idea or opinion that is shared by all the people in a group 共识

例 Scientists have not reached a **consensus** on the cause of the disease.

单词助记【同义词】agreement，concurrence，accord，unity，unanimity

procure [prəˈkjʊə(r)]

vt. to get (something) by some action or effort (设法)获得

例 She managed to **procure** a ticket to the concert.

wreck [rek]

❶ *n*. a vehicle，airplane，etc.，that has been badly damaged or destroyed 残骸

例 Firefighters pulled him from the car **wreck**.

❷ *vt.* to damage (something) so badly that it cannot be repaired 破坏，毁坏

例 Many houses were **wrecked** by the hurricane.

fraction [ˈfrækʃən]

❶ *n.* a part or amount of something 一部分

例 The new program will provide similar benefits at a **fraction** of the cost of the old one.

❷ *n.* a number which indicates that one number is being divided by another 分数

例 The students had a grasp of decimals，percentages and **fractions**.

lubricate [ˈluːbrɪkeɪt]

vt. to make (something) smooth or slippery：to apply a lubricant to (something, such as a machine or a part of a machine) 使润滑

例 **lubricate** a car engine

lag [læg]

❶ *n.* a space of time between two events 间隔；延迟

例 There's a time **lag** between infection with HIV and developing AIDS.

❷ *vi.* to fall behind in movement，progress，development，etc. 落后

例 His company has **lagged** behind its competitors in developing new products.

momentum [məʊˈmentəm]

n. the strength or force that allows something to continue or to grow stronger or faster as time passes 势头

例 The campaign slowly gathered some **momentum**.

culminate [ˈkʌlmɪneɪt]

❶ *vi.* to reach the end or the final result of something 告终，达到高潮

例 Their efforts have **culminated** in the discovery of a new cancer treatment.

❷ *vt.* to be the end or final result of (something) 使告终，使达到高潮

例 Their marriage **culminated** their long friendship.

temporary [ˈtempərərɪ]

adj. continuing for a limited amount of time：not permanent 暂时的

例 The drug will give you **temporary** relief from the pain.

单词助记【同义词】brief，short-lived，momentary，fleeting

infusion [ɪnˈfjuːʒən]

n. the addition of something (such as money) that is needed or helpful 注入，灌输

例 The company has received an **infusion** of cash/capital.

stature [ˈstætʃə(r)]

❶ *n.* a person's natural height 身高

例 She was a little short in **stature**.

❷ *n.* importance or reputation gained by ability or achievement 名望

例 The university has grown/gained in **stature** during her time as president.

adjust [əˈdʒʌst]

❶ *vt.* to change (something) in a minor way so that it works better 调整，调节

例 I **adjusted** the volume on the radio.

❷ *vi.* to change in order to work or do better in a new situation 适应（环境等）

例 Our eyes gradually **adjusted** to the darkness of the cave.

render [ˈrendə(r)]

❶ *vt.* to cause (someone or something) to be in a specified condition 使成为，使变

得

例 The sight of her **rendered** him speechless.

❷ *vt*. to give（something）to someone 提供，给予

例 He witnessed a car accident and stopped to **render** assistance.

❸ *vt*. to present or perform（something）艺术上呈现（如演奏、表演、描绘等）

例 He **rendered** the landscapes of the Netherlands with great skill and artistry.

discipline [ˈdɪsɪplɪn]

❶ *n*. a field of study：a subject that is taught 学科

例 She has received training in several academic **disciplines**.

❷ *n*. control that is gained by requiring that rules or orders be obeyed and punishing bad behavior 纪律

例 The teacher has a hard time maintaining **discipline** in the classroom.

❸ *n*. punishment for bad behavior 处罚

例 Some parents feel that the school's principal has been too harsh in meting out **discipline**.

❹ *vt*. to punish（someone）as a way of making sure that rules or orders are obeyed 处罚

例 He seems unwilling or unable to **discipline** his children.

sedentary [ˈsedəntərɪ]

❶ *adj*. doing or involving a lot of sitting：not doing or involving much physical activity 久坐的，不（或极少）活动的

例 Editing dictionary is a **sedentary** job.

❷ *adj*. staying or living in one place instead of moving to different places 定居的

例 **sedentary** tribes/people

【反义词】nomadic

单词助记

List 18

weave [wiːv]

vt. to make something (such as cloth) by crossing threads or other long pieces of material over and under each other 织

例 He **wove** a basket from the branches.

allocate [ˈæləʊkeɪt]

vt. to divide and give out (something) for a special reason or to particular people, companies, etc. 分配,划拨

例 We need to determine the best way to **allocate** our resources.

单词助记 【同义词】allot, assign, distribute, apportion, dispense

countervail [ˌkaʊntəˈveɪl]

❶ *vt.* to act against with equal power, force, or effect; counteract 抵消

例 **countervailing** influences

❷ *vt.* to furnish an equivalent of or a compensation for 补偿

例 The policy has many faults and many **countervailing** virtues.

pronounced [prəˈnaʊnst]

adj. very noticeable 明显的,显著的

例 There has been a **pronounced** improvement in her condition.

biography [baɪˈɒgrəfɪ]

n. the story of a real person's life written by someone other than that person 传记

例 a new **biography** of Abraham Lincoln

overt [ˈəʊvɜːt]

adj. easily seen; not secret or hidden; obvious 公开的,明显的

例 Although there is no **overt** hostility, black and white students do not mix much.

【反义词】covert

underscore [ˌʌndəˈskɔː(r)]

❶ *vt.* to draw a line under (something); underline 在……下面画线

例 She **underscored** the most important points.

❷ *vt.* to emphasize (something) or show the importance of (something) 强调

例 These failures **underscore** the difficulty of what we're attempting to do.

单词助记

merit [ˈmerɪt]

❶ *n.* a good quality or feature that deserves to be praised 优点,价值

例 The study has no scientific **merit**.

❷ *vt*. to deserve（something，such as attention or good treatment）by being important or good 值得，应受到

例 Both ideas **merit** further consideration.

intuitive ［ɪnˈtjuːɪtɪv］

adj. based on or agreeing with what is known or understood without any proof or evidence：known or understood by intuition 直觉的

例 She has an **intuitive** understanding of the business.

单词助记【同义词】instinctive

wagon ［ˈwægən］

n. a vehicle with four wheels that is used for carrying heavy loads or passengers and that is usually pulled by animals（such as horses）四轮马车

例 Pioneers crossed the American Midwest in **wagons**.

tame ［teɪm］

❶ *adj*. not wild：trained to obey people 养驯的，驯服的

例 The deer never became **tame**；they would run away if you approached them.

单词助记【同义词】domesticated，domestic，docile

❷ *vt*. to make（an animal）tame 驯服，驯化

例 It took a while to **tame** the horse.

candid ［ˈkændɪd］

adj. expressing opinions and feelings in an honest and sincere way 坦率的

例 He was quite **candid** about his past.

单词助记【同义词】frank，outspoken，forthright，straightforward

demise ［dɪˈmaɪz］

❶ *n*. an end of life：death 死亡

例 There are several theories about what caused the **demise** of the dinosaurs.

❷ *n*. the end of something that is thought of as being like a death 终止，终结

例 Losing this game will mean the team's **demise**.

descendant ［dɪˈsendənt］

n. a plant or animal that is related to a particular plant or animal that lived long ago 后代，后裔

例 Recent evidence supports the theory that birds are the modern **descendants** of dinosaurs.

单词助记【同义词】successor，heir；offspring，progeny

capital ［ˈkæpɪtəl］

❶ *n*. a city in which the main offices of a government are located：a **capital** city 首都，首府

例 Austin is the **capital** of Texas.

❷ *n*. money，property，etc.，that is used to start or operate a business 资本

例 Does he have the **capital** to start a new business?

synonym ［ˈsɪnənɪm］

n.【同义词】a word that has the same meaning as another word in the same language

例 Can you think of a **synonym** for "original"?

entity ［ˈentɪtɪ］

n. something that exists by itself：something that is separate from other things 实

体，组织，机构

例 One division of the company was broken off as a separate **entity**.

splash [splæʃ]

vi. of a liquid：to move, fall, or hit something in a noisy or messy way 飞溅，溅落，发出溅泼声

例 The hot oil **splashed** out of the pot.

hinder [ˈhɪndə(r)]

vt. to make（something, such as a task or action）slow or difficult 阻碍

例 It's not clear whether the change will help or **hinder** our project.

单词助记【同义词】hamper，obstruct，impede，inhibit，retard，balk

juvenile [ˈdʒuːvənaɪl]

❶ *adj.* relating to or meant for young people 青少年的

例 **Juvenile** crime is increasing at a terrifying rate.

❷ *adj.* not yet fully grown 幼小的，幼年的

例 **juvenile** birds/animals

nominate [ˈnɒmɪneɪt]

vt. to choose（someone or something）as a candidate for receiving an honor or award 提名

例 He was **nominated** for an Academy Award for his role in the film.

substitute [ˈsʌbstɪtjuːt]

❶ *n.* a person or thing that takes the place of someone or something else 替代物

例 Watching the movie is a poor **substitute** for reading the book.

❷ *vt.* to put or use（someone or something）in place of someone or something else 以……代替

例 You can sometimes **substitute** applesauce for vegetable oil in cake recipes.

❸ *vi.* to do the job of someone else or serve the function of something else 代替

例 I found someone to **substitute** for me.

quest [kwest]

n. a long and difficult search for something 搜寻，探求

例 They went on a **quest** for gold.

eminent [ˈemɪnənt]

❶ *adj.* successful，well-known and respected 卓越的，有名望的

例 an **eminent** physician

单词助记【同义词】prominent，preeminent，renowned，illustrious

❷ *adj.* standing out so as to be readily perceived or noted 明显的

例 an **eminent** blemish

单词助记【同义词】conspicuous

escalate [ˈeskəleɪt]

❶ *vt./vi.* to become worse or to make（something）worse or more severe（使）加剧，恶化

例 The conflict has **escalated** into an all-out war.

❷ both *vt./vi.* to become greater or higher or to make（something）greater or higher（使）增长，加强

例 The president promised to **escalate** the government's program to combat the dreaded disease.

拓展 *n.* escalation [ˌeskəˈleɪʃən]

例 "Come on," Will said，setting down his omelet in case there was an **escalation** in hostilities.

epic [ˈepɪk]

n. a long book，poem，movie，etc.，that usually tells a story about exciting events or adventures 史诗

例 Homer's ancient Greek **epic** "*The Odyssey*"

revive [rɪˈvaɪv]

vt./vi. to become or make（someone or something）become strong，healthy，or active again 恢复，复兴

例 The government is trying to **revive** the economy.

slender ['slendə(r)]

adj. thin especially in an attractive or graceful way 修长的，苗条的

例 She has a **slender** figure.

单词助记【同义词】thin

precipitation [prɪˌsɪpə'teɪʃn]

❶ *n*. water that falls to the ground as rain，snow，etc. 降水，降雪

例 The weather forecast calls for some sort of frozen **precipitation** tomorrow—either snow or sleet.

❷ *n*. the process of separating a solid substance from a liquid 沉淀，沉析

例 Minerals are separated from the seawater by **precipitation**.

decimate ['desɪmeɪt]

vt. to destroy a large number of（plants，animals，people，etc.）大批杀死

例 This kind of moth is responsible for **decimating** thousands of trees in our town.

trauma ['trɔːmə]

n. a very difficult or unpleasant experience that causes someone to have mental or emotional problems usually for a long time（精神上的）创伤

例 She never fully recovered from the **traumas** she suffered during her childhood.

converse [kən'vɜːs]

❶ *adj*. opposite or reverse 相反的

例 One must also consider the **converse** case.

❷ *vi*. engage in conversation 交流

例 He fell in beside her and they began to **converse** amicably.

diagnose ['daɪəgnəʊz]

vt. to recognize（a disease，illness，etc.）by examining someone or to recognize a disease，illness，etc.，in（someone）诊断

例 She was **diagnosed** as/with having cancer.

scurry ['skʌrɪ]

vi. to move quickly and with short steps 疾走，急促跑

例 She **scurried** to the office.

单词助记【同义词】hurry，hasten，run，rush，dash，scamper

rational ['ræʃənl]

adj. based on facts or reason and not on emotions or feelings 理性的

例 I'm sure there is a **rational** explanation for his decision.

embody [ɪm'bɒdɪ]

❶ *vt*. to represent（something）in a clear and obvious way：to be a symbol or example of（something）体现，象征

例 He is a leader who **embodies** courage.

❷ *vt*. to include（something）as a part or feature 包含，收录

例 The new car **embodies** many improvements.

pervasive [pə'veɪsɪv]

adj. existing in every part of something：spreading to all parts of something 普遍的，弥漫的

例 television's **pervasive** influence on our culture

static [ˈstætɪk]

adj. showing little or no change，action，or progress 静止的，不变地

例 Culture is not **static**.

单词助记【同义词】stationary，motionless，immobile，unmoving，still

impermeable [ɪmˈpɜːmɪəbl]

❶ *adj.* not allowing something（such as a liquid）to pass through 无法渗透的

例 The canoe is made from an **impermeable** wood.

❷ *adj.* not liable to be affected by pain or distress；insusceptible or imperturbable 不为所动的

例 women who appear **impermeable** to pain.

单词助记【同义词】insusceptible

inevitable [ɪnˈevɪtəbl]

adj. sure to happen 不可避免的，必然发生的

例 Some criticism was **inevitable**. / If the case succeeds，it is **inevitable** that other trials will follow.

upright [ˈʌpraɪt]

❶ *n.* a board or pole placed in a vertical position to support something 立柱

例 The **uprights** of the structure were embedded in concrete.

❷ *adj.* positioned to be straight up; vertical 笔直的

例 Put your seat back in the **upright** position.

❸ *adj.* always behaving in an honest way; having high moral standards 正直的

例 a very **upright**, trustworthy man

fortify [ˈfɔːtɪfaɪ]

vt. to strengthen (a place) by building military defenses (such as walls, trenches, etc.) （常通过筑墙、挖沟等）巩固（某地）

例 He remains barricaded inside his heavily-**fortified** mansion.

genuine [ˈdʒenjʊɪn]

❶ *adj.* actual, real, or true; not false or fake 真正的,非伪造的

例 The signature is **genuine**.

❷ *adj.* sincere and honest 真诚的

例 She showed a **genuine** interest in our work.

❸ *adv.* genuinely

例 He was **genuinely** surprised.

eradicate [ɪˈrædɪkeɪt]

vt. to remove (something) completely; to eliminate or destroy (something harmful) 根除

例 His ambition is to **eradicate** poverty in his community.

restrain [rɪˈstreɪn]

vt. to keep (something) under control 抑制,限制

例 The manufacturer took measures to **restrain** costs.

penchant [ˈpentʃənt]

n. a strong liking for something or a strong tendency to behave in a certain way 强烈倾向,嗜好

例 He has a **penchant** for asking stupid questions.

单词助记【同义词】preference, inclination, bent, bias, proclivity, predilection

anticipate [ænˈtɪsɪpeɪt]

vt. to think of (something that will or might happen in the future) 预料,预期

例 The cost turned out to be higher than **anticipated**.

circumvent [ˌsɜːkəmˈvent]

❶ *vt.* to avoid by going around 绕行

例 **circumvent** the traffic jam by taking an alternate route

❷ *vt.* to get around (something) in a clever and sometimes dishonest way 回避

例 We **circumvented** the problem by using a different program.

frank [fræŋk]

adj. used to say that someone is speaking or writing in a very direct and honest way 坦率的

例 Don't be afraid to be completely **frank** with me.

单词助记【同义词】candid，forthright，straightforward，explicit

plummet [ˈplʌmɪt]

❶ *vi.* to fall suddenly straight down especially from a very high place 垂直落下

例 The car **plummeted** to the bottom of the canyon.

单词助记【同义词】plunge

❷ *vi.* to fall or drop suddenly in amount，value，etc.（数量、价格等）暴跌

例 Temperatures are expected to **plummet** this weekend.

luminous [ˈluːmɪnəs]

adj. producing or seeming to produce light：shining 发光的，发亮的

例 **luminous** stars/galaxies

court [kɔːt]

❶ *n.* a tribunal presided over by a judge，judges，or a magistrate in civil and criminal cases 法庭

例 There was a large group of protesters outside the **court**.

❷ *n.* a quadrangular area，either open or covered，marked out for ball games such as tennis or basketball 球类运动场（如网球，篮球）

例 a basketball/tennis **court**

❸ *v.* be involved with romantically，typically with the intention of marrying 追求

例 The couple **courted** for two years before marrying.

harness [ˈhɑːnɪs]

vt. to use（something）for a particular purpose 利用

例 Engineers are finding new ways to **harness** the sun's energy to heat homes.

surpass [səˈpɑːs]

vt. to be better or greater than（someone or something）超过

例 Attendance is expected to **surpass** last year's record.

spite [spaɪt]

n. a desire to hurt，annoy，or offend someone 恶意

例 He is jealous and full of **spite**.

单词助记【同义词】malice，malevolence，animus，enmity

wane [weɪn]

❶ *vi.* of the moon：to appear to become thinner or less full（月）亏，缺

例 The moon waxes and then **wanes**.

❷ *vi.* to become smaller or less：to decrease in size，amount，length，or quality 变小，减少

例 The scandal caused her popularity to **wane**.

单词助记

infringe [ɪnˈfrɪndʒ]

    vt. / *vi.* to wrongly limit or restrict (something, such as another person's rights) 侵犯

    例 Her rights must not be **infringed**.

stringent [ˈstrɪndʒənt]

    adj. very strict or severe 严格的

    例 He announced that there would be more **stringent** controls on the possession of weapons.

doctrine [ˈdɒktrɪn]

    n. a set of ideas or beliefs that are taught or believed to be true 信条，学说

    单词助记【同义词】creed，credo，dogma，tenet，maxim，canon

herbicide [ˈhɜːbɪsaɪd]

    n. a chemical used to destroy plants or stop plant growth 除草剂

    例 The amount of toxic **herbicide** now used on soy has public health implications.

inherent [ɪnˈhɪərənt]

adj. belonging to the basic nature of someone or something 内在的，固有的

例 She believes that goodness is **inherent** in all people.

contemplate [ˈkɒntempleɪt]

❶ *vi.* to think deeply 沉思

例 I'd like some time to just sit and **contemplate**.

❷ *vt.* to think about doing（something）考虑

例 She's **contemplating** moving to the city.

ingenuous [ɪnˈdʒenjʊəs]

adj.（of a person or action）innocent and unsuspecting 天真的；单纯的

例 He seemed too **ingenuous** for a reporter.

urge [ɜːdʒ]

❶ *n.* a strong need or desire to have or do something 强烈欲望

例 He fought the **urge** to cry.

❷ *vt.* to try to persuade（someone）in a serious way to do something 力劝，敦促

例 I **urge** you to reconsider.

linger [ˈlɪŋɡə(r)]

❶ *vi.* to stay somewhere beyond the usual or expected time 徘徊，继续逗留

例 She **lingered** at the art exhibit.

❷ *vi.* to continue to exist as time passes 继续存留

例 The smell of her perfume **lingered**.

gravel [ˈɡrævəl]

n. small pieces of rock 砂砾，碎石

例 a layer of **gravel**

sole [səʊl]

❶ *adj.* The sole thing or person of a particular type is the only one of that type. 惟一的，独特的

例 He became the **sole** heir to the property.

❷ *n.* the part of an item of footwear on which the sole rests and upon which the wearer treads 鞋底

例 shoe **sole**

robust [rəʊˈbʌst]

❶ *adj.* strong and healthy 健壮的

例 More women than men go to the doctor. Perhaps men are more **robust** or worry less?

❷ *adj.* strongly held and forcefully expressed（观点）强有力的

例 She offered a **robust** argument against the plan.

leak [liːk]

❶ *vi.* of a liquid，gas，etc.：to come in or go out through a hole in a surface 渗漏

例 Water was **leaking** through a hole in the roof.

❷ *n*. a hole in a surface that lets something（such as a liquid or gas）pass in or out 漏洞，裂缝

例 The landlord said he would fix the **leak** in the roof.

coarse [kɔːs]

adj. having a rough quality 粗糙的

例 The fabric varies in texture from **coarse** to fine.

solitary [ˈsɒlɪtərɪ]

adj. tending to live or spend time alone 单独的，独自的

例 We tend to think of cats as kind of **solitary**.

retrieve [rɪˈtriːv]

vt. to get and bring（something）back from a place 找回，取回

例 Police **retrieved** his stolen car.

hygienic [haɪˈdʒiːnɪk]

adj. clean and likely to maintain good health；having or showing good hygiene 卫生的

例 The **hygienic** conditions of the operating room are maintained by the nursing staff.

traverse [trəˈvɜːs]

vt. to move across（an area）横穿，越过

例 The river **traverses** the county.

boost [buːst]

❶ *vt*. to push or shove（something or someone）up from below 抬，托，举

例 She **boosted** the boy onto his father's shoulders.

❷ *vt*. to increase the force，power，or amount of（something）促进，增强，提高

例 The farm has **boosted** wheat production by 25 percent.

shortcoming [ˈʃɔːtkʌmɪŋ]

n. a bad feature；a flaw or defect in something 缺点

例 The main **shortcoming** of this camera is that it uses up batteries quickly.

【单词助记】【同义词】defect，fault，flaw，drawback，weakness，foible

rotation [rəʊˈteɪʃən]

❶ *n*. the act or process of moving or turning around a central point 旋转，转动

例 The Earth makes one **rotation** every day.

❷ *n*. the act of regularly changing something by replacing it with something else 轮流，交替

例 Alfalfa and corn are planted in **rotation**.

【单词助记】

supreme [sjuːˈpriːm]

❶ *adj*. highest in rank or authority 最高的，最权威的

例 the **Supreme** Court

❷ *adj*. highest in degree or quality：greatest or highest possible（性质、程度等）最高的，最大的

例 She has an air of **supreme** confidence about her.

amateur [ˈæmətə(r)]

❶ *n*. a person who does something（such as a sport or hobby）for pleasure and not as a job 业余爱好者

例 These photos were taken by both **amateurs** and professionals.

单词助记【同义词】nonprofessional，nonspecialist，dilettante

❷ *adj*. 业余的

例 At college he studied English and did **amateur** boxing.

divert [daɪˈvɜːt；〈美〉-ˈvɜːrt]

vt. to change the direction or use of（something）使偏离，使改道

例 The stream was **diverted** toward the farmland.

embrace [ɪmˈbreɪs]

❶ both *vt.* / *vi.* to hold someone in your arms as a way of expressing love or friendship 拥抱

例 He **embraced** her tenderly.

❷ *vt.* to accept (something or someone) readily or gladly 欣然接受

例 These ideas have been widely **embraced** by the scientific community.

intricate [ˈɪntrɪkɪt]

adj. having many parts 复杂的，精细的

例 The **intricate** network of canals.

单词助记【同义词】complex，complicated，convoluted，tangled，entangled，twisted

constellation [ˌkɒnstəˈleɪʃən]

❶ *n.* a group of stars that forms a particular shape in the sky and has been given a name 星座

例 The **constellation** Ursa Major contains the stars of the Big Dipper.

❷ *n.* a group of people or things that are similar in some way 一系列，一群

例 The patient presented a **constellation** of symptoms.

despondent [dɪˈspɒndənt]

adj. very sad and without hope 沮丧的

例 He grew increasingly **despondent** about her illness.

entrench [ɪnˈtrentʃ]

vt. to place (someone or something) in a very strong position that cannot easily be changed 确保，牢固树立

例 These dictators have **entrenched** themselves politically and are difficult to move.

intermittent [ˌɪntəˈmɪtənt]

adj. starting，stopping，and starting again：not constant or steady 断断续续的

例 The forecast is for **intermittent** rain.

devour [dɪˈvaʊə(r)]

vt. to quickly eat all of (something) especially in a way that shows that you are very hungry 狼吞虎咽地吃

例 The lions **devoured** their prey.

impediment [ɪmˈpedɪmənt]

n. something that makes it difficult to do or complete something：something that interferes with movement or progress 阻碍，障碍物

例 There were no legal **impediments** to the deal.

remedy [ˈremədɪ]

❶ *n.* a medicine or treatment that relieves pain or cures a usually minor illness 治疗方法；药物

例 The store now sells herbal remedies.

❷ *n.* a way of solving or correcting a problem 解决办法

例 Building more roads isn't always the best **remedy** for traffic congestion.

trample [ˈtræmpl]

vt./vi. to cause damage or pain by walking or stepping heavily on something or someone 践踏，踩坏

例 The workmen **trampled** on my flower bed. / Her glasses were **trampled** underfoot by the crowd.

command [kəˈmɑːnd]

❶ *n.* an order given to a person or animal to do something 命令，指示

例 We are expected to obey his **commands**.

❷ *v.* give an authoritative order 控制，管理

例 He **commanded** that work should cease

constrain [kənˈstreɪn]

vt. to limit or restrict (something or someone) 限制

例 Teenagers often feel **constrained** by rules.

bode [bəʊd]

vt. to be a sign of (a future event or situation) 为……的预兆

例 This could **bode** disaster for all involved.

单词助记 【同义词】augur，portend，herald，presage，foretell，prophesy，forebode

acquire [əˈkwaɪə(r)]

vt. to get (something)：to come to have (something) 获得

例 The old word has **acquired** a new meaning.

integrate [ˈɪntɪɡreɪt]

vt./vi. to make (something) a part of another larger thing (使)融入，(使)结合

例 He feels that these books should be **integrated** into the curriculum.

ravage [ˈrævɪdʒ]

n. to damage or harm (something) very badly 破坏，摧毁

例 The village was **ravaged** by the plague.

deficient [dɪˈfɪʃənt]

adj. not having enough of something that is important or necessary 缺乏的，不足的

例 a nutritionally **deficient** diet / a man who is deficient in judgment

sue [suː]

vt./vi. to bring a lawsuit against someone or something 控告，起诉

例 They've threatened to **sue** the company.

monotonous [məˈnɒtənəs]

adj. used to describe something that is boring because it is always the same 单调的

例 It's **monotonous** work，like most factory jobs.

refine [rɪˈfaɪn]

❶ *vt.* to remove the unwanted substances in (something) 精制，提纯

例 Oil is **refined** to remove naturally occurring impurities.

❷ *vt.* to improve (something) by making small changes 改进，完善

例 The inventor of the machine spent years **refining** the design.

List 23

mania [ˈmeɪnɪə]

n. extreme enthusiasm for something that is usually shared by many people 狂热

例 The band was part of the early rock-and-roll **mania**.

inhibit [ɪnˈhɪbɪt]

❶ *vt*. to prevent or slow down the activity or occurrence of（something）抑制，阻碍

例 Strict laws are **inhibiting** economic growth.

单词助记【同义词】impede，hinder，hamper，retard，curb，check，check，suppress

❷ *vt*. to keep（someone）from doing what he or she wants to do 禁止，阻止

例 Fear can **inhibit** people from expressing their opinions.

pest [pest]

n. an animal or insect that causes problems for people especially by damaging crops 害虫；有害动物

例 These insects/birds are **pests** for farmers.

temperate [ˈtempərɪt]

adj. having temperatures that are not too hot or too cold（气候或地区）温和的

例 The Nile Valley keeps a **temperate** climate throughout the year.

单词助记【同义词】mild，clement，benign，balmy

submerge [səbˈmɜːdʒ]

vt. to make（someone or something）go under the surface of water or some other liquid：to cover（someone or something）with a liquid 使浸没，淹没

例 The town was **submerged** by the flood.

timid [ˈtɪmɪd]

adj. feeling or showing a lack of courage or confidence 胆怯的

例 She's very **timid** and shy when meeting strangers.

单词助记【同义词】apprehensive，timorous，scared，frightened，cowardly

miracle [ˈmɪrəkl]

n. a very amazing or unusual event，thing，or achievement 奇迹

例 The bridge is a **miracle** of engineering.

negligible [ˈneglɪdʒəbl]

adj. very small or unimportant 极小的，微不足道的

例 The grant covered only a **negligible** part of the cost.

intermediary [ˌɪntəˈmiːdjərɪ]

❶ *n*. a person who works with opposing sides in an argument or dispute in order to bring about an agreement 中间人

例 He served as an **intermediary** between the workers and the executives.

❷ *adj*. 中间的，中间人的

例 He was an **intermediary** agent in the negotiations.

juncture [ˈdʒʌŋktʃə(r)]

❶ *n.* a place where things join；junction 连接；连接处

例 the **juncture** of two rivers

❷ *n.* an important point in a process or activity 关键时刻

例 At this **juncture** it looks like they are going to get a divorce.

swamp [swɒmp]

❶ *n.* land that is always wet and often partly covered with water 沼泽

例 Alligators live in the lowland **swamps**.

❷ *n.* a difficult or troublesome situation or subject 困境

例 I am trapped in the **swamp**.

❸ *vt.* to cause (someone or something) to have to deal with a very large amount of things or people at the same time 使应接不暇

例 I'm **swamped** with work right now.

turbulence ['tɜːbjʊləns]

❶ *n.* sudden, violent movements of air or water 湍流，紊流

例 The plane hit quite a bit of **turbulence** during our flight.

❷ *n.* a state of confusion，violence，or disorder 混乱，动荡

例 A period of **turbulence** preceded the riots.

repudiate [rɪ'pjuːdɪeɪt]

❶ *vt.* to refuse to accept；especially：to reject as unauthorized or as having no binding force 拒绝接受；拒不履行

例 The new government **repudiated** the treaty signed by the former government.

❷ *vt.* to reject as untrue or unjust 否认，驳斥

例 He **repudiated** the charge of having taken bribes.

resurrect [ˌrezə'rekt]

vt. to cause (something that had ended or been forgotten or lost) to exist again，to be used again，etc. 使复苏

例 He is trying to **resurrect** his acting career.

virtuoso [ˌvɜːtjʊ'əʊsəʊ]

n. a person who does something in a very skillful way 大师（尤指乐器演奏高手）

例 She's a piano **virtuoso**.

deflate [dɪ'fleɪt]

vt./ vi. When something such as a tyre or balloon deflates，or when you deflate it，all the air comes out of it. （使）放气

例 We **deflate** the tyres to make it easier to cross the desert.

vagary ['veɪɡərɪ]

n. an unpredictable or erratic action，occurrence，course，or instance 变幻莫测，反复无常

例 I take an assortment of clothes on holiday，as a provision against the **vagaries** of the weather.

idiosyncrasy [ˌɪdɪə'sɪnkrəsɪ]

❶ *n.* an unusual way in which a particular person behaves or thinks 习性，癖好

例 Her habit of using "like" in every sentence was just one of her **idiosyncrasies**.

❷ *n.* an unusual part or feature of something 特性

例 The current system has a few **idiosyncrasies**.

prolific [prə'lɪfɪk]

adj. producing a large amount of something 多产的

例 She is a **prolific** writer of novels and short stories.

单词助记【同义词】plentiful，abundant，profuse，copious，lush，fecund

comprehensible [ˌkɒmprɪˈhensəbl]

adj. able to be understood；intelligible 可理解的

例 They spoke in barely **comprehensible** slang.

modest [ˈmɒdɪst]

❶ *adj.* not very large in size or amount 不太大的,不太多的

例 He earns a **modest** income.

❷ *adj.* free from ostentation or showy extravagance 朴实的,朴素的

例 They own a **modest** cottage near the beach.

❸ *adj.* not too proud or confident about yourself or your abilities: not showing or feeling great or excessive pride 谦虚的,谦逊的

例 She's very **modest** about her achievements.

dormant [ˈdɔːmənt]

adj. not doing anything at this time: not active but able to become active 休眠的

例 The seeds will lie **dormant** until the spring.

resilient [rɪˈzɪliənt]

❶ *adj.* able to become strong, healthy, or successful again after something bad happens 有复原力的

例 The local economy is remarkably **resilient**.

❷ *adj.* able to return to an original shape after being pulled, stretched, pressed, bent, etc. 有弹性的

例 Cotton is more resistant to being squashed and polyester is more **resilient**.

percussion [pəˈkʌʃən]

n. musical instruments (such as drums, cymbals, or xylophones) that you play by hitting or shaking 打击乐器

例 The marimba is a **percussion** instrument.

cumbersome [ˈkʌmbəsəm]

adj. hard to handle or manage because of size or weight 笨重的

例 Although the machine looks **cumbersome**, it is actually easy to use.

【反义词】manageable

prompt [prɒmpt]

❶ *vt.* to cause (someone) to do something 促使

例 Curiosity **prompted** her to ask a few questions.

❷ *adj.* done or given without delay 立即的

例 The victims need **prompt** medical assistance.

roam [rəʊm]

vt./vi. to go to different places without having a particular purpose or plan 闲逛,漫游

例 Goats **roam** free on the mountain.

单词助记【同义词】wander, rove, ramble, drift, walk, tramp

noble [ˈnəʊbl]

❶ *adj.* having, showing, or coming from personal qualities that people admire (such as honesty, generosity, courage, etc.) 高尚的

例 He was a man of **noble** character.

❷ *adj*. of，relating to，or belonging to the highest social class：of，relating to，or belonging to the nobility 高贵的，贵族的

例 She married a man of **noble** birth/rank.

prior [ˈpraɪə(r)]

adj. existing earlier in time：previous 事先的，较早的

例 The job requires **prior** experience in advertising.

contemporary [kənˈtempərəri]

❶ *adj*. happening or beginning now or in recent times 当代的

例 The story is old，but it has importance to **contemporary** audiences.

单词助记【同义词】modern

❷ *adj*. existing or happening in the same time period：from the same time period 同时代的

例 The book is based on **contemporary** accounts of the war.

❸ *n*. a person who lives at the same time or is about the same age as another person 同时代的人

例 He was a **contemporary** of George Washington.

pinnacle [ˈpɪnəkl]

n. the best or most important part of something：the point of greatest success or achievement 顶峰

例 Winning the championship was the **pinnacle** of his career.

单词助记【同义词】peak，apex，zenith，apogee，acme

circuitous [səˈkjuːɪtəs]

adj. not straight，short，and direct 迂回的

例 He took a **circuitous** route to town.

thrill [θrɪl]

❶ *vt*. to cause (someone) to feel very excited or happy 使激动

例 Circus performers still **thrill** audiences today.

❷ *adj*. very exciting 激动人心的

例 It was **thrilling** to see her win the race.

obstruct [əbˈstrʌkt]

❶ *vt*. to be in front of (something)：to make (something) difficult to see 挡住(视线等)

例 His neighbors built a wall that **obstructed** his view of the ocean.

❷ *vt*. to block (something，such as a pipe or street) so that things cannot move through easily 阻塞(道路等)

例 A large tree **obstructed** the road.

lax [læks]

adj. not careful enough：not strict enough 马马虎虎的，不严谨的

例 Security has been **lax**.

steadfast [ˈstedfɑːst]

adj. very devoted or loyal to a person，belief，or cause：not changing 坚定的

例 He was **steadfast** in his support of the governor's policies.

单词助记【同义词】loyal，faithful，committed，devoted，dedicated，steady

rear [rɪə(r)]

71

❶ *n*. the back part of something 后部

例 The store is in the **rear** of the building.

❷ *adj*. at or near the back of something 后部的

例 He slipped and fell on his **rear**. / He settled back in the **rear** of the taxi.

chisel [ˈtʃɪzəl]

❶ *n*. a metal tool with a flat, sharp end that is used to cut and shape a solid material (such as stone, wood, or metal) 凿子

例 a hammer and **chisel**

❷ *vt*. to cut or shape (something) with a chisel 凿，雕刻

例 He set out to **chisel** a dog out of sandstone.

imminent [ˈɪmɪnənt]

adj. happening very soon 即将发生的

例 These patients are facing **imminent** death.

单词助记【同义词】impending

tangible [ˈtændʒəbl]

adj. able to be touched or felt 可触摸的，有实体的

例 **tangible** objects

单词助记【同义词】touchable，palpable

preeminent [ˌpriˈemənənt]

❶ *adj.* standing above others in rank，importance，or achievement 卓越的，超群的

例 The poem is a **preeminent** example of his work.

单词助记 【同义词】distinguished，prominent，eminent，renowned

❷ *adj.* coming before all others in importance 首要的

例 the **preeminent** reason for the booming economy

coalesce [ˌkəʊəˈles]

vi. to come together to form one group or mass 合并

例 The ice masses **coalesced** into a glacier over time.

satisfy [ˈsætɪsfaɪ]

❶ *vt.* to cause (someone) to be happy or pleased 使满意

例 The movie's ending failed to **satisfy** audiences.

❷ *vt.* to provide，do，or have what is required by (someone or something) 满足（要求）

例 She **satisfied** all conditions for approval of the loan.

perplex [pəˈpleks]

vt. to confuse (someone) very much 使困惑

例 Questions about the meaning of life have always **perplexed** humankind.

cherish [ˈtʃerɪʃ]

❶ *vt.* to feel or show great love for (someone or something) 珍爱，珍视

例 They **cherish** their native land.

❷ *vt.* to keep in one's mind or heart 怀有，抱有

例 She **cherished** in her heart the hope that her husband would return sooner or later.

suppress [səˈpres]

❶ *vt.* to end or stop (something) by force 镇压，压制

例 Political dissent was brutally **suppressed**.

单词助记 【同义词】subdue，repress，crush，quell，quash，squash

❷ *vt.* to stop yourself from expressing (an emotion or a reaction) 抑制（情感或反应）

例 He struggled to **suppress** his feelings of jealousy.

splendid [ˈsplendɪd]

❶ *adj.* very impressive and beautiful 壮观的，壮丽的

例 The balcony gave us a **splendid** view of the river.

❷ *adj.* very good；excellent 极好的

例 I have some **splendid** news.

applaud [əˈplɔːd]

vt./vi. to strike the hands together over and over to show approval or praise 鼓掌；为……鼓掌以示同意

例 The audience stood and **applauded** at the end of the show.

seam [siːm]

❶ *n*. a line where two pieces of cloth or other material are sewn together 缝合线

例 the **seams** of a dress

❷ *n*. a layer of coal, rock, etc., that is between two other layers of rock underground （煤）层

例 coal **seams**

excrete [eksˈkriːt]

vt. to pass (waste matter) from the body or from an organ in the body 排出，分泌（废物或有害物）

例 The kidneys **excrete** toxins.

单词助记 【同义词】secrete

excavate [ˈekskəveɪt]

vt. to uncover (something) by digging away and removing the earth that covers it 挖掘

例 They **excavated** an ancient city.

单词助记 【同义词】empty out

secession [sɪˈseʃən]

n. the act of separating from a nation or state and becoming independent 退出，脱离

例 the **secession** of the Southern states

humiliate [hjuːˈmɪlɪeɪt]

vt. to make (someone) feel very ashamed or foolish 使丢脸，使出丑

例 He accused her of trying to **humiliate** him in public.

postulate [ˈpɒstjʊleɪt]

vt. to suggest (something, such as an idea or theory) especially in order to start a discussion 假定，假设

例 The theory **postulates** that carbon dioxide emissions contribute to global warming.

employ [ɪmˈplɔɪ]

❶ *vt*. to provide (someone) with a job that pays wages or a salary 雇用

例 He's **employed** by the local drugstore.

❷ *vt*. to use (something) for a particular purpose or to do something 使用

例 The company is accused of **employing** questionable methods to obtain the contract.

feast [fiːst]

n. a special meal with large amounts of food and drink 盛宴

例 Every guest brought a different dish to the party, and we had quite a **feast**.

ephermeral [ɪˈfemərəl]

adj. lasting for a very short time 短暂的

例 Fashions are **ephemeral**.

单词助记 【同义词】brief, short, short-lived, fleeting, passing, transient

momentary [ˈməʊməntərɪ]

adj. lasting for a very short time; brief 短暂的

例 He experienced a **momentary** loss of consciousness.

单词助记 【同义词】brief, short, transient, transitory, ephemeral, evanescent

stipulate [ˈstɪpjʊleɪt]

vt. to demand or require（something）as part of an agreement 规定，明确要求

例 The cease-fire was **stipulated** by the treaty.

plunge ［plʌndʒ］

❶ *vi.* to fall or jump suddenly from a high place 落下，跳下

例 The rocket **plunged** toward the Earth.

❷ *vi.* to fall or drop suddenly in amount，value，etc.：plummet（数量、价格等）暴跌

例 The moose population has **plunged** in recent years.

List 26

aspirant [əsˈpaɪərənt]

n. a person who has ambitions to achieve something 有抱负的人

例 He is among the few **aspirants** with administrative experience.

scrub [skrʌb]

❶ *vt./vi*. to rub (something) hard with a rough object or substance and often with soap in order to clean it 擦洗，擦净

例 She **scrubbed** the potatoes.

❷ *n*. a stunted tree or shrub 矮树

例 There is an area of scrub and woodland beside the railway line.

spur [spɜː(r)]

❶ *vt*. to encourage (someone) to do or achieve something 激励

例 The reward spurred them to work harder.

❷ *vt*. to cause (something) to happen or to happen more quickly 推动，使加速

例 Lower interest rates should spur economic growth.

sufficient [səˈfɪʃənt]

adj. having or providing as much as is needed：enough 足够的

例 Her explanation was not sufficient to **satisfy** the police.

regime [reɪˈʒiːm]

n. a form of government 政体，政权

volatile [ˈvɒlətaɪl]

❶ *adj*. easily becoming a gas at a fairly low temperature 易挥发的

例 It's thought that the blast occurred when **volatile** chemicals exploded.

❷ *adj*. likely to change in a very sudden or extreme way 易变的，反复无常的

例 The stock market can be very **volatile**.

单词助记 【同义词】mercurial, capricious, whimsical, fickle, flighty, impulsive

单词助记

recede [rɪˈsiːd]

vi. to move away gradually 后退，远离

例 The floods gradually **receded** from the fields.

orchestra [ˈɔːkɪstrə]

n. a group of musicians who play usually classical music together and who are led by a conductor 管弦乐队

例 He plays violin in the school **orchestra**.

exhale [eks'heɪl]

vt./vi. to breathe out 呼出；呼气

例 She inhaled deeply and **exhaled** slowly，trying to relax.

sanctuary ['sæŋktʃʊərɪ]

❶ *n.* a place of refuge or safety 庇护所

例 People automatically sought a **sanctuary** in time of trouble.

单词助记 【同义词】refuge，haven，harbor，shelter，hideaway，hideout

❷ *n.* a holy place；a temple or church 圣所

例 The **sanctuary** contains the altar of sacrifice.

precipitate [prɪ'sɪpɪteɪt]

❶ *vt.* to cause（something solid）to become separated from a liquid especially by a chemical process【化学】使沉淀；使从溶液中分离

例 **precipitate** minerals from seawater

❷ *vt.* to cause（vapor）to condense and fall or deposit【气象学】使（水蒸气）凝结

例 An ice-filled glass **precipitates** moisture from the air.

❸ *vt.* to cause（something）to happen quickly or suddenly 使……突然发生

例 Her death **precipitated** a family crisis.

commemorate [kə'meməreɪt]

vt. to do something special in order to remember and honor（an important event or person from the past）纪念

例 All of the director's films will be shown to **commemorate** the 50th anniversary of his death.

inordinate [ɪ'nɔːdɪnɪt]

adj. going beyond what is usual，normal，or proper 过度的

例 I waited an **inordinate** amount of time.

sloth [sləʊθ]

❶ *n.* reluctance to work or make an effort；laziness 懒惰

例 He admitted a lack of motivation and a feeling of **sloth**.

❷ *n.* a slow-moving tropical American mammal that hangs upside down from the branches of trees using its long limbs and hooked claws 树懒

advocate ['ædvəkeɪt]

❶ *vt.* to support or argue for（a cause，policy，etc.）提倡

例 He **advocates** traditional teaching methods.

❷ *n.* ['ædvəkət] a person who argues for or supports a cause or policy 倡导者

例 He was a strong **advocate** of free market policies and a multi-party system.

单词助记 【同义词】champion，supporter，backer，proponent，exponent，campaigner

undermine [ˌʌndə'maɪn]

vt. to make（someone or something）weaker or less effective usually in a secret or gradual way 削弱

例 She tried to **undermine** my authority by complaining about me to my boss.

grasp [ɡrɑːsp]

❶ *vt.* to take and hold（something）with your fingers，hands，etc. 抓住，抓紧

例 I **grasped** the rope by its end.

❷ *vt.* to understand（something that is complicated or difficult）理解，掌握

例 The government has not yet **grasped** the seriousness of the crisis.

extol [ɪkˈstɔl]

    vt. to praise (someone or something) highly 高度赞扬

    例 The health benefits of exercise are widely **extolled**.

单词助记【同义词】acclaim，exalt，eulogize，adulate

efface [ɪˈfeɪs]

    vt. to cause (something) to fade or disappear 消除，抹去

    例 He struggled to **efface** his unhappy memories.

intimate [ˈɪntɪmət]

    ❶ *adj.* having a very close relationship：very warm and friendly 亲密的

    例 We have an **intimate** friendship with our neighbors.

    ❷ *n.* a very close friend 密友

    例 His coworkers knew him as "Robert"，but his **intimates** called him "Robbie".

单词助记【同义词】best friend，confidant，confidante

abolish [əˈbɒlɪʃ]

    vt. to officially end or stop（something，such as a law）；to completely do away with（something）废除

    例 He is in favor of **abolishing** the death penalty.

    单词助记【同义词】terminate，eliminate，exterminate，destroy，annihilate，extinguish

sovereign [ˈsɒvrɪn]

    ❶ *n*. a king or queen 君主

    例 a Spanish **sovereign**

    ❷ *adj*. having unlimited power or authority（权力）至高无上的

    例 **Sovereign** power will continue to lie with the Supreme People's Assembly.

    ❸ *adj*. highest and most important 最重大的

    例 The government's **sovereign** duty is to protect the rights of its citizens.

prototype [ˈprəʊtəʊtaɪp]

    n. an original or first model of something from which other forms are copied or developed 原型

    例 They tested the **prototype** of the car.

    单词助记【同义词】paradigm，typical example，archetype，exemplar

contiguous [kənˈtɪgjʊəs]

    adj. used to describe things that touch each other or are immediately next to each other 相接的；邻近的

    例 She's visited each of the 48 **contiguous** states in the U.S.，but she hasn't been to Alaska or Hawaii yet.

anonymous [əˈnɒnɪməs]

    adj. not named or identified 匿名的

    例 The donor wishes to remain **anonymous**.

fusion [ˈfjuːʒən]

    n. the process or result of joining two or more things together to form a single entity 融合，合并

    例 A large amount of energy is released when（nuclear）**fusion** occurs.

affluent [ˈæflʊənt]

    adj. having a large amount of money and owning many expensive things：rich，wealthy 富裕的，丰富的

    例 His family was more **affluent** than most.

    【同义词】prosperous，wealthy

abrasion [əˈbreɪʒən]

    n. the act or process of damaging or wearing away something by rubbing，grinding，or scraping 磨损，磨耗

    例 **abrasion** of rocks by wind and water

auspicious [ɔːsˈpɪʃəs]

adj. showing or suggesting that future success is likely 吉利的，有望成功的

例 It was an **auspicious** time to open a new business.

appall [əˈpɔːl]

vt. to cause (someone) to feel fear, shock, or disgust 使惊骇，使震惊

例 She was **appalled** by their behavior.

clement [ˈklemənt]

adj. not too hot or too cold（气候）温和的

例 The country is known for its **clement** weather.

单词助记【同义词】mild

abound [əˈbaʊnd]

vi. to be present in large numbers or in great quantity 大量存在

例 Good fish **abound** in the North Sea.

antiquity [ænˈtɪkwətɪ]

❶ *n*. very great age 古老

例 It indicates the **antiquity** of the tradition.

❷ *n*.〈antiquities〉objects from ancient times 古物

例 a museum of Roman **antiquities**

assess [əˈses]

vt. to make a judgment about (something) 评估

例 The school will **assess** the students' progress each year.

pristine [ˈprɪstaɪn]

❶ *adj*. not changed by people：left in its natural state 原始状态的

例 **pristine** mountain snow

❷ *adj*. in perfect condition：completely clean, fresh, neat, etc. 崭新的，清新的，干净的

例 My office is a mess but her office is always **pristine**.

dictate [dɪkˈteɪt]

❶ *vt*. to say or state (something) with authority or power 命令，规定

例 They insisted on being able to **dictate** the terms of surrender.

❷ *vt*. If one thing dictates another, the first thing causes or influences the second thing. 决定，对……有决定性影响

例 Our choice of activities will likely be **dictated** by the weather.

revolve [rɪˈvɒlv]

vt./*vi*. to turn around a center point or line：rotate 旋转，转动

例 The Earth **revolves** on its axis.

scent [sent]

❶ *n*. a pleasant smell that is produced by something 香味

例 The flower has a wonderful **scent**.

❷ *n*. a smell that is left by an animal or person and that can be sensed and followed by some animals（such as dogs）气味

例 The dogs followed the fox's **scent**.

单词助记【同义词】odor

expel [ɪksˈpel]

❶ *vt*. to officially force (someone) to leave a place or organization 逐出；开除

例 She was **expelled** from school for bad behavior.

❷ *vt*. to push or force (something) out 排出

例 As the lungs exhale this waste，gas is **expelled** into the atmosphere.

jettison [ˈdʒetɪsn]

vt. to get rid of (something) 丢弃，处理掉

例 We should **jettison** these old computers and get new ones.

List 28

scratch [skrætʃ]

vt. to make a line or mark in the surface of（something）by rubbing or cutting it with something rough or sharp 刮，擦，挖

例 Someone **scratched** the paint on my car.

arbitrary [ˈɑːbɪtrərɪ]

❶ *adj.* not planned or chosen for a particular reason：not based on reason or evidence 随意的

例 An **arbitrary** number has been assigned to each district.

❷ *adj.* done without concern for what is fair or right 武断的

例 Although **arbitrary** arrests are illegal，they continue to occur in many parts of the country.

immune [ɪˈmjuːn]

adj. not capable of being affected by a disease 免疫的

例 Most people are **immune** to the disease.

pertinent [ˈpɜːtɪnənt]

adj. relating to the thing that is being thought about or discussed 相关的

例 His comments weren't **pertinent**（to the discussion）.

congeal [kənˈdʒiːl]

vi. of a liquid：to become thick or solid 凝结，凝固

例 The gravy began to **congeal** in the pan.

单词助记 【同义词】coagulate，clot，thicken

rapport [ræˈpɔː(r)]

n. a friendly relationship 友善关系

例 She works hard to build **rapport** with her patients.

paradigm [ˈpærədaɪm]

n. a model or pattern for something that may be copied 范例

例 Her recent book provides us with a new **paradigm** for modern biography.

legitimate [lɪˈdʒɪtɪmət]

❶ *adj.* allowed according to rules or laws 合法的

例 The government will not seek to disrupt the **legitimate** business activities of the defendant.

❷ *adj.* fair or reasonable 合理的

例 We think her concern/excuse is **legitimate**.

grudging [ˈɡrʌdʒɪŋ]

adj. said，done，or given in an unwilling or doubtful way 勉强的

例 Her theories have begun to win **grudging** acceptance in the scientific community.

convention [kənˈvenʃən]

❶ *n.* a large meeting of people who come to a place for usually several days to talk about their shared work or other interests or to make decisions as a group 大型会

议

例 The conference was held at the new **convention** center.

单词助记【同义词】conference，meeting，congress，assembly，summit

❷ *n*. a custom or a way of acting or doing things that is widely accepted and followed 习俗

例 It's important to follow the **conventions** of punctuation in a paper for school.

单词助记【同义词】custom，norm

elusive [ɪˈluːsɪv]

❶ *adj*. hard to find or capture 难抓住的，难找到的

例 **elusive** creatures / The causes of unemployment remain **elusive**.

❷ *adj*. hard to understand，define，or remember 难（理解、形容、记）的

例 an **elusive** concept/idea/name

annihilate [əˈnaɪəleɪt]

vt. to destroy（something or someone）completely 毁灭，消灭

例 Bombs **annihilated** the city.

endeavor [ɪnˈdevə(r)]

n. a serious effort or attempt 努力，尝试

例 She is involved in several artistic **endeavors**.

单词助记【同义词】effort，exertion，industry

venture [ˈventʃə(r)]

❶ *n*. a new activity，project，business，etc.，that typically involves risk 冒险，风险项目

例 a space **venture**

❷ *vi*. to go somewhere that is unknown，dangerous，etc. 冒险去（某处）

例 We **ventured** out into the woods.

❸ *vi*. to start to do something new or different that usually involves risk 冒险（做某事）

例 The company is **venturing** into the computer software industry.

halt [hɔːlt]

vt./*vi*. to stop（something or someone）from moving or continuing；to stop moving or happening （使）停住；（使）停止

例 The fighting **halted** briefly.

terminal [ˈtɜːmɪnəl]

❶ *adj*. a building where buses or trains regularly stop so that passengers can get on and off：station 终点站

例 I will meet you outside the bus **terminal**.

❷ *adj*. at the end：forming or coming at the end of something 末端的，结尾的

例 The **terminal** stop for this line is Boston.

crumble [ˈkrʌmbl]

vt./*vi*. If something **crumbles**，or if you crumble it，it breaks into a lot of small pieces. 弄碎；碎裂

例 The recipe calls for the herbs to be **crumbled**.

单词助记【同义词】disintegrate，collapse，fragment，decay，deteriorate

laden [ˈleɪdn]

adj. loaded heavily with something：having or carrying a large amount of something

充满的，满载的

例 The following summer the peach tree was **laden** with fruit.

deliberate [dɪˈlɪbərət]

❶ *adj*. done or said in a way that is planned or intended：done or said on purpose 故意的

例 I don't think that was a mistake；I think it was **deliberate**.

单词助记【同义词】intentional，calculated，conscious，intended

❷ *adj*. done or decided after careful thought 深思熟虑的

例 a **deliberate** choice/decision

❸ both *vt*./*vi*. to think about or discuss something very carefully in order to make a decision 仔细考虑；慎重商议

例 They will **deliberate** the question. / The six-person jury deliberated about two hours before returning with the verdict.

拓展 *adv*. **deliberately** [dɪˈlɪbərətlɪ] 故意地

例 He **deliberately** tricked them.

twist [twɪst]

❶ *vt*. to bend or turn（something）in order to change its shape 扭曲

例 The antenna was **twisted** out of shape.

单词助记【同义词】writhe

❷ *vt*. to turn a part of your body around：to change your position 转动（身体某部分）

例 She **twisted** her head sideways and looked toward the door.

❸ *vt*. to hurt（your ankle，knee，wrist，etc.）by turning it too far 扭伤（脚踝或手腕等）

例 I **twisted** my ankle playing softball.

incision [ɪnˈsɪʒən]

n. a surgical cut made in skin or flesh 切口

例 The technique involves making a tiny **incision** in the skin.

repel [rɪˈpel]

❶ *vt*. to force (an enemy, attacker, etc.) to stop an attack and turn away 击退

例 Their superior forces **repelled** the invasion.

❷ *vt*. to keep (something) out or away 抗,防

例 The candle **repels** insects.

comprehensive [ˌkɒmprɪˈhensɪv]

adj. complete; including all or nearly all elements or aspects of something 全面的,全方位的

例 The Rough Guide to Nepal is a **comprehensive** guide to the region.

jar [dʒɑː(r)]

n. a clay container that has a wide opening 罐子,坛子

例 a pottery **jar**

protagonist [prəˈtæɡənɪst]

❶ *n*. an advocate or champion of a particular cause or idea 倡导者,支持者

例 the main **protagonists** of their countries' integration into the world market

单词助记【同义词】champion, advocate, upholder, proponent, exponent, campaigner

❷ *n*. the leading character or one of the major characters in a drama, movie, novel, or other fictional text 主人公

judge [dʒʌdʒ]

❶ *vt*./*vi*. to form an opinion about (something or someone) after careful thought 判断,估计

例 It can be difficult to **judge** sizes accurately. / Judging from this schedule, we have a busy week ahead.

❷ *n*. a person who has the power to make decisions on cases brought before a court of law 法官

例 She's one of the strictest **judges** in the state.

❸ *n*. a person who decides the winner in a contest or competition 裁判员,评委

例 He served as a **judge** at the baking contest.

outbreak [ˈaʊtbreɪk]

n. a sudden start or increase of fighting or disease (暴动、疾病等的) 爆发

例 They are preparing for an **outbreak** of the virus.

senate [ˈsenɪt]

n. the smaller group of the two groups of people who meet to discuss and make the laws of a country, state, etc. 参议院

例 the New York State **Senate** / The **Senate** voted to repeal the tax cut.

expediency [ɪksˈpiːdɪənsɪ]

n. 权宜,便利

例 The **expediency** of such a plan is questionable.

单词助记【同义词】convenient

cylinder [ˈsɪlɪndə(r)]

❶ n. a shape that has straight sides and two circular ends 圆柱

例 It was recorded on a wax **cylinder**.

❷ n. a tube in which a piston of an engine moves 汽缸

例 a four- **cylinder** engine

versatile [ˈvɜːsətaɪl]

adj. able to adapt or be adapted to many different functions or activities 有多种技能的,多才多艺的

例 She is a **versatile** athlete who participates in many different sports.

单词助记【同义词】adaptable,flexible,resourceful

stunning [ˈstʌnɪŋ]

adj. very surprising or shocking 令人震惊的

例 Researchers have made a **stunning** discovery.

imperial [ɪmˈpɪəriəl]

adj. of or relating to an empire or an emperor 帝国的,皇帝的

例 They executed Russia's **imperial** family in 1918.

confidential [ˌkɒnfɪˈdenʃəl]

adj. intended to be kept secret 机密的;秘密的

例 These documents are completely/strictly **confidential**.

单词助记【同义词】secret

单词助记

taper [ˈteɪpə(r)]

vi. to become gradually smaller toward one end 逐渐变细

例 Her slacks **taper** at the ankle.

concord [ˈkɒnkɔːd]

n. agreement or harmony between people or groups 和谐

例 They lived in peace and **concord**.

单词助记 来自"chord"

facet [ˈfæsɪt]

❶ n. a small, flat surface on a jewel (宝石的)刻面

例 the **facets** of a diamond

❷ n. a part or element of something 方面

例 Which **facet** of his character is most appealing?

rim [rɪm]

n. the outer edge of a usually round object 边，边缘

例 There were chips on the **rim** of the plate.

shun [ʃʌn]

vt. to avoid（someone or something）回避

例 After his divorce he found himself being **shunned** by many of his former friends.

【同义词】avoid，evade，eschew

supervise [ˈsuːpɚˌvaɪz]

vt. to be in charge of（someone or something）：to watch and direct（someone or something）监督，管理

例 She **supervises** a staff of 30 workers.

List 30

aggregate [ˈæɡrɪɡeɪt]

❶ both *vt.* / *vi.* to join or combine into a single group （使）聚集

例 These insects tend to aggregate in dark，moist places.

单词助记 【同义词】congregate

❷ *adj.* [ˈæɡrɪɡət] formed by adding together two or more amounts：total 合计的

例 The university receives more than half its **aggregate** income from government sources.

ambiguous [æmˈbɪɡjuəs]

adj. able to be understood in more than one way：having more than one possible meaning 模棱两可的，意义不明确的

例 We were confused by the **ambiguous** wording of the message.

单词助记 【同义词】equivocal

victim [ˈvɪktɪm]

n. someone or something that is harmed by an unpleasant event 受害者

例 He was the **victim** of an error.

vent [vent]

n. an opening through which air，steam，smoke，liquid，etc.，can go into or out of a room，machine，or container 出口（如通风口）

例 There was a small air **vent** in the ceiling.

evade [ɪˈveɪd]

vt. to stay away from（someone or something）：to avoid（someone or something）逃避

例 His criminal activities somehow **evaded** detection.

单词助记 【同义词】elude，avoid，dodge，sidestep

vt. to avoid dealing with or facing（something）回避

例 Mr Portillo denied he was **evading** the question.

shield [ʃiːld]

❶ *n.* a large piece of metal，wood，etc.，carried by someone（such as a soldier or police officer）for protection 盾

例 **shield** volcano 盾状火山

❶ *vt.* to cover and protect（someone or something）遮挡，保护

例 She lifted her hand to **shield** her eyes from the glare.

单词助记

lucrative [ˈluːkrətɪv]

adj. producing money or wealth 赚钱的，有利可图的

例 The business has proved to be highly **lucrative**.

inflict [ɪnˈflɪkt]

vt. to cause someone to experience or be affected by (something unpleasant or harmful) 造成，使遭受

例 These insects are capable of **inflicting** a painful sting.

secrete [sɪˈkriːt]

❶ *v.* (of a cell, gland, or organ) produce and discharge (a substance) 分泌

例 The sweat glands **secrete** water.

例 Insulin is **secreted** in response to rising levels of glucose in the blood.

❷ *v.* conceal；hide 藏匿

例 He **secreted** the money under the mattress.

pacify [ˈpæsɪfaɪ]

vt. to cause (someone who is angry or upset) to become calm or quiet 安抚

例 She resigned from her position to **pacify** her accusers.

apprentice [əˈprentɪs]

❶ *n.* a person who learns a job or skill by working for a fixed period of time for someone who is very good at that job or skill 学徒

例 He left school at 15 and trained as an **apprentice** carpenter.

❷ *vt.* to make (someone) an apprentice 使做学徒

例 He was **apprenticed** to a carpenter at the age of 15.

aberrant [æˈberənt]

adj. different from the usual or natural type；unusual 反常的，异常的

例 Ian's rages and **aberrant** behaviour worsened.

intertwine [ˌɪntəˈtwaɪn]

vt./vi. to twist together or around (使)缠绕，交织

例 The branches are **intertwined** with each other and grow into a solid wall.

scant [skænt]

adj. very small in size or amount 少量的，不足的

例 She paid scant attention to the facts.

单词助记 反义词：abundant，ample，sufficient

grace [greɪs]

❶ *n.* a way of moving that is smooth and attractive and that is not stiff or awkward 优美

例 She walked across the stage with effortless grace.

❷ *n.* a controlled，polite，and pleasant way of behaving 风度

例 He has shown remarkable **grace** during this crisis.

concede [kənˈsiːd]

vt. to say that you accept or do not deny the truth or existence of (something)；to admit (something) usually in an unwilling way (常指不情愿地)承认

例 When she noted that the economy was actually improving, he reluctantly **conceded** the point.

privilege [ˈprɪvɪlɪdʒ]

❶ *n.* a right or benefit that is given to some people and not to others 特权

例 Good health care should be a right and not a **privilege**

❷ *n.* a special opportunity to do something that makes you proud 荣幸

例 Meeting the President was a **privilege**.

spawn [spɔːn]

❶ *vt.* to produce or lay eggs in water — used of animals such as fish or frogs（鱼、蛙等）产卵

例 Salmon **spawn** in late summer or fall.

❷ *vt.* to cause (something) to develop or begin 引起, 造成

例 Tyndall's inspired work **spawned** a whole new branch of science.

perpetual [pəˈpetjʊəl]

adj. happening all the time or very often 长期的, 反复不断的

例 Lack of government funding has been a **perpetual** problem for the organization.

champion [ˈtʃæmpjən]

❶ *n.* someone or something (such as a team or an animal) that has won a contest or competition especially in sports 冠军

例 Kasparov became world **champion**.

❷ *vt.* to fight or speak publicly in support of (a person, belief, cause, etc.) 拥护, 捍卫

例 Our senator **championed** the idea of lowering taxes.

List 31

hesitate [ˈhezɪteɪt]

vi. to stop briefly before you do something especially because you are nervous or unsure about what to do 犹豫

例 She **hesitated** and waited for her friend to say something.

单词助记 【同义词】pause，delay，wait，temporize，equivocate

ambitious [æmˈbɪʃəs]

❶ *adj*. having ambition：having a desire to be successful，powerful，or famous（人）雄心勃勃的

例 The company was created by two very **ambitious** young men in the early 1900s.

❷ *adj*. not easily done or achieved：requiring or showing ambition（想法、计划）宏大的

例 Your plans for the future are very **ambitious**.

kinetic [kɪˈnetɪk]

adj. of or relating to the movement of physical objects 运动的，动力的

例 **kinetic** energy/theory

devoid [dɪˈvɔɪd]

adj. entirely lacking or free from 缺乏的，全无的，免于

例 Lisa kept her voice **devoid** of emotion.

trim [trɪm]

❶ *vt*. to cut（something）off something else or to make（something）neat by cutting it 修剪

例 She **trimmed** away the dead branches.

❷ *vt*. to make the size，amount，or extent of（something）smaller 削减，压缩

例 They are looking for ways to **trim** the budget.

tactic [ˈtæktɪk]

n. an action or method that is planned and used to achieve a particular goal 策略，战术

例 We may need to change **tactics**.

blank [blæŋk]

adj. without any writing，marks，or pictures 空白的

例 Leave that line **blank**.

单词助记 反义词：full

shivery [ˈʃɪvərɪ]

adj. shaking because of cold，fear，illness，etc. 颤抖的

例 He woke up feeling sweaty and **shivery**.

homogeneous [ˌhɒməʊˈdʒiːnɪəs]

adj. made up of the same kind of people or things 同类的，同质的

例 The unemployed are not a **homogeneous** group.

conspicuous [kənˈspɪkjʊəs]

adj. very easy to see or notice 明显的，显眼的

例 There were a number of **conspicuous** changes to the building.

单词助记【同义词】visible, noticeable, discernible, perceptible, obvious, manifest

flexible [ˈfleksəbl]

❶ *adj*. capable of bending or being bent 易弯曲的，柔韧的

例 a material that is both strong and **flexible**

单词助记【同义词】pliable, supple, bendable, pliant, plastic, elastic

❷ *adj*. able to change or to do different things 灵活的

例 This computer program has to be **flexible** to meet all our needs.

单词助记【同义词】adaptable, adjustable, variable, versatile

perspire [pəˈspaɪə(r)]

vi. to produce a clear liquid from your skin when you are hot or nervous：sweat 出汗，流汗

例 She ran two miles and wasn't even **perspiring**.

morose [məˈrəʊs]

adj. sullen and ill-tempered 忧郁的，孤僻的

例 She was **morose**, pale, and reticent.

单词助记【同义词】sullen, sulky, gloomy, moody, melancholy, melancholic

单词助记 摸到玫瑰会很扎手，所以郁闷了

plague [pleɪɡ]

❶ *n*. a disease that causes death and that spreads quickly to a large number of people 瘟疫

例 A cholera **plague** had been killing many prisoners of war at the time.

❷ *vt*. to cause constant or repeated trouble, illness, etc., for（someone or something）使困扰

例 The new plane has been **plagued** with mechanical problems.

autobiography [ˌɔːtəbaɪˈɒɡrəfɪ]

n. a biography written by the person it is about 自传

例 He published his **autobiography** last autumn.

conventional [kənˈvenʃənl]

adj. used and accepted by most people：usual or traditional 传统的

例 Today, many patients seek healing through both alternative medicine and **conventional** medicine.

单词助记【同义词】orthodox, traditional, customary

expire [ɪksˈpaɪə(r)]

vi. to end：to no longer be valid after a period of time 到期，失效

例 My driver's license has **expired**.

flush [flʌʃ]

❶ *vi*.（of a person's skin or face）become red and hot, typically as the result of illness or strong emotion 发红，脸红

例 Mr. Cunningham **flushed** angrily.

❷ *vt*./*vi*. cleanse（something, especially a toilet）by causing large quantities of water to pass through it 冲

例 The nurse **flushed** out the catheter.

transient [ˈtrænzɪənt]

adj. not lasting long 短暂的

例 In most cases，pain is **transient**.

单词助记【同义词】transitory，temporary，ephemeral，impermanent，brief，momentary

confide [kənˈfaɪd]

v. tell someone about a secret or private matter while trusting them not to repeat it to others 吐露

例 He **confided** his secret to a friend.

bold [bəʊld]

❶ *adj.* not afraid of danger or difficult situations 大胆的，无畏的

例 The area was settled by **bold** pioneers.

❷ *adj.* very noticeable or easily seen 鲜明地，醒目的

例 The painting is done in **bold** colors.

secluded [sɪˈkluːdɪd]

adj. hidden from view：private and not used or seen by many people 僻静的，隐蔽的

例 We looked for a **secluded** spot in the park to have our picnic.

pursue [pəˈsjuː]

❶ *vt.* to follow and try to catch or capture（someone or something）for usually a long distance or time 追赶

例 The hounds **pursued** the fox for miles.

❷ *vt.* to try to get or do（something）over a period of time 追求，致力于

例 She wants to **pursue** a legal career.

probe [prəʊb]

vt. If you probe a place，you search it in order to find someone or something that you are looking for. 探索，探寻

例 A flashlight beam **probed** the underbrush only yards away from their hiding place.

minimum [ˈmɪnɪməm]

n. the lowest number or amount that is possible or allowed 最小值，最少量

例 She will serve a **minimum** of 10 years in jail.

symphony [ˈsɪmfənɪ]

n. an elaborate musical composition for full orchestra 交响乐

例 **symphony** orchestra

opt [ɒpt]

vi. to choose one thing instead of another 选择

例 She was offered a job but **opted** to go to college instead.

offset [ˈɒfset]

vt. to cancel or reduce the effect of（something）：to create an equal balance between two things 抵消，补偿

例 Gains in one area **offset** losses in another.

faith [feɪθ]

n. strong belief or trust in someone or something 信心，信赖

例 His parents have always had **faith** in him.

collaborate [kəˈlæbəreɪt]

vi. to work with another person or group in order to achieve or do something 合作

例 Several doctors **collaborated** in the project.

overwhelming [ˌəʊvəˈwelmɪŋ]

adj. very great in number，effect，or force 势不可挡的，压倒之势的

例 The party won an **overwhelming** victory in Burma's general elections last May.

contentious [kənˈtenʃəs]

❶ *adj*. likely to cause people to argue or disagree 有争议的

例 I think it's wise to avoid such a highly **contentious** topic at a dinner party.

❷ *adj*. exhibiting an often perverse and wearisome tendency to quarrels and disputes 好争辩的

例 a man of a most **contentious** nature

petrify [ˈpetrɪfaɪ]

❶ *vt*. change（organic matter）into a stony concretion 使石化

例 **petrified** fossil

❷ *vt*. make（someone）so frightened that they are unable to move or think 把……吓呆

例 His icy controlled quietness **petrified** her.

merge [mɜːdʒ]

❶ *vt*. to cause（two or more things，such as two companies）to come together and become one thing 使合并

例 Their music **merges** different styles from around the world..

❷ *vi*. to become joined or united 合并

例 The two banks **merged** to form one large institution.

hub [hʌb]

n. the central and most active part or place（活动等的）中枢，中心

例 The island is a major tourist **hub**.

erratic [ɪˈrætɪk]

adj. acting，moving，or changing in ways that are not expected or usual：not consistent or regular 不规则的，不稳定的

例 The light flashes at **erratic** intervals.

单词助记【同义词】unpredictable，inconsistent，changeable，variable，inconstant，irregular

indispensable [ˌɪndɪsˈpensəbl]

adj. extremely important and necessary 不可或缺的，必需的

例 She is **indispensable** to the team.

scrutinize [ˈskruːtɪnaɪz]

vt. to examine（something）carefully especially in a critical way 仔细观察（检查）

例 I closely **scrutinized** my opponent's every move.

rupture [ˈrʌptʃə(r)]

❶ *n*. a crack or break in something（such as a pipe）破裂

例 A **rupture** in the pipeline resulted in major water damage.

❷ both *vt*./*vi*. to break or burst（使）破裂

例 The pipe **ruptured** because of high water pressure.

mediocre [ˌmiːdɪˈəʊkə(r)]

adj. of average quality 平庸的

例 The critics dismissed him as a **mediocre** actor.

accelerate [əkˈseləreɪt]

❶ both *vt.*/*vi.* to move faster；to gain speed（使）加速

例 The plane **accelerated** down the runway.

❷ both *vt.*/*vi.* to cause（something）to happen sooner or more quickly 促进

例 He says that cutting taxes will help to **accelerate** economic growth.

acute [əˈkjuːt]

❶ *adj.* very serious or dangerous；requiring serious attention or action 严峻的，激烈的

例 The labour shortage is becoming **acute**.

❷ *adj.* having or showing an ability to think clearly and to understand what is not obvious or simple about something 敏锐的

例 In the dark my sense of hearing becomes so **acute**.

❸ *adj.* becoming very severe very quickly 急性的

例 an **acute** disease

circulate [ˈsɜːkjʊleɪt]

both *vt.*/*vi.* to move without stopping through a system，place，etc. 循环，流动

例 Blood **circulates** through the body.

keen [kiːn]

❶ *adj.* having or showing an ability to think clearly and to understand what is not obvious or simple about something 敏锐的

例 She's a very **keen** observer of the political world.

❷ *adj.* very strong and sensitive；highly developed 灵敏的

例 The dog has a **keen** sense of smell.

❸ *adj.* very excited about and interested in something 热衷的

例 She's a **keen** tennis player.

❹ *adj.* strong or intense（感觉）强烈的，深切的

例 After his death，she felt a **keen** sense of loss.

拓展 *adv.* keenly

例 They were **keenly** interested in how well I was doing.

pale [peɪl]

❶ *adj.* light in color 浅色的；苍白的

例 The walls were painted a **pale** blue. / Her illness had left her **pale** and weak.

❷ *vi.* to appear less important，good，serious，etc.，when compared with something else 显得逊色

例 His accomplishments **pale** beside those of his father.

obliterate [əˈblɪtəreɪt]

vt. to destroy (something) completely so that nothing is left 摧毁

例 The tide eventually **obliterated** all evidence of our sand castles.

dilute [daɪˈljuːt]

❶ *vt.* to make (a liquid) thinner or less strong by adding water or another liquid 稀释

例 You can **dilute** the medicine with water.

❷ *vt.* to lessen the strength of (something) 削弱

例 The hiring of the new CEO **diluted** the power of the company's president.

diameter [daɪˈæmɪtə(r)]

n. the distance through the center of something from one side to the other 直径

例 Dig a hole that's two feet deep and three feet in **diameter**.

precarious [prɪˈkeərɪəs]

adj. not safe, strong, or steady 不稳定的，危险的

例 He earned a **precarious** livelihood by gambling.

单词助记【反义词】secure, stable, steady, reliable

enact [ɪˈnækt]

vt. to make (a bill or other legislation) officially become part of the law 通过（法案）

例 The authorities have failed so far to **enact** a law allowing unrestricted emigration.

aid [eɪd]

❶ both *vt./vi.* to provide what is useful or necessary：help 帮助

例 The research **aided** in establishing new theories.

❷ *n.* the act of helping someone：help or assistance given to someone 帮助

例 The project was completed with the **aid** of several students.

❸ *n.* money that is given to a student to help pay for the cost of attending a school 援助

例 She applied for financial **aid** in order to go to college.

enduring [ɪnˈdjʊərɪŋ]

adj. to continue to exist in the same state or condition 持久的

例 **enduring** friendships

单词助记【同义词】abiding, durable, persisting, eternal, perennial, permanent, unending, everlasting, constant

instigate [ˈɪnstɪɡeɪt]

❶ *vt.* to rouse to strong feeling or action 唆使，怂恿

例 The scene in the movie had **instigated** teenagers to commit similar acts.

❷ *vt.* to cause (something) to happen or begin 发起，煽动

例 The government has **instigated** an investigation into the cause of the accident.

conscious [ˈkɒnʃəs]

❶ *adj.* aware of something (such as a fact or feeling)：knowing that something exists or is happening 意识到的

例 We are **conscious** of the risks involved in the procedure.

❷ *adj.* done after thinking about facts and reasons carefully 故意的

例 I don't think we ever made a **conscious** decision to have a big family.

拓展 adv. consciously 自觉地，有意识地

例 I wasn't **consciously** aware of having laughed.

enigma [ɪˈnɪgmə]

n. someone or something that is difficult to understand or explain 难解之谜

例 Iran remains an **enigma** for the outside world.

单词助记【同义词】puzzle，riddle，conundrum，paradox，problem，quandary

intuition [ɪnˌtjuːˈɪʃən]

n. a natural ability or power that makes it possible to know something without any proof or evidence；a feeling that guides a person to act a certain way without fully understanding why 直觉

例 I trusted my **intuition** and ended the relationship.

单词助记【同义词】instinct

predicament [prɪˈdɪkəmənt]

n. a difficult or unpleasant situation 困境

例 The governor has gotten himself into quite a **predicament**.

单词助记【同义词】plight，quandary，dilemma

proliferate [prəˈlɪfəreɪt]

vi. to increase in number or amount quickly 激增

例 New problems have **proliferated** in recent months.

单词助记【同义词】multiply，rocket，mushroom，snowball，burgeon

institution [ˌɪnstɪˈtjuːʃən]

❶ *n.* an established organization 机构

例 The Hong Kong Bank is Hong Kong's largest financial **institution**.

❷ *n.* a custom，practice，or law that is accepted and used by many people 习俗；制度

例 She's not interested in the **institution** of marriage.

gratify [ˈgrætɪfaɪ]

vt. to make（someone）happy or satisfied 使高兴，使满意

例 He's **gratified** by the response he's been getting.

List 34

leisure [ˈleʒə(r)]

    n. time when you are not working: time when you can do whatever you want to do 空闲时间

    例 In his **leisure**, he paints and sculpts.

endure [ɪnˈdjʊə(r)]

    ❶ *vt.* to experience (pain or suffering) for a long time 忍受，忍耐

    例 The refugees have **endured** more hardship than most people can imagine.

    ❷ *vi.* to continue to exist in the same state or condition 持续，继续存在

    例 This tradition has **endured** for centuries.

bizarre [bɪˈzɑː(r)]

    adj. very unusual or strange 怪异的

    例 His behavior was **bizarre**.

    单词助记【同义词】strange，peculiar，odd，outlandish，abnormal，eccentric

sanction [ˈsæŋkʃən]

    ❶ *n.* official permission or approval 批准，认可

    例 The country acted without the **sanction** of the other nations.

    ❷ *n.* an action that is taken or an order that is given to force a country to obey international laws by limiting or stopping trade with that country，by not allowing economic aid for that country，etc. 制裁

    例 The United Nations has decided to impose trade **sanctions** on the country.

intermingle [ˌɪntəˈmɪŋgl]

    both *vt./vi.* to mix together （使）掺和，（使）混合

    例 In her short stories，science fiction and romance **intermingle**.

congregate [ˈkɒŋgrɪgeɪt]

    vi. to come together in a group or crowd 聚集

    例 Students began to **congregate** in the hall.

    单词助记【同义词】aggregate

limb [lɪm]

    n. a leg or arm 肢（腿或臂）

    例 Many soldiers died in the battle，and many lost **limbs**.

fidelity [fɪˈdelətɪ]

    ❶ *n.* loyalty to a person，organization，or set of beliefs 忠诚，尽责

    例 She began to doubt her husband's **fidelity**.

    ❷ *n.* the degree to which a device (such as a CD player，radio，or television) correctly reproduces sounds，pictures，etc. 保真度

    例 The movie's director insisted on total **fidelity** to the book.

entry [ˈentrɪ]

    ❶ *n.* the act of entering something 进入

    例 His friends were surprised by his **entry** into politics.

❷ *n*. something that is entered in a book, list, etc. 条目

例 Many **entries** relate to the two world wars.

❸ *n*. a person or thing that is entered in a contest 参赛的人（或作品）

例 The race has attracted a record number of **entries**.

buoyant [ˈbɔɪənt]

❶ *adj*. able to float 能浮起的

例 This was such a small and **buoyant** boat.

❷ *adj*. cheerful and optimistic 开心的，乐观的

例 The conference ended with the party in a **buoyant** mood.

单词助记【同义词】cheerful, cheery, happy, lighthearted, carefree, merry

shelter [ˈʃeltə(r)]

❶ *n*. a structure that covers or protects people or things 遮蔽物，躲藏处

例 We made a **shelter** from branches.

❷ *vt*. to protect (someone) from danger, bad weather, etc.; to provide shelter for (someone) 遮蔽

例 A cave **sheltered** the climbers during the storm.

subsist [səbˈsɪst]

vi. to exist or continue to exist 存在；生存

例 Some doubt still **subsists** in his mind.

repress [rɪˈpres]

vt. to not allow yourself to do or express (something) 抑制，忍住

例 He **repressed** his anger.

disposition [ˌdɪspəˈzɪʃən]

❶ *n*. the act or the power of disposing or the state of being disposed 处置

例 **disposition** notice

单词助记【同义词】inclination, tendency, proneness, propensity, proclivity.

❷ *n*. the usual attitude or mood of a person or animal 性情

例 Your sunny **disposition** was a way of rubbing off on those around you.

agile [ˈædʒaɪl]

adj. able to move quickly and easily 敏捷的

例 Ruth was a **agile** as monkey.

单词助记【同义词】nimble, lithe, supple, limber

propagate [ˈprɒpəgeɪt]

❶ both *vt./vi*. to produce (a new plant) 繁殖

例 Most plants **propagate** by seed.

❷ *vt*. to transmit (hereditary features or elements) to, or through, offspring. 遗传（特征等）

例 Scientists were hoping to **propagate** the best qualities of both types of sheep.

❸ *vt*. to make (something, such as an idea or belief) known to many people 宣传

例 They **propagated** political doctrines which promised to tear apart the fabric of British society.

obscure [əbˈskjʊə(r)]

❶ *adj*. difficult to understand; likely to be understood by only a few people 复杂难懂的

例 The movie is full of **obscure** references that only pop culture enthusiasts will understand.

【同义词】abstruse，recondite，arcane，esoteric，mystifying，puzzling

❷ *vt*. to make (something) difficult to understand or know：to make (something) obscure 使……难懂

例 The true history has been **obscured** by legends about what happened.

❸ *vt*. to hide or cover (something)：to be in front of (something) so that it cannot be seen 遮掩

例 The mountains were **obscured** by low clouds.

chronic [ˈkrɒnɪk]

❶ *adj*. continuing or occurring again and again for a long time 慢性的，长期的

例 He suffers from **chronic** arthritis/pain.

❷ *adj*. always or often doing something specified 习惯性的，积习难改的

例 Anyone who does not believe that smoking is an addiction has never been a **chronic** smoker.

拓展 *adv*. **chronically** [ˈkrɑːnɪklɪ]

例 He is **chronically** short of money.

foster [ˈfɒstə(r)]

vt. to help (something) grow or develop 促进，培养

例 We are trying to **foster** a sense of community.

equivalent [ɪˈkwɪvələnt]

❶ *adj*. having the same value，use，meaning，etc. 相同的；等效的

例 Allowing him to leave prison now would be **equivalent** to saying that his crime was not serious.

❷ *n*. something that has the same value，use，meaning，etc.，as another thing 相等物；等效物

例 His newspaper column is the journalistic **equivalent** of candy.

【同义词】counterpart

aggravate [ˈægrəveɪt]

❶ *vt.* to make (an injury, problem, etc.) more serious or severe 使恶化

例 The symptoms were **aggravated** by drinking alcohol.

❷ *vt.* to make (someone) angry：to annoy or bother (someone) 激怒，使恼火

例 Our neighbors were **aggravated** by all the noise.

subdue [səbˈdjuː]

❶ *vt.* to get control of (a violent or dangerous person or group) by using force, punishment, etc. 征服，制服

例 The troops were finally able to **subdue** the rebel forces after many days of fighting.

❷ *vt.* to get control of (something, such as a strong emotion) 克制（感情）

例 She struggled to **subdue** her fears.

vital [ˈvaɪtl]

❶ *adj.* extremely important：crucial 至关重要的，生死攸关的

例 He played a **vital** role in guiding the project.

❷ *adj.* very lively or energetic 有生命力的，充满活力的

例 Their music still seems fresh and **vital** after all these years.

单词助记【反义词】insignificant，trivial unimportant，useless

incisive [ɪnˈsaɪsɪv]

adj. accurate and sharply focused 切中要害的

例 She's known for her **incisive** mind and quick wit.

inventory [ˈɪnvəntərɪ]

n. a complete list of the things that are in a place 清单

例 We made an **inventory** of the library's collection.

revolution [ˌrevəˈluːʃən]

❶ *n.* an instance of revolving 旋转，公转

例 The period of **revolution** of the Earth around the Sun is equal to one year.

❷ *n.* a forcible overthrow of a government or social order in favor of a new system 革命

例 This new theory could cause a **revolution** in elementary education.

glaze [ɡleɪz]

❶ *n.* a liquid mixture that is put on the surface of something and that becomes shiny and smooth when it is dry 釉

例 The pot is covered with a bright red **glaze**.

❷ *vt.* to give a smooth and shiny coating to (something) 给（陶器等）上釉

例 **glazed** ceramic pots

inclination [ˌɪnklɪˈneɪʃən]

n. a feeling of wanting to do something：a tendency to do something 倾向，意向

例 He has an **inclination** to brag.

【单词助记】【同义词】tendency，propensity，proclivity，leaning，predisposition，disposition

knit [nɪt]

❶ *vt*./*vi*. to make (a piece of clothing) from yarn or thread by using long needles or a special machine 编织

例 She **knit** a sweater for me.

❷ *vt*. to closely join or combine (things or people) 紧密连接

例 Her novels **knit** together science and fantasy.

【单词助记】

detach [dɪ'tætʃ]

vt./*vi*. to separate (something) from something larger 拆卸，分离

例 During the accident the trailer was **detached** from the car.

pierce [pɪəs]

❶ *vt*./*vi*. to make a hole in or through (something) 刺穿

例 The bullet **pierced** his lung.

❷ *vt*./*vi*. to go through or into (something) in a forceful or noticeable way 穿过

例 A scream **pierced** through the air.

bulk [bʌlk]

n. the large size of someone or something 大块

例 The sheer weight and **bulk** of the car makes it safe to drive.

propel [prə'pel]

vt. to push or drive (someone or something) forward or in a particular direction 推进

例 The train is **propelled** by steam.

【单词助记】【同义词】drive，shoot，thrust launch，push

inject [ɪn'dʒekt]

vt. to force (a liquid) into something 注射，注入

例 The medicine is **injected** directly into the muscle.

candidate ['kændɪdeɪt]

n. a person who is being considered for a job, position, award, etc. 候选人

例 He seemed like an unlikely **candidate** for the job.

burnish ['bɜːnɪʃ]

vt. to make (something, such as metal or leather) smooth and shiny by rubbing it: polish 擦亮，使有光泽

例 **burnished** gold/leather

【单词助记】【同义词】polish

mock [mɒk]

❶ *vt*. to laugh at or make fun of (someone or something) especially by copying an action or a way of behaving or speaking（为了取笑）模仿

例 He made the other boys laugh by **mocking** the way the teacher spoke.

【单词助记】【同义词】parody，mimic

❷ *vt*. to criticize and laugh at（someone or something）for being bad，worthless，or unimportant 嘲笑，轻蔑

例 He **mocks** art only because he doesn't understand it.

单词助记【同义词】jeer，scoff

anchor ［ˈæŋkə(r)］

❶ *n*. a heavy device that is attached to a boat or ship by a rope or chain and that is thrown into the water to hold the boat or ship in place 锚

例 The ship dropped **anchor** in a secluded harbor.

❷ *vt*. to connect（something）to a solid base：to hold（something）firmly in place 使固定

例 The roots **anchor** the plant in the earth.

单词助记

revenue ［ˈrevənjuː］

n. money that is collected for public use by a government through taxes（政府等）收入

例 Government officials have reported a decrease in **revenue**.

serene ［sɪˈriːn］

adj. calm and peaceful 宁静的；安详的

例 He didn't speak much，he just smiled with that **serene** smile of his.

单词助记【同义词】peaceful，tranquil，quiet，still，relaxing，undisturbed

erroneous [ɪˈrəʊnɪəs]

adj. not correct 错误的

例 Some people have the **erroneous** notion that one can contract AIDS by giving blood.

donate [dəʊˈneɪt]

vt. to give (money, food, clothes, etc.) in order to help a person or organization 捐赠

例 The computers were **donated** by local companies.

discard [dɪsˈkɑːd]

vt. to throw (something) away because it is useless or unwanted 丢弃

例 Read the manufacturer's guidelines before **discarding** the box.

evoke [ɪˈvəʊk]

❶ *vt.* to bring (a memory, feeling, image, etc.) into the mind 唤起(回忆、情感)

例 The old house **evoked** memories of his childhood.

❷ *vt.* to cause (a particular reaction or response) to happen 引起(反应)

例 Her remarks have **evoked** an angry response.

outdated [ˌaʊtˈdeɪtɪd]

adj. no longer useful or acceptable；not modern or current 过时的

例 Caryl Churchill's play about Romania is already **outdated**.

【同义词】old-fashioned, out of fashion, unfashionable, behindhand, obsolete, antiquated

allege [əˈledʒ]

vt. to state without definite proof that someone has done something wrong or illegal 指称，声称

例 He **alleged** that the mayor has accepted bribes.

【同义词】claim, assert, declare, state, contend, argue, affirm, maintain

preliminary [prɪˈlɪmɪnərɪ]

adj. coming before the main part of something 初步的

例 **Preliminary** studies show that the drug could help patients with skin cancer.

meticulous [məˈtɪkjʊləs]

adj. very careful about doing something in an extremely accurate and exact way

例 He is **meticulous** about keeping accurate records. 一丝不苟的，谨小慎微的

【同义词】careful, punctilious, painstaking, detailed, fastidious

拓展 *adv.* meticulously [meˈtɪkjʊləslɪ]

例 It's a beautiful Victorian house, **meticulously** restored.

concise [kənˈsaɪs]

adj. using few words；not including extra or unnecessary information 简洁的

例 Burton's text is **concise** and informative.

circumstance [ˈsɜːkəmstəns]

n. a condition or fact that affects a situation 情形，情况

例 If our business is to survive, we must be able to adapt to changing **circumstances**.

mutilate [ˈmjuːtɪleɪt]

❶ *vt.* to cause severe damage to (the body of a person or animal) 使伤残

例 Her arm was **mutilated** in a car accident.

❷ *vt.* to ruin the beauty of (something); to severely damage or spoil (something) 毁坏

例 Brecht's verdict was that his screenplay had been **mutilated**.

intrinsic [ɪnˈtrɪnsɪk]

adj. belonging to the essential nature of a thing; occurring as a natural part of something 内在的，本质的

例 Creativity is **intrinsic** to human nature.

拓展 *adv.* **intrinsically** [ɪnˈtrɪnzɪklɪ]

例 Sometimes I wonder if people are **intrinsically** evil.

单词助记【反义词】extrinsic, acquired, learned

heterogeneous [ˌhetəˈrɒdʒənɪəs]

adj. made up of parts that are different 混杂的，由不同成分组成的

例 an ethnically **heterogeneous** population

adverse [ˈædvɜːs]

adj. bad or unfavorable; not good 不利的

例 Many fear that budget cuts will have an **adverse** effect on education.

corroborate [kəˈrɒbəreɪt]

vt. to support or help prove (a statement, theory, etc.) by providing information or evidence 证实，确证

例 Two witnesses **corroborated** his story.

inhale [ɪnˈheɪl]

vt./vi. to breathe in 吸入；吸气

例 She **inhaled** the fresh country air.

peer [pɪə(r)]

❶ *n.* a person who belongs to the same age group or social group as someone else 同辈，同龄人

例 teenagers spending time with their **peer** groups.

❷ *v.* look keenly or with difficulty at someone or something 仔细看

例 Blake screwed up his eyes, trying to **peer** through the fog.

exertion [ɪgˈzɜːʃən]

❶ *n.* physical or mental effort 努力

例 He was panting from the **exertion** of climbing the stairs.

单词助记【同义词】effort, strain, struggle, toil, endeavor.

❷ *n.* the application of a force, influence, or quality 施加

例 He was flabby and untidy, his face was red and his hair wet with **exertion**.

elliptical [ɪˈlɪptɪkəl]

❶ *adj.* relating to or having the form of an ellipse 椭圆的

例 The moon follows an **elliptical** path around the Earth.

❷ *adj.* difficult to understand 晦涩的

例 He spoke only briefly and **elliptically** about the mission.

单词助记 【同义词】cryptic，abstruse，ambiguous，obscure，oblique

preposterous [prɪˈpɒstərəs]

    adj. extremely unreasonable and foolish 荒谬的，可笑的

    例 The whole idea is **preposterous**!

单词助记 【同义词】absurd，ridiculous，ludicrous

inflate [ɪnˈfleɪt]

both *vt.*/ *vi.* If you inflate something such as a balloon or tyre，or if it inflates，it becomes bigger as it is filled with air or a gas. (使)充气,(使)膨胀

例 The balloon slowly **inflated**.

单词勋记

discrete [dɪsˈkriːt]

adj. separate and different from each other 分离的,独立的

例 The process can be broken down into a number of **discrete** steps.

antagonist [ænˈtægənɪst]

n. a person who opposes another person 敌手,对手

例 He faced his **antagonist** in a series of debates.

wax [wæks]

❶ *vi.* of the moon：to appear to become larger or more full (月亮)渐圆,渐盈

例 The moon **waxes** and then wanes.

❷ *vi.* to become larger or more：to increase in amount，size，etc. 渐渐变大;渐渐增多

例 Interest in the story seems to **wax** and wane depending on other news.

scorn [skɔːn]

vt. to show that you think（someone or something）is not worthy of respect or approval 轻蔑,鄙视

例 He **scorns** anyone who earns less money than he does.

单词勋记 【同义词】scoff，despise

rueful [ˈruːfʊl]

adj. showing or feeling regret for something done 悔恨的

例 He gave me a **rueful** smile and apologized.

拓展 *adv.* ruefully [ˈruːfəlɪ]

例 "I still have a scar from the accident," he said **ruefully**.

单词勋记 【同义词】regretful，remorseful，contrite，repentant，penitent

inspect [ɪnˈspekt]

❶ *vt.* to look at（something）carefully in order to learn more about it，to find problems，etc. 检查,检验

例 The border guard **inspected** their passports.

❷ *vt.* to officially visit a school，hospital，etc.，in order to see if rules are being followed and things are in their proper condition 视察

例 The Public Utilities Commission **inspects** us once a year.

avid [ˈævɪd]

adj. very eager：enthusiastic，keen 热切的，热衷的

例 He is an **avid** admirer of horror movies.

retreat [rɪˈtriːt]

❶ *vi*. If you retreat，you move away from something or someone. 后退，远离

例 As the temperatures warm，the glaciers begin to **retreat**.

❷ *n*. 后退，远离

例 Studies show the glaciers are in **retreat**.

❸ *vi*. If you retreat from something such as a plan or a way of life，you give it up，usually in order to do something safer or less extreme. 躲避，退避

例 She **retreated** from public life.

❹ *n*. 躲避，退避

例 Some of her friends were surprised by her **retreat** from public life following her defeat in the election.

furious [ˈfjʊərɪəs]

adj. very angry 狂怒的

例 He is **furious** at the way his wife has been treated.

单词助记 【同义词】enraged，infuriated，raving，seething，outraged

comprehend [ˌkɒmprɪˈhend]

❶ *v*. grasp mentally；understand 理解

例 He is able to fully **comprehend**.

❷ *v*. include，comprise，or encompass 包括

例 Education **comprehends** the training of many kinds of ability.

precede [prɪˈsiːd]

vt. to happen，go，or come before（something or someone）先于……而发生（存在）

例 Riots **preceded** the civil war.

formidable [ˈfɔːmɪdəbl]

❶ *adj*. very powerful or strong：deserving serious attention and respect 可怕的，令人畏惧的

例 a **formidable** enemy/opponent/weapon.

❷ *adj*.的 large or impressive in size or amount 庞大的；令人惊叹

例 He had a **formidable** array of compositions to his credit.

marvel [ˈmɑːvəl]

❶ *vi*. to feel great surprise，wonder，or admiration 惊叹，赞叹

例 The audience **marveled** at the magician's skill.

❷ *n*. someone or something that is extremely good，skillful，etc.；a wonderful or marvelous person or thing 奇迹

例 The bridge is a **marvel** of engineering.

constrict [kənˈstrɪkt]

❶ *vt*./*vi*. to become or cause（something）to become narrower，smaller，or tighter（使）收缩

例 The drug causes the blood vessels to **constrict**.

❷ *vt.* to prevent or keep（something or someone）from developing freely 约束,限制

例 The declining economy has **constricted** job opportunities

拓展 *n.* constriciton［kənˈstrɪkʃən］收缩

例 The drug causes **constriciton** of blood vessels.

confine［kənˈfaɪn］

vt. to keep（someone or something）within limits；to prevent（someone or something）from going beyond a particular limit，area，etc. 限定范围,限制

例 Please **confine** your comments to 200 words.

prerequisite［ˌpriːˈrekwɪzɪt］

n. something that you officially must have or do before you can have or do something else 先决条件

例 The introductory course is a **prerequisite** for the advanced-level courses.

crest［krest］

n. the highest part or point of something（such as a hill or wave）顶峰

例 We stood on the **crest** of the hill/mountain.

单词助记【同义词】summit，peak，pinnacle，apex

circumstantial［ˌsɜːkəmˈstænʃəl］

adj. based on information which suggests that something is true but does not prove that it is true 好像发生过却无法证明的

例 Fast work by the police had started producing **circumstantial** evidence.

majestic［məˈdʒestɪk］

adj. large and impressively beautiful 壮丽的,雄伟的

例 **majestic** mountains/trees

SSAT

强化词汇

List 38

circumscribe [ˈsɜːkəmskraɪb]

❶ *v.* to draw a shape around (another shape) 在……周围画线

例 The circle is **circumscribed** by a square.

❷ *v.* to limit the size or amount of (something) 限制

例 There are laws **circumscribing** the right of individual citizens to cause bodily harm to others.

单词助记 【同义词】restrict，curb，confine，restrain

embroider [ɪmˈbrɔɪdə(r)]

v. to sew a design on a piece of cloth; to make (a story, the truth, etc.) more interesting by adding details that are not true or accurate 刺绣；装饰

例 She **embroidered** tiny flowers on the baby's scarf.

单词助记 【同义词】sew，stitch，cross-stitch

lackadaisical [ˌlækəˈdeɪzɪkl]

adj. feeling or showing a lack of interest or enthusiasm 无精打采的，不决断的，不热心的

例 His teachers did not approve of his **lackadaisical** approach to homework.

单词助记 【同义词】lazy，apathetic

abject [ˈæbdʒekt]

adj. sunk to or existing in a low state or condition（指境况）凄惨的；绝望的

例 They live in **abject** misery.

单词助记 【同义词】wretched，degrading

absolve [əbˈzɒlv]

v. to make (someone) free from guilt, responsibility, etc. 宣布免除

例 No remorse will **absolve** shoplifters who are caught, and all cases will be prosecuted to the full extent of the law.

单词助记 【同义词】acquit，discharge，excuse，forgive，pardon

bereft [bɪˈreft]

adj. lacking something needed，wanted，or expected 丧失的

例 The **bereft** woman seemed to be taking the sudden death of her rich husband amazingly well.

单词助记 【同义词】deprived，deserted

quell [kwel]

v. to end or stop (something) usually by using force（用武力）制止，结束，镇压，使平静

例 The National Guard was called in to help **quell** the late-night disturbances downtown.

单词助记 【同义词】quiet，suppress

permeable [ˈpɜːmɪəbl]

adj. allowing liquids or gases to pass through 可渗透的，具渗透性的

例 The cell has a **permeable** membrane.

treacherous [ˈtretʃərəs]

adj. not able to be trusted; showing that someone cannot be trusted 骗人的,不可信的,靠不住的,危险的

例 They were not prepared to hike over such **treacherous** terrain.

单词助记 【同义词】untrustworthy，disloyal，dangerous，unreliable

exquisite [ˈekskwɪzɪt]

adj. finely done or made; very beautiful or delicate 优美的,高雅的,精致的

例 Her singing voice is truly **exquisite**.

单词助记 【同义词】beautiful，attractive，gorgeous

blatant [ˈbleɪtənt]

adj. very obvious and offensive 公然的,露骨的

例 He showed a **blatant** disregard for the safety of other drivers.

单词助记 【同义词】flagrant，glaring，obvious，undisguised，unconcealed

moisture [ˈmɔɪstʃə(r)]

n. a small amount of a liquid (such as water) that makes something wet or moist 潮湿,湿气,湿度

例 Wool socks will pull **moisture** away from your skin.

单词助记 【同义词】dampness，wetness，humidity

esteem [ɪˈstiːm]

n. respect and affection 尊敬

例 She has won **esteem** for her work with cancer patients.

tangential [tænˈdʒenʃəl]

adj. diverging from a previous course or line; erratic 离题的;不相干

例 Their romance is **tangential** to the book's main plot.

单词助记 【同义词】digressing

anarchy [ˈænəkɪ]

n. a situation of confusion and wild behavior in which the people in a country，group，organization，etc.，are not controlled by rules or laws 混乱,(尤指)政治混乱

例 When the teacher was absent，there was **anarchy** in the classroom.

单词助记 【同义词】chaos

mendicant [ˈmendɪkənt]

n. beggar 乞丐

例 wandering **mendicants**

单词助记 【同义词】beggar

单词助记

scathing [ˈskeɪθɪŋ]

adj. very harsh or severe (言辞、文章)严厉的,尖刻的,不留情的

例 Republican senators were **scathing** in their criticism of today's hearing.

pernicious [pəˈnɪʃəs]

adj. causing great harm or damage often in a way that is not easily seen or noticed 很有害的，恶性的

例 More **pernicious** still has been the acceptance of the author's controversial ideas by the general public.

单词助记【同义词】dangerous

polygon [ˈpɒlɪɡən]

n. a flat shape that has three or more straight lines and angles 多角形，多边形

例 Pentagons，hexagons，and octagons are all kinds of **polygons**.

stagger [ˈstæɡə(r)]

v. to move or cause（someone）to move unsteadily from side to side 摇晃，蹒跚

例 She **staggered** over to the sofa.

单词助记【同义词】sway

knot [nɒt]

n. an interlacement of the parts of one or more flexible bodies forming a lump or knob（绳的）结,（树的）节

例 One lace had broken and been tied in a **knot**.

单词助记

candor [ˈkændə(r)]

n. the quality of being open and honest in expression；frankness 率直,坦白

例 He was quite **candid** about his past.

单词助记【同义词】frankness，honesty，candidness，truthfulness，sincerity，forthrightness

bend [bend]

v. to use force to cause（something，such as a wire or pipe）to become curved 弯, 弯曲

例 His glasses got **bent** when he dropped them.

单词助记【同义词】stoop；bow；bend over

arbitrator [ˈɑːbɪtreɪtə(r)]

n. an independent person or body officially appointed to settle a dispute 仲裁人

例 Both sides agreed to accept a decision by an impartial **arbitrator**.

单词助记【同义词】adjudicator，arbiter，judge，referee，umpire

endorse [ɪnˈdɔːs]

❶ *v*. to publicly or officially say that you support or approve of（someone or something）公开支持

例 I can **endorse** their opinion wholeheartedly.

❷ *v*. to publicly say that you like or use（a product or service）in exchange for money 代言

例 That brand of sneaker is **endorsed** by several basketball stars.

epitome [ɪˈpɪtəmɪ]

❶ *n*. a perfect example；an example that represents or expresses something very well 缩影,典型的人或事物

例 The golden rule is often cited as the **epitome** of moral conduct："Do unto others as you would have them do unto you."

❷ *n*. a summary of a written work（书、演讲等的）摘要

单词助记【同义词】summary

brazen [ˈbreɪzən]

adj. acting or done in a very open and shocking way without shame or embarrassment 无耻的，无礼的

例 He exhibited a **brazen** disregard for other people's feelings.

单词助记【同义词】bold，impudent，impertinent，insolent，barefaced，blatant

ratify [ˈrætɪfaɪ]

v. to make (a treaty，agreement，etc.) official by signing it or voting for it 批准，签认(合约等)

例 A number of countries have refused to **ratify** the treaty.

单词助记【同义词】approve formally，confirm，verify

chicanery [ʃɪˈkeɪnərɪ]

n. actions or statements that trick people into believing something that is not true：deception or trickery 耍花招哄骗别人(尤指于法律事务中)；不诚实的行为

例 He wasn't above using **chicanery** to win votes.

单词助记【同义词】trickery，subterfuge

therapeutic [ˌθerəˈpjuːtɪk]

❶ *adj.* producing good effects on your body or mind 有益于健康的

例 Gardening can be very **therapeutic**.

单词助记【同义词】healing，relaxing，beneficial.

❷ *adj.* of or relating to the treatment of illness 治疗(学)的，疗法的

例 the **therapeutic** effects of radiation

contagious [kənˈteɪdʒəs]

adj. having a sickness that can be passed to someone else by touching；able to be passed from one person or animal to another by touching (接触)传染的

例 I'm sick，but the doctor says I'm not **contagious**.

单词助记【同义词】infectious

pellucid [peˈljuːsɪd]

adj. very clear 透明的，清澈的

例 Her poetry has a **pellucid** simplicity that betrays none of the sweat that went into writing it.

单词助记【同义词】transparent，lucid

denounce [dɪˈnaʊns]

v. to publicly state that someone or something is bad or wrong：to criticize (someone or something) harshly and publicly 公开指责，抨击

例 The government called on the group to **denounce** the use of violence.

单词助记【同义词】condemn

chop [tʃɒp]

v. to cut into or sever usually by repeated blows of a sharp instrument 砍，伐

例 When I was a boy，my father taught me how to **chop** wood.

单词助记【同义词】cut up

rebuke [rɪˈbjuːk]

v. to speak in an angry and critical way to (someone) 责难或指责

例 The father **rebuked** his son for the spendthrift ways he had adopted since his arrival at college.

单词助记【同义词】scold，reprimand

incandescent [ˌɪnkæn'desənt]

❶ *adj.* white or glowing because of great heat 白热的，白炽的

例 **incandescent** gases

❷ *adj.* producing bright light when heated 十分明亮的，耀眼的

例 The sun blazed down from an **incandescent** sky.

❸ *adj.* very impressive, successful, or intelligent 感情强烈的，激情的

例 She was **incandescent** with rage.

agenda [ə'dʒendə]

n. a list of things to be considered or done 议程

例 The committee set the **agenda** for the next several years of research.

单词助记【同义词】programme；schedule；plan

indulgent [ɪn'dʌldʒənt]

adj. willing to allow someone to have or enjoy something even though it may not be proper，healthy，appropriate，etc. 放纵的，纵容的

例 He gave the child an **indulgent** smile.

单词助记【同义词】permissive；kind；lenient

filament ['fɪləmənt]

n. a thin thread or hair 细丝，长丝

例 The cable was made up of fine **filaments** twisted together.

单词助记【同义词】thread；strand；string

glib [glɪb]

adj. speaking in a smooth，easy way that is not sincere 口齿伶俐的，油嘴滑舌的

例 Politicians need to do more than provide **glib** answers to difficult questions.

List 40

wretched [ˈretʃɪd]

adj. very unhappy，ill，etc.；very bad or unpleasant 很不愉快的，不幸的，沮丧的

例 I don't know what's wrong with her，but she looks **wretched**.

单词助记【同义词】contemptible

embezzle [ɪmˈbezl]

v. to steal money that you have been trusted with 侵吞；盗用，监守自盗；贪污

例 He was caught **embezzling** money from his clients.

corpulence [ˈkɔːpjʊləns]

n. the state of being fat 肥胖

例 The doctor warned that the patient's **corpulence** was unhealthy and not merely unattractive.

单词助记【同义词】fatness，obesity

单词助记

fractious [ˈfrækʃəs]

adj. causing trouble；hard to manage or control；full of anger and disagreement 易怒的，脾气坏的

例 The **fractious** crowd grew violent.

单词助记【同义词】irritable；peevish；restless

tease [tiːz]

n. a joking remark that criticizes someone in a friendly way；a teasing remark 逗笑，戏弄

例 The lower rate is just a **tease** to attract new customers.

tepid [ˈtepɪd]

adj. not hot and not cold 温的，不冷不热的

例 My suggestion was given a **tepid** response.

单词助记【同义词】lukewarm

intrepid [ɪnˈtrepɪd]

adj. feeling no fear；very bold or brave 无畏的；勇敢的

例 He is an **intrepid** explorer who probed parts of the rain forest never previously attempted.

单词助记【同义词】fearless，courageous

amenable [əˈmiːnəbl]

adj. able to be controlled，organized，or affected by something 易控制的，顺从的

例 Whatever you decide to do，I'm **amenable**—just let me know.

单词助记 【同义词】agreeable

gruesome [ˈɡruːsəm]

adj. causing horror or disgust 可憎的，可怕的

例 The police report described the scene in **gruesome** detail.

单词助记 【同义词】causing horror，grisly

articulate [ɑːˈtɪkjʊlə]

❶ *adj*. able to express ideas clearly and effectively in speech or writing 表达能力强的

例 She's an intelligent and **articulate** speaker.

单词助记 【同义词】eloquent，fluent，effective，persuasive，lucid

❷ *v*. to express (something, such as an idea) in words 清楚地表达

例 He had some trouble **articulating** his thoughts.

deviate [ˈdiːvɪeɪt]

v. to do something that is different or to be different from what is usual or expected 偏离；越轨

例 Sailors were forced to **deviate** from their course in order to avoid the storm.

单词助记 【同义词】differ，depart，diverge

obstacle [ˈɒbstəkl]

n. something that makes it difficult to do something 障碍（物），妨碍

例 He overcame the **obstacles** of poverty and neglect.

单词助记 【同义词】hindrance

intervene [ˌɪntəˈviːn]

v. to occur, fall, or come between points of time or events 干涉，干预；调解

例 The prisoner asked me to **intervene** with the authorities on his behalf.

单词助记 【同义词】interfere，arbitrate，mediate

mangle [ˈmæŋɡl]

v. to injure with deep disfiguring wounds by cutting, tearing, or crushing 严重损毁

例 His body was crushed and **mangled** beyond recognition.

单词助记 【同义词】crush，mash，smash

pretext [ˈpriːtekst]

n. a reason that you give to hide your real reason for doing something 借口

例 She went back to her friend's house on the **pretext** that she had forgotten her purse.

单词助记 【同义词】excuse

conquer [ˈkɒŋkə(r)]

v. to gain control of (a problem or difficulty) through great effort 征服，战胜，攻克

例 The city was **conquered** by the ancient Romans.

单词助记 【同义词】seize，take，capture

intractable [ɪnˈtræktəbl]

adj. not easily managed, controlled, or solved 难驾驭（管理、指挥）的；倔强的；难处理的

例 He is an **intractable** child who deliberately does the opposite of whatever he is told.

单词助记 【同义词】unruly，stubborn

exotic [ɪɡˈzɒtɪk]

adj. introduced from another country; very different, strange, or unusual 异国的；独特的，不一样的

例 She's known for her **exotic** tastes.

单词助记【同义词】foreign

spontaneous [spɒnˈteɪnɪəs]

adj. done or said in a natural and often sudden way and without a lot of thought or planning; doing things that have not been planned but that seem enjoyable and worth doing at a particular time 自发的，无意识的，自然的

例 The comment was completely **spontaneous**.

单词助记【同义词】impulsive, unprompted

amiable [ˈeɪmɪəbl]

adj. friendly and pleasant 和蔼的

例 Everyone knew him as an **amiable** fellow.

单词助记【同义词】friendly, affable, amicable, cordial, warmhearted, agreeable

ossify [ˈɒsɪfaɪ]

v. to become or to cause something to become unable to change 骨化，硬化；使僵化

例 The cartilage will **ossify**，becoming bone.

单词助记【同义词】harden，turn bone

swagger [ˈswægə(r)]

v. walk or behave in a very confident and typically arrogant or aggressive way 大摇大摆地走

例 He **swaggered** into the shop like he owned the place.

单词助记【同义词】strut，parade，stride

malice [ˈmælɪs]

n. a desire to cause harm to another person 恶意，蓄意害人

例 She claimed that her criticisms were without **malice**.

raze [reɪz]

v. to destroy（something，such as a building）completely 彻底摧毁，将……夷为平地

例 The developer **razed** the old school building and built a high-rise condominium complex.

whisper [ˈwɪspə(r)]

v. to speak very softly or quietly 低语，耳语

例 She leaned over and **whispered** to the girl next to her.

单词助记【同义词】rumor；word；gossip

circumspect [ˈsɜːkəmspekt]

adj. thinking carefully about possible risks before doing or saying something 谨慎小心的，周到的

例 She has a reputation for being quiet and **circumspect** in investigating charges of child abuse.

单词助记【同义词】cautious，wary，careful，chary

avarice [ˈævərɪs]

n. a strong desire to have or get money 贪婪

例 The corporate world is plagued by **avarice** and a thirst for power.

单词助记【同义词】greed

flicker [ˈflɪkə(r)]

❶ *v.* to burn or glow in an unsteady way：to produce an unsteady light（通常指灯光）闪烁

例 The overhead light kept **flickering** off and on.

❷ *v.* to move irregularly or unsteadily 摇曳，颤动

例 In a moment her eyelids **flickered**，then opened.

alacrity [əˈlækrəti]

n. a quick and cheerful readiness to do something 敏捷，爽快

例 She accepted the invitation with an **alacrity** that surprised me.

单词助记【同义词】eagerness；speed

surreptitious [ˌsʌrəpˈtɪʃəs]

adj. done in a secret way 偷偷摸摸的，暗中进行的

例 She had a **surreptitious** relationship with her employee.

单词助记【同义词】done in secrecy

nostalgic [nɒsˈtældʒɪk]

adj. unhappy at being away and longing for familiar things or persons 对往事怀恋的，怀旧的

例 Although we still depict **nostalgic** snow scenes on Christmas cards，winters are now very much warmer.

单词助记【同义词】sentimental，wistful，misty

tycoon [taɪˈkuːn]

n. a very wealthy and powerful business person 巨头，大亨

例 a newspaper **tycoon**

单词助记【同义词】magnate，mogul，industrialist

procrastinate [prəˈkræstɪneɪt]

v. to be slow or late about doing something that should be done：to delay doing something until a later time because you do not want to do it，because you are lazy，etc. 拖延，耽搁

例 He **procrastinated** and missed the submission deadline.

incentive [ɪnˈsentɪv]

n. something that encourages a person to do something or to work harder 激励某人做某事的事物，诱因，动机

例 The rising cost of electricity provides a strong **incentive** to conserve energy.

单词助记【同义词】motive，stimulus

counsel [ˈkaʊnsəl]

❶ *n.* advice given to someone 忠告，劝告

例 The student sought **counsel** from her teacher.

单词助记【同义词】advise，recommend，advocate，encourage，urge，warn

❷ *v.* to give advice to（someone）劝告，建议

例 She **counseled** him not to accept the offer.

hutch [hʌtʃ]

n. an enclosed area or cage for an animal 养小动物的圈栏（尤指兔箱），笼；茅屋，小舍

例 The rabbit popped out as soon as we opened the **hutch**.

consummate [kənˈsʌmət]

❶ *v.* to make（something）perfect or complete 使完美

例 Their happiness was **consummated** when their son was born.

单词助记【同义词】complete；perfect.

❷ *v.* finish，complete 使结束

例 The bargaining process went on for a few days，but the deal was never **consummated**.

jaded [ˈdʒeɪdɪd]

adj. feeling or showing a lack of interest and excitement caused by having done or experienced too much of something 精疲力竭的，厌腻了的

例 He became **jaded** from years of work as a police officer.

单词助记【同义词】bored，world-weary，tired

sentry [ˈsentrɪ]

n. a soldier who guards a door，gate，etc. 哨兵，步兵

例 The general placed an armed **sentry** at the bridge.

soporific [ˌsɒpəˈrɪfɪk]

❶ *n*. a soporific agent 催眠的物质、药剂等

例 a substance used as a **soporific**

单词助记【同义词】sleep-inducing.

❷ *adj*. causing a person to become tired and ready to fall asleep 催眠的

例 This medication is **soporific**，so do not drive after taking it.

单词助记【同义词】boring，tedious，tired，dreary

List 42

drool [druːl]

❶ *v.* to let saliva flow out from the mouth 流口水

例 The dog **drooled** when we put the steak down on the floor.

单词助记【同义词】dribble，salivate，slobber.

❷ *v.* to show admiration or desire for something in an exaggerated way 表示过分兴奋

例 Everyone was **drooling** over his new car.

narcissistic [ˌnɑːsɪˈsɪstɪk]

adj. characteristic of those having an inflated idea of their own importance 自恋的，自我陶醉的

例 He was insufferable at times — self-centred and **narcissistic**.

单词助记【同义词】egoistic

confound [kənˈfaʊnd]

v. to surprise and confuse (someone or something) 使惊惶；弄糊涂

例 The murder case has **confounded** investigators.

单词助记【同义词】confuse，muddle，mix up

medley [ˈmedlɪ]

n. a mixture of different people or things 混合物，混杂

例 There is a **medley** of snack foods available on the buffet table.

单词助记【同义词】assortment，mixture

disseminate [dɪˈsemɪneɪt]

v. to cause (something, such as information) to go to many people 散布，传播

例 The Internet allows us to **disseminate** information faster.

单词助记【同义词】scatter；spread

eligible [ˈelɪdʒəbl]

adj. able to be chosen for something；able to do or receive something 有资格当选的，有条件被选中的

例 I'd like to join but I'm not **eligible** yet.

单词助记【同义词】entitled，qualified

altruistic [ˌæltrʊˈɪstɪk]

adj. showing unselfish concern for the welfare of others 利他的，无私心的

例 Such **altruistic** behavior is one of the noblest attributes of our species.

单词助记【同义词】unselfish，humane，selfless

contend [kənˈtend]

❶ *v.* to argue or state (something) in a strong and definite way 争夺，竞争

例 A number of groups are **contending** (with each other) for power in the new government.

单词助记【同义词】compete，struggle，argue.

❷ *v.* maintain，assert 声称，主张

例 These people **contend** that they have earned the right to the land.

poignant [ˈpɔɪnjənt]

adj. causing a strong feeling of sadness 伤心至极的，痛切的

例 The photograph was a **poignant** reminder of her childhood.

单词助记【同义词】touching

discerning [dɪˈsɜːnɪŋ]

adj. able to see and understand people，things，or situations clearly and intelligently 有识别力的；有眼力的；有洞察力的

例 She has a **discerning** eye for good art.

caricature [ˈkærɪkətʃə(r)]

❶ *n*. a drawing that makes someone look funny or foolish because some part of the person's appearance is exaggerated 夸张的描绘或模仿

例 An artist was doing **caricatures** in the park.

单词助记【同义词】exaggerated portrait，cartoon

❷ *v*. to do a caricature of (someone or something)：to draw or describe (someone or something) in a funny or exaggerated way 用漫画表现或夸张描述、模仿……

例 The press **caricatured** him as clumsy and forgetful.

olfactory [ɒlˈfæktəri]

adj. of，relating to，or connected with the sense of smell 嗅觉的

例 We think this indicates that the missing sections had some **olfactory** cue—or cues—that the females had used for recognizing their nests.

acrid [ˈækrɪd]

adj. bitter and unpleasant in taste or smell 辛辣的，刺鼻的

例 Thick，**acrid** smoke rose from the factory.

单词助记【同义词】bitter，harsh

inane [ɪˈneɪn]

adj. very silly or stupid 无意义的，无比愚蠢的

例 The film's plot is **inane** and full of clichés.

单词助记【同义词】lacking sense，silly

circumlocution [ˌsɜːkəmləˈkjuːʃən]

n. the use of many words to say something that could be said more clearly and directly by using fewer words 迂回说法

例 I'm trying to avoid **circumlocutions** in my writing.

antagonize [ænˈtæɡənaɪz]

v. to cause (someone) to feel hostile or angry：to irritate or upset (someone) 敌对，对抗

例 Her comments **antagonized** many people.

单词助记【同义词】provoke，irritate，annoy，oppose

felicitous [fɪˈlɪsɪtəs]

adj. very well suited for some purpose or situation（措辞等）恰当的，贴切的

例 A **felicitous** accompaniment to dinner is provided by a harpist on weekends at the restaurant.

itinerant [aɪˈtɪnərənt]

adj. traveling from place to place：staying in a place for only a short amount of time 巡回的，流动的

例 An **itinerant** musician can see a lot of the world.

单词助记 【同义词】traveling

spurious [ˈspjʊərɪəs]

adj. not genuine, sincere, or authentic; based on false ideas or bad reasoning 伪造的，欺骗性的

例 One reiterated theme of his book is that the electoral process can be the most dangerous of delusions, tending to confer a **spurious** legitimacy on those most willing to corrupt it. —Hilary Mantel, New York Review, 21 Sept. 2006

单词助记 【同义词】false，counterfeit，not genuine

pandemic [pænˈdemɪk]

❶ *adj.* (of a disease) prevalent over a whole country or the world 大范围流行的

例 a **pandemic** virus/disease

单词助记 【同义词】widespread，prevalent，pervasive

❷ *n.* an outbreak of a pandemic disease 大流行病

例 The 1918 flu **pandemic** claimed millions of lives.

List 43

succumb [səˈkʌm]

　　v. to stop trying to resist something 不再抵抗（诱惑、疾病、攻击等），屈从

　　例 They will pressure you, and you must try not to **succumb**.

salient [ˈseɪlɪənt]

　　adj. very important or noticeable 显著的，重要的，主要的

　　例 Chronic fatigue is also one of the **salient** features of depression.

　　单词助记【同义词】prominent, conspicuous

choreographer [ˈkɒrɪəɡrɑːfə]

　　n. someone who decide how a dancer or group of dancers will move during a performance 舞蹈指导

　　例 My **choreographer** keeps chiseling away at me, hoping to shape me into perfection.

turmoil [ˈtɜːmɔɪl]

　　n. a state of confusion or disorder 混乱

　　例 The country has been in **turmoil** for the past 10 years.

　　单词助记【同义词】chaos; disorder; confusion

diplomatic [ˌdɪpləˈmætɪk]

　　adj. having or showing an ability to deal with people in a sensitive and effective way 得体的，圆通的

　　例 We need to find a **diplomatic** way to say no.

　　单词助记【同义词】tactful, delicate, judicious, nonconfrontational, prudent, politic, skillful

discursive [dɪsˈkɜːsɪv]

　　adj. talking or writing about many different things in a way that is not highly organized 东拉西扯的，离题的

　　例 The speaker's **discursive** style made it difficult to understand his point.

　　单词助记【同义词】rambling, digressive, meandering, wandering, maundering

compile [kəmˈpaɪl]

　　❶ *v.* to create (a CD, book, list, etc.) by gathering things (such as songs or pieces of writing or information) 收集

　　例 He **compiled** a book of poems.

　　❷ *v.* to put together (various songs, pieces of writing, facts, etc.) in a publication or collection 编辑，编制

　　例 They took the best submissions and **compiled** them in a single issue of the magazine.

distinct [dɪsˈtɪŋkt]

　　adj. different in a way that you can see, hear, smell, feel, etc.; noticeably different 截然不同的，完全分开的

　　例 Each herb has its own **distinct** flavor.

单词助记 【同义词】specific，distinctive

vacuous [ˈvækjʊəs]

adj. having or showing a lack of intelligence or serious thought；lacking meaning，importance，or substance 空虚的，内容贫乏的，无意义的

例 He had a **vacuous** expression on his face.

单词助记 【同义词】empty，void

tout [taʊt]

v. to try to persuade people to buy your goods or services 兜售，贩卖

例 The company is running advertisements **touting** the drug's effectiveness.

bewildered [bɪˈwɪldəd]

adj. perplexed by many conflicting situations or statements 迷惑的

例 Some shoppers looked **bewildered** by the sheer variety of goods for sale.

adhere [ədˈhɪə(r)]

v. to stick to something；to attach firmly to something 黏附，附着

例 The stamp failed to **adhere**.

epicure [ˈepɪkjʊə(r)]

n. a person who appreciates fine food and drink 讲究饮食的人，美食家

例 Thomas Jefferson was one of America's first great **epicures**.

assimilate [əˈsɪmɪleɪt]

v. to learn (something) so that it is fully understood and can be used；to cause (a person or group) to become part of a different society，country，etc. 吸收，同化

例 Many of these religious traditions have been **assimilated** into the culture.

lampoon [læmˈpuːn]

❶ *n*. a piece of writing，a cartoon，etc.，that mocks or makes fun of a well-known person or thing 讽刺文章或言辞

例 He said such ridiculous things that he was often the target of **lampoons** in the press.

单词助记 【同义词】ridicule

❷ *v*. to publicly criticize (someone or something) in a way that causes laughter 冷嘲热讽，奚落

例 He was **lampooned** for his short stature and political views.

unprincipled [ʌnˈprɪnsəpld]

adj. not having or showing concern for what is right 没道理的，无原则的，不合人道的

例 The **unprincipled** businessman made a lot of money and didn't care how he did it.

单词助记 【同义词】dishonest，corrupt，amoral

nominal [ˈnɒmɪnl]

adj. existing as something in name only；not actual or real 名义上的，有名无实的

例 Her title of vice president had been **nominal** only.

单词助记 【同义词】supposed，ostensible，so-called

exacerbate [ɪgˈzæsəbeɪt]

v. to make (a bad situation，a problem，etc.) worse 使恶化；使加重

例 The proposed factory shutdown would only **exacerbate** our unemployment problems.

单词助记 【同义词】aggravate，worsen

arcane [ɑːˈkeɪn]

adj. secret or mysterious: known or understood by only a few people 秘密的，神秘的

例 Grammatical rules seem **arcane** to generations of students who were never taught grammar in the first place.

单词助记【同义词】mysterious，secret；enigmatic，esoteric，cryptic，obscure，recondite

pundit [ˈpʌndɪt]

n. a person who knows a lot about a particular subject and who expresses ideas and opinions about that subject publicly（such as by speaking on television and radio shows）某一学科的权威，专家

例 The new mini laptop has gotten a thumbs-up from industry **pundits**.

List 44

lucid [ˈluːsɪd]

❶ *adj.* very clear and easy to understand 清楚的，易懂的

例 He is able to recognize his wife in his **lucid** moments.

单词助记【同义词】clear, easily understood

❷ *adj.* suffused with light: luminous 清澈的，透明的

例 a **lucid** account of the history of mankind

invigorate [ɪnˈvɪɡəreɪt]

v. to give life and energy to (someone) 使生气勃勃，使精力充沛，使健壮

例 A brisk walk in the cool morning air always **invigorates** me.

单词助记【同义词】refresh, energize, revitalize

abstinence [ˈæbstɪnəns]

n. the practice of not doing or having something that is wanted or enjoyable 节制，节欲

例 The program promoted sexual **abstinence** for young people.

单词助记【同义词】self-denial, self-restraint, self-discipline

acumen [əˈkjuːmən]

n. the ability to think clearly and make good decisions 敏锐，聪明

例 Her political **acumen** won her the election.

单词助记【同义词】shrewdness

ballad [ˈbæləd]

n. a kind of poem or song that tells a story (such as a story about a famous person from history) 民歌（特别指叙述故事的歌），民谣

例 He is listening to a haunting **ballad** about lost love and loneliness.

单词助记【同义词】popular/romantic song or poem

dueling [ˈdjuːəlɪŋ]

n. a formal fight between two people in which they use guns or swords in order to settle a quarrel 决斗

例 They had been **dueling** for hours and finally called a draw.

pithy [ˈpɪθɪ]

adj. using few words in a clever and effective way 简练的，精辟的，简洁扼要的

例 The book is filled with **pithy** sayings about love and loss.

单词助记【同义词】profound；concise；meaningful

unleash [ʌnˈliːʃ]

v. to allow or cause (something very powerful) to happen suddenly 释放，引发

例 The storm **unleashed** its fury. / The editorial unleashed a flood of angry responses.

insolent [ˈɪnsələnt]

adj. rude or impolite: having or showing a lack of respect for other people 倨慢的，无礼的

例 **Insolent** behavior will not be tolerated.

单词助记 【同义词】offensive；insulting

lush [lʌʃ]

adj. growing vigorously especially with luxuriant foliage 茂盛的

例 The frequent rainfall encourages the **lush** growth of trees，ferns，and shrubs.

boorish [ˈbʊərɪʃ]

adj. resembling or befitting a boor（as in crude insensitivity）粗野的

例 His behavior，too，became steadily more outrageous，sometimes descending into the pointlessly provocative or **boorish**.

单词助记 【同义词】rude，ill-mannered，impolite

intransigent [ɪnˈtrænsɪdʒənt]

adj. completely unwilling to change：very stubborn 不让步的，不妥协的；难和解的，势不两立的

例 He has remained **intransigent** in his opposition to the proposal.

单词助记 【同义词】uncompromising

bibliography [ˌbɪblɪˈɒɡrəfɪ]

n. a list of the books，magazines，articles，etc.，that are mentioned in a text 文献书，参考书目

例 The instructor provided the students with an excellent **bibliography** on local history.

单词助记 【同义词】list，index，appendix

aviary [ˈeɪvɪərɪ]

n. a place（such as a large cage or a building）where many birds are kept 大鸟笼，鸟舍

例 The zoo has a new outdoor **aviary**.

tumult [ˈtjuːmʌlt]

n. a state of noisy confusion or disorder 激动的吵闹声

例 We had to shout to be heard over the **tumult**.

单词助记 【同义词】confusion，disorder

perfunctory [pəˈfʌŋktərɪ]

adj. used to describe something that is done without energy or enthusiasm because of habit or because it is expected 敷衍的，马虎的

例 The violinist delivered a **perfunctory** performance that displayed none of the passion and warmth he was once known for.

单词助记 【同义词】routine

hatch [hætʃ]

v. to produce young by incubation 孵化

例 The young disappeared soon after they were **hatched**.

单词助记

fervid [ˈfɜːvɪd]

adj. having or showing feelings that are very strong or too strong 充满激情的，热烈的

例 At the school board meeting the librarian delivered a **fervid** speech defending the classic novel against would-be censors.

单词助记 【同义词】intense，passionate

slovenly ['slʌvənlɪ]

adj. untidy especially in personal appearance 不修边幅的

例 He dressed in a **slovenly** manner.

单词助记 【同义词】careless；dishevelled；untidy

furnish ['fɜːnɪʃ]

❶ *v*. to supply or give（something）to someone or something 提供

例 They'll be able to **furnish** you with the rest of the details.

单词助记 【同义词】supply，provide，equip

❷ *v*. to provide（a room or building）with furniture（用家具）布置

例 He has enough money to **furnish** the apartment nicely.

competent ['kɒmpɪtənt]

adj. having the necessary ability or skills; able to do something well or well enough to meet a standard 有能力的,能胜任的

例 The defendant was declared **competent** to stand trial.

单词助记【同义词】capable, fit

bolster ['bəʊlstə(r)]

v. to make (something) stronger or better; to give support to (something) 给予必要的支持,鼓励

例 She came with me to **bolster** my confidence.

单词助记【同义词】support, uphold

fulcrum ['fʌlkrəm]

n. the support on which a lever moves when it is used to lift something 杠杆支点

例 We unconsciously assume the center of a picture corresponds to a **fulcrum**.

单词助记【同义词】pivot, hinge, swivel

impugn [ɪm'pjuːn]

v. to criticize (a person's character, intentions, etc.) by suggesting that someone is not honest and should not to be trusted 批评;对……有怀疑

例 Her motives have been scrutinized and **impugned**.

单词助记【同义词】cast doubt upon, call in question

compassion [kəm'pæʃən]

n. a feeling of wanting to help someone who is sick, hungry, in trouble, etc. 怜悯,同情

例 She had the **compassion** to offer help when it was needed most.

单词助记【同义词】sympathy, empathy, concern, solicitude

subtle ['sʌtl]

adj. hard to notice or see; not obvious 不易察觉的

例 Racial discrimination still exists, only now it's more **subtle** than it once was.

translucent [trænz'luːsənt]

adj. not completely clear or transparent but clear enough to allow light to pass through 半透明的

例 The building is roofed entirely with **translucent** corrugated plastic.

oracle ['ɒrəkl]

n. an answer or message given by an oracle; a person (such as a priestess) through whom a god was believed to speak 神示,神谕;圣贤,哲人

例 I met her long before she had become the **oracle** of pop culture.

immaculate [ɪ'mækjʊlət]

adj. perfectly clean; having no flaw or error 整洁的,无污迹的

例 She had an **immaculate** record of service.

单词助记【同义词】tidy

pyramid [ˈpɪrəmɪd]

　　n. a very large structure built especially in ancient Egypt that has a square base and four triangular sides which form a point at the top; a shape, object, or pile that is wide near the bottom and narrows gradually as it reaches the top 金字塔

　　例 On a plate in front of him was piled a **pyramid** of flat white crackers.

debunk [diːˈbʌŋk]

　　v. to show that something (such as a belief or theory) is not true; to show the falseness of (a story, idea, statement, etc.) 揭穿真相,暴露

　　例 The article **debunks** the notion that life exists on Mars.

　　单词助记【同义词】discredit

extinguish [ɪkˈstɪŋgwɪʃ]

　　v. to cause (something) to stop burning 熄灭,扑灭

　　例 The fire department was called in to **extinguish** the blaze.

　　单词助记【同义词】douse, quench

equivocal [ɪˈkwɪvəkəl]

　　adj. having two or more possible meanings; not easily understood or explained 模棱两可的,模糊的,含糊的

　　例 He responded to reporters' questions with **equivocal** answers.

　　单词助记【同义词】ambiguous, indefinite, vague

prophesy [ˈprɒfɪsaɪ]

　　v. to state that something will happen in the future 预言,预报

　　例 The book claims that modern events were **prophesied** in ancient times.

affable [ˈæfəbl]

　　adj. friendly and easy to talk to 平易的,和蔼的

　　例 As the show's **affable** host, she keeps the freewheeling gabfest from getting out of hand.

　　单词助记【同义词】friendly, amiable, genial, congenial, cordial, warm

detain [dɪˈteɪn]

　　❶ *v*. to keep or prevent (someone) from leaving or arriving at the expected time 耽搁

　　例 We were **detained** for 15 minutes by a flat tire.

　　单词助记【同义词】delay; hold up; keep.

　　❷ *v*. to officially prevent (someone) from leaving a place; to hold or keep (someone) in a prison or some other place 扣押,拘留

　　例 They were **detained** by the police for questioning.

melancholy [ˈmelənkəlɪ]

　　n. a sad mood or feeling 忧郁,悲哀

　　例 The bleakness of winter sometimes gives me cause for **melancholy**.

　　单词助记【同义词】sadness, state of grief

jeer [dʒɪə(r)]

　　❶ *v*. to shout insulting words at someone; to laugh at or criticize someone in a loud and angry way 嘲笑

　　例 The prisoner was **jeered** by an angry mob.

　　❷ *n*. a jeering remark or sound 嘲讽

　　例 There was constant **jeer** and interruption from the floor.

disparity [dɪsˈpærətɪ]

    n. inequality or difference in some respect 不同；不一致

    例 The US has had an enormous amount of income **disparity** for quite some time.

单词助记【同义词】difference，inequality，discrepancy

pulp [pʌlp]

    ❶ *n.* the inner，juicy part of a fruit or vegetable 水果的肉质部分，果肉

    例 The fruit has sweet，juicy **pulp** and hard，black seeds.

    ❷ *n.* popular or sensational writing that is generally regarded as being of poor quality 粗制滥造的书籍

    例 The story is a mix of **pulp** fiction and Greek tragedy.

facetious [fəˈsiːʃəs]

adj. joking or jesting often inappropriately 诙谐的，爱开玩笑的，不当戏谑的

例 The essay is a **facetious** commentary on the absurdity of war as a solution for international disputes.

officious [əˈfɪʃəs]

adj. describe an annoying person who tries to tell other people what to do in a way that is not wanted or needed 过分殷勤的，爱管闲事的

例 That **officious** little man always tells everyone else how to do their jobs.

单词助记【同义词】overly helpful, bossy

anesthetic [ˌænɪsˈθetɪk]

❶ *adj.* lacking awareness or sensitivity 麻醉的

例 the **anesthetic** properties of a drug.

❷ *n.* a substance that produces anesthesia 麻醉剂

例 The doctor gave him the stitches without an **anesthetic**.

posthumously [ˈpɒstjuməslɪ]

adv. after death 死后地

例 This has been cited as the reason she was not included with the others：The Nobel Prize is not awarded **posthumously**.

scoff [skɒf]

❶ *n.* an expression of scorn, derision, or contempt：gibe 嘲笑；嘲弄的话

例 His army was the **scoff** of all Europe.

单词助记【同义词】jeer, scorn

❷ *v.* to show contempt by derisive acts or language 嘲笑，嘲弄

例 Industry executives continued to **scoff** at the idea of Apple being considered a serious games company.

coddle [ˈkɒdl]

v. to treat (someone) with too much care or kindness 悉心照料，娇惯

例 The judges were accused of **coddling** criminals.

单词助记【同义词】baby

单词助记 可以和 cuddle：搂抱，记在一起。

nadir [ˈneɪˌdɪə(r)]

n. the worst or lowest point of something 天底，最低点；最压抑、消沉等的时刻

例 The relationship between the two countries reached a **nadir** in the 1920s.

droll [drəʊl]

adj. having an odd and amusing quality 有趣的，滑稽的

例 his unique brand of **droll** self-mockery

单词助记【同义词】amusing, funny, comic

infuriate [ɪnˈfjʊərɪeɪt]

v. to make (someone) very angry：to make (someone) furious 激怒，使发怒

例 I was **infuriated** by his arrogance.

单词助记【同义词】annoy，irritate

tractable [ˈtræktəbl]

adj. easily managed or controlled 易处理的，驯服的，温顺的

例 This new approach should make the problem more **tractable**.

fluctuate [ˈflʌktʃʊeɪt]

v. to change level，strength，or value frequently 波动，涨落，起伏

例 His popularity has **fluctuated** during his term in office.

单词助记【同义词】vary，alter，ebb and flow

pertinacious [ˌpɜːtɪˈneɪʃəs]

adj. adhering resolutely to an opinion，purpose，or design；perversely persistent 坚持的，固执的，坚决的

例 Whenever they encounter something，they manage to see it through，striving forward toward it and dealing with it confidently with indomitable will and **pertinacious** perseverance.

单词助记【同义词】resolute，stubborn，obstinate

boisterous [ˈbɔɪstərəs]

adj. very noisy and active in a lively way 狂暴的，喧闹的

例 A large and **boisterous** crowd attended the concert.

contrite [ˈkɒntraɪt]

adj. feeling or showing regret for bad behavior 悔悟的，由悔悟引发的

例 Being **contrite** is not enough to spare you an arrest if you're caught shoplifting.

单词助记【同义词】sorry，repentant

hapless [ˈhæplɪs]

adj. having no luck；very unfortunate 不幸的，倒霉的

例 She plays the **hapless** heroine who is unlucky in love.

单词助记【同义词】unfortunate，unlucky，luckless

fawn [fɔːn]

❶ *n.* a deer that is less than a year old（未满一岁的）幼鹿；浅黄褐色

例 The **fawn** ran to the top of the ridge.

❷ *v.* to try to get the approval of an important or powerful person by giving that person praise，special attention，etc. 巴结，奉承，讨好

例 The waiters were **fawning**（all）over the celebrity.

❸ *adj.* a light brown color 浅黄褐色的

例 Tania was standing there in her light **fawn** coat.

单词助记

debilitate [dɪˈbɪlɪteɪt]

v. to make（someone or something）weak；to reduce the strength of（someone or something) 使（人或人的身体）非常虚弱

例 The virus **debilitates** the body's immune system.

单词助记【同义词】enfeeble，enervate，devitalize，sap

congregation [ˌkɒŋgrɪˈgeɪʃən]

n. an assembly of persons 集合在一起的群众

例 She is a member of a small **congregation**.

单词助记【同义词】church-goers，audience，flock

curvature [ˈkɜːvətʃə(r)]

n. the act of curving：the state of being curved 弯曲

例 The lenses have different **curvatures**.

contemptuous [kənˈtemptjʊəs]

adj. feeling or showing deep hatred or disapproval：feeling or showing contempt 蔑视的；鄙视的；表示轻蔑的

例 He made some **contemptuous** comments about the baseball team's pathetic showings.

单词助记【同义词】scornful，disdainful，disrespectful，insulting，insolent，derisive

nocturnal [nɒkˈtɜːnl]

adj. active mainly during the night 夜间的,夜间发生的

例 He bought a new telescope so he could pursue his favorite **nocturnal** hobby of astronomy.

eternal [ɪˈtɜːnəl]

adj. having no beginning and no end in time; lasting forever; existing at all times; always true or valid 永久的,不朽的

例 When will his **eternal** whining stop?

单词助记【同义词】everlasting; undying; unending

tangle [ˈtæŋgəl]

n. a tangled twisted mass; snarl; a complicated or confused state or condition 缠结,纠缠

例 They got caught in a legal/financial **tangle**.

单词助记【同义词】mass; jumble; knot

parry [ˈpærɪ]

❶ v. to defend yourself by turning or pushing aside (a punch, a weapon, etc.) 挡开,避开

例 She cleverly **parried** the reporters' questions.

单词助记【同义词】deflect, block, fend off.

❷ n. an act or instance of skillfully avoiding something 挡开,避开,闪避

例 Her question met with a **polite** parry.

estranged [ɪsˈtreɪndʒd]

adj. caused to be unloved 疏远的,不和的

例 Sometimes I will be angry and when I am, I will try to tell you openly so that I need not hate our differences or feel **estranged**.

单词助记【同义词】alienated, separated, apart

sensible [ˈsensəbl]

adj. having or showing good sense or judgment 明智的,合情理的,切合实际的

例 She was **sensible** enough to stop driving when she got too tired.

单词助记【同义词】reasonable, practical

levity [ˈlevɪtɪ]

n. a lack of seriousness; excessive or unseemly frivolity 欠考虑,不慎重,轻率,轻浮

例 They managed to find some **levity** in the situation.

单词助记【同义词】light-heartedness

filch [fɪltʃ]

v. to steal (something that is small or that has little value) 偷(尤指小的或不贵重的物品)

例 He **filched** a pack of gum when no one was looking.

单词助记【同义词】steal

disputatious [ˌdɪspjuːˈteɪʃəs]

adj. inclined or showing an inclination to dispute or disagree，even to engage in law suits 争辩的，好争辩的

例 He is a **disputatious** professor who could give you an argument on just about anything.

abundant [əˈbʌndənt]

adj. existing or occurring in large amounts 丰富的，大量的

例 Rainfall is more **abundant** in summer.

单词助记【同义词】plentiful，copious，rich

bleach [bliːtʃ]

❶ *v*. to remove color or dirt and stains from（hair，clothing，etc.）especially through the effect of sunlight or by using chemicals 漂白

例 Those pants will look nicer if you **bleach** them.

单词助记【同义词】lighten；peroxide；blanch.

❷ *n*. a strong chemical that is used to make something clean or white 漂白剂

例 **Bleach** keeps the white clothes from yellowing.

mutiny [ˈmjuːtɪnɪ]

n. an open rebellion against the proper authorities 叛乱

例 The **mutiny** was led by the ship's cook.

单词助记【同义词】insurrection，rebellion，revolt，riot

herbivorous [hɜːˈbɪvərəs]

adj. feeding on plants 食草的

例 The camel is a **herbivorous** animal.

bombastic [bɒmˈbæstɪk]

adj. marked by or given to a speech or writing that is meant to sound important or impressive but is not sincere or meaningful 夸夸其谈的，空洞浮夸的

例 She gave a **bombastic** speech intended to impress the voters in her congressional district.

urbane [ɜːˈbeɪn]

adj. polite and confident 彬彬有礼的，温文尔雅的

例 The dialogue is witty and **urbane**.

单词助记【同义词】courteous

conglomerate [kənˈɡlɒmərɪt]

n. a composite mass or mixture 聚合物

例 Our small company must compete with the big **conglomerates**.

futile [ˈfjuːtaɪl]

adj. having no result or effect：pointless or useless 无效的，无用的

例 All our efforts proved **futile**.

gigantic [dʒaɪˈɡæntɪk]

adj. extremely large 巨大的，巨人似的

例 A raccoon got into the trash and now there's a **gigantic** mess in our backyard.

单词助记【同义词】huge，enormous，massive

precocious [prɪˈkəʊʃəs]

adj. of a child：having or showing the qualities or abilities of an adult at an unusually early age 早熟的,较早具备某种能力的,超常的,较早显出的,(儿童)老气的

例 A **precocious** musician，he was giving concerts when he was seven.

acrimony [ˈækrɪmənɪ]

    n. angry and bitter feelings 尖刻,刻薄

    例 The dispute began again with increased **acrimony**.

单词助记【同义词】bitterness，anger

deleterious [ˌdelɪˈtɪərɪəs]

　　adj. damaging or harmful 有害的，有毒的

　　例 The chemical is **deleterious** to the environment.

　　单词助记【同义词】harmful, damaging, detrimental, injurious

temperance [ˈtempərəns]

　　n. the practice of always controlling your actions, thoughts, or feelings so that you do not eat or drink too much, become too angry, etc.; the practice of drinking little or no alcohol 节制（尤指饮食），戒酒

　　例 My father attributes his ripe old age to **temperance** in all things, especially eating and drinking.

　　单词助记【同义词】moderation, self-control

tirade [taɪˈreɪd]

　　n. a long and angry speech 长篇激烈的演说

　　例 The coach directed a **tirade** at the team after the loss.

timorous [ˈtɪmərəs]

　　adj. easily frightened 胆怯的，羞怯的

　　例 He spoke with a **timorous** voice.

　　单词助记【同义词】fearful

decipher [dɪˈsaɪfə(r)]

　　v. to find the meaning of (something that is difficult to read or understand); decode 解开（疑团），破译（密码）

　　例 I couldn't **decipher** his sloppy handwriting.

　　单词助记【同义词】decode, decrypt, interpret

celestial [sɪˈlestɪəl]

　　adj. of or relating the sky or heavens 天空的；天堂的

　　例 The late afternoon sunlight gave the room a **celestial** glow.

assiduous [əˈsɪdjʊəs]

　　adj. showing great care, attention, and effort 专心致志的，勤勉的

　　例 They were **assiduous** in their search for all the latest facts and figures.

　　单词助记【同义词】diligent, persistent

soothe [suːð]

　　v. gently calm (a person or their feelings) 安慰；平息

　　例 The waiter tried to **soothe** the angry customer.

cursory [ˈkɜːsərɪ]

　　adj. done or made quickly but carelessly 粗略的，草率的，仓促的

　　例 Only a **cursory** inspection of the building's electrical wiring was done.

　　单词助记【同义词】perfunctory, desultory, casual, superficial

rustic [ˈrʌstɪk]

adj. of, relating to, or suitable for the country or people who live in the country 有农村或村民特色的

例 The inn has a **rustic** atmosphere.

单词助记 【同义词】rural

limpid [ˈlɪmpɪd]

adj. perfectly clear 清澈的

例 Her eyes are the blue of a **limpid** stream of water.

单词助记 【同义词】transparent，clear，translucent

evict [ɪˈvɪkt]

v. to force (someone) to leave a place (依法从房屋里或土地上)驱逐，赶出

例 His landlord has threatened to **evict** him if he doesn't pay the rent soon.

单词助记 【同义词】throw out，kick out，expel

mar [mɑː(r)]

v. to ruin the beauty or perfection of (something)：to hurt or damage the good condition of (something) 毁坏，损坏，玷污

例 Her acting **mars** an otherwise great movie.

单词助记 【同义词】disfigure，spoil

ailment [ˈeɪlmənt]

n. a sickness or illness 疾病

例 The doctor treated him for a variety of **ailments**.

单词助记 【同义词】illness，sickness，disease

charlatan [ˈʃɑːlətən]

n. a person who falsely pretends to know or be something in order to deceive people 冒充内行者，骗子

例 The famed faith healer turned out to be a **charlatan**.

单词助记 【同义词】fake，impostor

empirical [ɪmˈpɪrɪkəl]

adj. based on testing or experience 以观察或实验为依据的

例 They collected plenty of **empirical** data from their experiments.

单词助记 【同义词】experiential，experimental，firsthand

captivate [ˈkæptɪveɪt]

v. to attract and hold the attention of (someone) by being interesting，pretty，etc. 迷惑

例 The play has been **captivating** audiences for years.

单词助记 【同义词】attract，charm，enchant

rancorous [ˈræŋkərəs]

adj. marked by rancor：deeply malevolent 深恨的，怀恶意的

例 It is a **rancorous** autobiography in which the author heaps blame on just about everyone who had the misfortune of knowing him.

duplicity [djuːˈplɪsətɪ]

n. dishonest behavior that is meant to trick someone 表里不一，欺骗，欺诈

例 He exposed the spy's **duplicity**.

单词助记 【同义词】deception，trickery

ardent [ˈɑːdənt]

adj. having or showing very strong feelings 热心的，热情的

例 He made **ardent** declarations of love to the woman he someday hoped to marry.

单词助记 【同义词】passionate，enthusiastic，keen

List 49

paradox [ˈpærədɒks]

n. a seemingly absurd or self-contradictory statement or proposition that when investigated or explained may prove to be well founded or true 悖论，矛盾的事物

例 It is a **paradox** that computers need maintenance so often, since they are meant to save people time.

单词助记 【同义词】contradiction，incongruity，conflict

stagnant [ˈstægnənt]

adj. not active, changing, or progressing 不流动的，停滞的

例 Many people who make their living in academia are reasonably well insulated from financial devastation. For most tenured faculty, the worst they are likely to experience is **stagnant** pay and deferred retirement.

单词助记 【同义词】still，motionless，quiet

capricious [kəˈprɪʃəs]

adj. changing often and quickly; especially: often changing suddenly in mood or behavior 无定见的，变幻莫测的

例 The court ruled that the punishment was arbitrary and **capricious**.

单词助记 【同义词】fickle，mercurial，volatile，unpredictable，temperamental，whimsical

clairvoyant [kleəˈvɔɪənt]

❶ *adj*. able to see beyond the range of ordinary perception 透视的，有洞察力的

例 In order to reach these higher levels, some **clairvoyant** ability is required. This can be developed, or natural ability.

❷ *n*. one having the ability to ability to communicate with dead people, to predict future events, or to know about things that you did not actually see happen or hear about 透视者，千里眼的人

例 You did not have to be a **clairvoyant** to see that the war would go on.

deride [dɪˈraɪd]

v. to talk or write about (someone or something) in a very critical or insulting way: to say that (someone or something) is ridiculous or has no value 取笑，嘲笑

例 My brothers **derided** our efforts, but they were forced to eat their words when we won first place.

单词助记 【同义词】ridicule，mock，scoff，jibe

inertia [ɪˈnɜːʃə]

❶ *n*. lack of movement or activity especially when movement or activity is wanted or needed 惯性

例 **Inertia** carried the plane onto the ground.

❷ *n*. a feeling of not having the energy or desire that is needed to move, change, etc. 无力

例 He blames governmental **inertia** for the holdup.

单词助记 【同义词】apathy，inactivity，torpor

splice [splaɪs]

v. to join ropes，wires，etc.，by weaving or twisting them together 接合

例 Film editors used to **splice** reels of film together to make a whole movie.

mitigate [ˈmɪtɪɡeɪt]

v. to make (something) less severe，harmful，or painful 温和，缓和，减轻

例 Emergency funds are being provided to help **mitigate** the effects of the disaster.

单词助记【同义词】lessen

flounder [ˈflaʊndə(r)]

❶ *v*. to struggle to move or obtain footing (常指在水中)挣扎

例 He was **floundering** around in the pool like an amateur.

单词助记【同义词】stumble，fall，sink

❷ *n*. a type of fish that has a flat body and that is eaten as food 比目鱼

sonorous [səˈnɔːrəs]

adj. having a sound that is deep，loud，and pleasant 圆润低沉的(尤指语言、文字等)感人的，堂皇的

例 He has a deep，**sonorous** voice.

somnolent [ˈsɒmnələnt]

adj. tired and ready to fall asleep 瞌睡的，困的，昏昏欲睡的

例 The professor is trying to teach **somnolent** students on a very hot day.

单词助记【同义词】sleepy

prattle [ˈprætl]

❶ *v*. to talk for very long about something that is not important or interesting (小孩般)天真无邪地说话，闲扯，东拉西扯

例 They **prattled** on into the night，discussing school，music，and friends.

单词助记【同义词】babble

❷ *n*. trifling or empty talk 闲扯，东拉西扯，(小孩般)咿咿呀呀的话

例 Your **prattle** begins to annoy me.

gregarious [ɡrɪˈɡeərɪəs]

❶ *adj*. (of a person) fond of company；sociable 爱交际的

例 She is outgoing and **gregarious**.

单词助记【同义词】sociable，convivial，affable，amiable

❷ *adj*. (of animals) living in flocks or loosely organized communities 群居的

例 Snow geese are very **gregarious** birds.

单词助记【同义词】sociable

hackneyed [ˈhæknɪd]

adj. not interesting，funny，etc.，because of being used too often：not fresh or original 不新奇的，陈腐的，常见的

例 It's **hackneyed**，but true—the more you save the more you earn.

clamor [ˈklæmə(r)]

❶ *n*. a loud continuous noise (such as the noise made when many people are talking or shouting) 喧闹，叫嚷，大声的要求

例 A **clamor** outside woke them up in the night.

单词助记【同义词】shouting

❷ *v*. to make a din 喧嚷，大声要求

例 The children **clamored** around them，singing songs and laughing.

larva [ˈlɑːvə]

n. a very young form of an insect that looks like a worm（昆虫）幼虫,（蠕虫）蚴

例 The **larva** of a butterfly is called a caterpillar.

hirsute [ˈhɜːsjuːt]

adj. having a lot of hair especially on the face or body 多毛的

例 The actor wore a **hirsute** mask as part of his werewolf costume.

单词助记【同义词】hairy，long-haired，unshaven

vilify [ˈvɪlɪfaɪ]

v. to say or write very harsh and critical things about（someone or something）中伤,诽谤

例 He was **vilified** in the press for his comments.

ravenous [ˈrævənəs]

adj. very hungry 极饿的

例 By the time dinner was ready，we were **ravenous**.

glistening [ˈɡlɪsənɪŋ]

adj. flashing，reflecting light 闪耀的,反光的

例 Deborah's face was white and **glistening** with sweat.

List 50

tactful [ˈtæktfəl]

adj. careful not to offend or upset other people；having or showing tact 圆通的，言行得体的

例 It was **tactful** of her not to criticize me in front of my boss.

preach [priːtʃ]

v. to make a speech about religion in a church or other public place；to deliver a sermon；to write or speak about (something) in an approving way 说教，布道，鼓吹

例 The minister **preached** to the congregation about the need for tolerance.

单词助记【同义词】sermon，proclaim，advocate

单词助记

banish [ˈbænɪʃ]

v. to send (someone or something) away 放逐，驱逐

例 The dictator **banished** anyone who opposed him.

单词助记【同义词】exile，expel，deport，eject，expatriate，ostracize

vivacious [vɪˈveɪʃəs]

adj. happy and lively in a way that is attractive 活泼的，快活的

例 Historically，in nations where city economies are dying and where，as well，cities are drained in service to transactions of decline，one city remains **vivacious** longest：the capital city. —Jane Jacobs，Cities and the Wealth of Nations，(1984) 1985

单词助记【同义词】lively

diffuse [dɪˈfjuːz]

❶ *adj.* spread out over a large space；not concentrated in one area 四散的，漫射的

例 The forest was filled with a soft，**diffuse** light.

单词助记【同义词】disperse，spread，disseminate

❷ *v.* to spread out：to move freely throughout a large area (使)扩散，(使)弥漫，(使)传播

例 The heat from the radiator **diffuses** throughout the room.

extravagant [ɪksˈtrævəgənt]

adj. more than is usual，necessary，or proper；very fancy；very expensive and not necessary 奢侈的；过度的；放肆的

例 The company has been making **extravagant** claims about the drug's effectiveness.

【同义词】wasteful, excessive

persevere [ˌpɜːsɪˈvɪə(r)]

　　v. to continue doing something or trying to do something even though it is difficult 坚忍,坚持

　　例 She **persevered** in her studies and graduated near the top of her class.

plethora [ˈpleθərə]

　　n. a very large amount or number; an amount that is much greater than what is necessary 过多,过剩,过量

　　例 There has been a **plethora** of plays in recent years whose claim to modernity is based on indicated rather than felt emotion.

【同义词】abundance, excess

eddy [ˈedɪ]

　　❶ *n.* a circular movement of air or water 旋涡

　　例 The boat was caught in a powerful **eddy**.

【同义词】current

　　❷ *v.* to move in a circle; to form an eddy (使)起旋涡

　　例 The dust whirled and **eddied** in the sunlight.

phobia [ˈfəʊbɪə]

　　n. an extremely strong dislike or fear of someone or something 恐惧,厌恶

　　例 His fear of crowds eventually developed into a **phobia**.

【同义词】fear, terror, dread

release [rɪˈliːs]

　　❶ *v.* to allow (a person or animal) to leave a jail, cage, prison, etc.; to set (someone or something) free; to stop holding (someone or something) 释放,放开

　　例 There is a lot of controversy over whether or not wolves should be **released** into the park.

【同义词】let go, set free

　　❷ *n.* relief or deliverance from sorrow, suffering, or trouble 释放,排放,解除

　　例 The prisoner was questioned before his **release**.

overwhelm [ˌəʊvəˈwelm]

　　v. to affect strike (someone) very strongly (强烈地影响而)使不知所措,压垮

　　例 The city was **overwhelmed** by the invading army.

【同义词】exhaust, defeat

conscientious [ˌkɒnʃɪˈenʃəs]

　　adj. very careful about doing what you are supposed to do; concerned with doing something correctly 认真的,勤奋的

　　例 He was **conscientious** about following the doctor's orders.

【同义词】diligent, industrious, punctilious, sedulous, assiduous

nonchalant [ˈnɒnʃələnt]

　　adj. relaxed and calm in a way that shows that you do not care or are not worried about anything 漠不关心的,无动于衷的

　　例 The team may have been somewhat **nonchalant** at the beginning of the season, but they now know that they need to work hard.

【同义词】casual, offhand, cool

fabricate [ˈfæbrɪkeɪt]

❶ *v*. invent or concoct（something），typically with deceitful intent 伪造

例 She was accused of **fabricating** data.

单词助记【同义词】concoct，make up，invent

❷ *v*. construct or manufacture（something，especially an industrial product），especially from prepared components 生产

例 Their plan is to **fabricate** the house out of synthetic materials.

单词助记【同义词】create，manufacture，assemble，fashion

whimsical [ˈwɪmzɪkəl]

adj. unusual in a playful or amusing way：not serious 异想天开的；古怪的；反复无常的

例 She has a **whimsical** sense of humor.

单词助记【同义词】unpredictable，capricious

inexorable [ɪnˈeksərəbl]

adj. not able to be stopped or changed 无情的，不可阻挡的

例 He made an **inexorable** demand.

单词助记【同义词】determined，relentless

truncate [trʌŋˈkeɪt]

v. to make（something）shorter 修剪；把……截短，删减，缩短

例 Sorry, the text is too long to edit. **Truncate** it to 255 characters?

单词助记【同义词】cut off

dissension [dɪˈsenʃən]

n. disagreement that causes the people in a group to argue about something that is important to them 意见不合，纠纷，争吵

例 The incident has caused a lot of **dissension** within the police department.

indomitable [ɪnˈdɒmɪtəbl]

adj. impossible to defeat or discourage 不屈服的，不气馁的，不可战胜的

例 An **indomitable** spirit was needed to endure the rigors of pioneer life.

单词助记【同义词】uncontrollable

taunt [tɔːnt]

n. a sarcastic challenge or insult 嘲笑

例 For years they suffered racist **taunts**.

单词助记 【同义词】mock，tease，jeer

thwart [θwɔːt]

v. to prevent (someone) from doing something or to stop (something) from happening 阻挠

例 The army **thwarted** the attempt at a coup.

单词助记 【同义词】frustrate，spoil，prevent

despicable [ˈdespɪkəbl]

adj. very bad or unpleasant：deserving to be despised 卑劣的，卑鄙的，可鄙的

例 She is a **despicable** traitor.

单词助记 【同义词】contemptible，loathsome，hateful，detestable，reprehensible，abhorrent

innuendo [ˌɪnjuːˈendəʊ]

n. a statement which indirectly suggests that someone has done something immoral，improper，etc. 含沙射影的话；暗讽

例 His reputation has been damaged by **innuendos** about his drinking and gambling.

单词助记 【同义词】insinuation

conflagration [ˌkɒnfləˈɡreɪʃən]

n. a large destructive fire 大火（灾）

例 A **conflagration** in 1947 reduced 90 percent of the houses to ashes.

单词助记 【同义词】fire，blaze，inferno

premonition [ˌpreməˈnɪʃən]

n. a feeling or belief that something is going to happen when there is no definite reason to believe it will 预先的警告（告诫），预感；前兆

例 She had a **premonition** that he would call.

pliant [ˈplaɪnt]

adj. able to bend without breaking；able to move freely 易弯的，柔韧的；能适应的

例 She's proud and stubborn，you know，under that **pliant** exterior.

单词助记 【同义词】flexible，pliable

punctuality [ˌpʌŋktjʊˈælətɪ]

n. the quality or habit of adhering to an appointed time 准时

例 The most lovable and hateful thing in him is his **punctuality**.

单词助记 【同义词】promptness，timekeeping，reliability

fidget [ˈfɪdʒɪt]

❶ *v.* to make a lot of small movements because you are nervous，bored，etc.；to move or act in a nervous or restless way 坐立不安

例 He was constantly **fidgeting** in his chair.

单词助记【同义词】 twitch，squirm，fret.

❷ *n*. uneasiness or restlessness as shown by nervous movements 坐立不安

例 The overwhelming **fidgets** keep him stay up all night.

effigy [ˈefɪdʒɪ]

n. an image or representation especially of a person；especially：a crude figure representing a hated person（人或动物的）雕像，模拟像，肖像

单词助记【同义词】 image，statue，figure

truculent [ˈtrʌkjʊlənt]

adj. easily annoyed or angered and likely to argue 好斗的，寻衅的

例 The hard work is to demonstrate exactly how the outsize Churchillian personality，so **truculent**，so impulsive，so often profoundly wrongheaded，became，in the dark spring of 1940，just what was needed for national survival.

单词助记【同义词】 aggressive，hostile，belligerent

democracy [dɪˈmɒkrəsɪ]

n. a form of government in which people choose leaders by voting 民主政治，民主主义

例 In a **democracy**，every citizen should have the right to vote.

fabulous [ˈfæbjʊləs]

adj. very good；resembling or suggesting a fable：of an incredible，astonishing，or exaggerated nature 难以置信的，寓言里的

例 He is making **fabulous** amounts of money.

单词助记【同义词】 excellent，wonderful，tremendous

ludicrous [ˈluːdɪkrəs]

adj. amusing or laughable through obvious absurdity，incongruity，exaggeration，or eccentricity 荒唐（滑稽）可笑的

例 Some of this censorship is trivial，some is **ludicrous**，and some is breathtaking in its power to dumb down what children learn in school.

单词助记【同义词】 absurd，ridiculous

summit [ˈsʌmɪt]

❶ *n*. the highest point of a hill or mountain 顶峰

例 The climbers failed to reach the **summit**.

单词助记【同义词】 acme，peak，height，pinnacle，zenith，climax.

❷ *n*. a meeting between heads of government 峰会

例 A **summit** on global warming was held that year.

单词助记【同义词】 meeting，negotiation，conference，talk(s)，discussion.

euphony [ˈjuːfənɪ]

n. pleasing or sweet sound；especially：the acoustic effect produced by words so formed or combined as to please the ear 声音；（尤指语音的）和谐，谐音

例 Even the too-near table of boisterous boys contributes to its **euphony**.

supercilious [ˌsjuːpəˈsɪlɪəs]

adj. having or showing the proud and unpleasant attitude of people who think that they are better or more important than other people 高傲的，傲慢的

例 The **supercilious** art dealer rolled her eyes when we asked if she had anything for under ＄1,000.

单词助记【同义词】 haughty，superior

dexterity [dekˈsterɪtɪ]

　　n. the ability to use your hands skillfully 纯熟，灵巧

　　例 The job requires manual **dexterity**.

　　单词助记【同义词】deftness，adroitness，skill

pollen [ˈpɒlən]

　　n. the very fine usually yellow dust that is produced by a plant and that is carried to other plants of the same kind usually by wind or insects so that the plants can produce seeds 花粉

　　例 The problem occurs because plants need to transfer **pollen** by wind and insect to reproduce.

drought [draʊt]

　　n. a long period of time during which there is very little or no rain 旱灾，干旱

　　例 The **drought** caused serious damage to crops.

　　单词助记【同义词】dearth，deficiency，famine

barricade [ˌbærɪˈkeɪd]

　　n. a temporary wall, fence, or similar structure that is built to prevent people from entering a place or area 障碍物

　　例 Police erected **barricades** to keep the crowds from approaching the crime scene.

　　单词助记【同义词】blockade, barrier, cordon

pugnacious [pʌgˈneɪʃəs]

　　adj. showing a readiness or desire to fight or argue 好战的, 好斗的

　　例 There's one **pugnacious** member on the committee who won't agree to anything.

　　单词助记【同义词】combative

　　单词助记

extemporaneous [eksˌtempəˈreɪnjəs]

　　adj. made up or done without special preparation（讲话或做事）毫无准备的, 临时的

　　例 Caught by surprise, I had to make an **extemporaneous** speech at the awards banquet.

　　单词助记【同义词】spontaneous, unrehearsed

prudent [ˈpruːdənt]

　　adj. having or showing careful good judgment 审慎的, 有先见之明的, 判断力强的

　　例 An endless war is not always the most moral or the most **prudent** course of action.

　　单词助记【同义词】wise

cherubic [tʃeˈruːbɪk]

　　adj. someone（such as a child）who is thought of as being like a small angel 天使的, 天真无邪的, 可爱的

　　例 The main photograph in the public domain shows a **cherubic**, smiling 11-year-old with a predisposition for his father's chubbiness.

　　单词助记【同义词】innocent, sweet, angelic

superfluous [sjʊˈpɜːfluəs]

　　adj. beyond what is needed: not necessary 过多的, 过剩的, 多余的

　　例 He cleared off all the **superfluous** stuff on his desk to make room for the new computer.

　　单词助记【同义词】unnecessary, excessive, extra

emaciated [ɪˈmeɪʃɪeɪtɪd]

　　adj. very thin especially from disease or hunger or cold 瘦弱的, 衰弱的

　　例 Up the road, a tall, **emaciated** figure came running toward him.

【单词助记】【同义词】scrawny

dilapidated [dɪˈlæpɪdeɪtɪd]

　　adj. in very bad condition because of age or lack of care 残破的，破烂的，失修的

　　例 He had a **dilapidated** car that had seen better days.

【单词助记】【同义词】decrepit，rundown，derelict

meek [miːk]

　　adj. having or showing a quiet and gentle nature：not wanting to fight or argue with other people 温顺的，驯服的

　　例 She may seem **meek** and mild but it is all an act.

poll [pəʊl]

　　n. an assessment of public opinion obtained by questioning a representative sample 民意调查

　　例 The magazine conducted a **poll** to find out the favorite 100 movies of all time.

renounce [rɪˈnaʊns]

　　❶ *v*. to say especially in a formal or official way that you will no longer have or accept（something）：to formally give up（something）放弃，抛弃；断然拒绝

　　例 She **renounced** her inheritance.

【单词助记】【同义词】abandon，disown，repudiate.

　　❷ *v*. to say in a formal or definite way that you refuse to follow，obey，or support（someone or something）any longer 与……断绝关系

　　例 Many of his former supporters have **renounced** him.

braggart [ˈbrægət]

　　n. a loud arrogant boaster 吹嘘的人

　　例 Her father was an old unmarried professor of mathematics，a brutal man and a **braggart**，who went out to give lessons in spite of his age.

precursor [prɪˈkɜːsə(r)]

　　n. something that comes before something else and that often leads to or influences its development 先驱，先行者；先兆，前兆

　　例 The 18th-century lyric poets like Robert Burns were **precursors** of the Romantics.

【单词助记】【同义词】forerunner，ancestor，predecessor

ascetic [əˈsetɪk]

　　❶ *adj*. relating to or having a strict and simple way of living that avoids physical pleasure 禁欲的，苦行的

　　例 She has never been close to her **ascetic**，workaholic father.

【单词助记】【同义词】austere，self-denying，abstinent，abstemious

　　❷ *n*. a person who practices strict self-denial as a measure of personal and especially spiritual discipline 苦行者，禁欲者

　　例 Throughout history power has been the vice of the **ascetic**.

gawky [ˈgɔːkɪ]

　　adj. awkward and clumsy 迟钝的，笨拙的

　　例 And many of the royals were surprised at how beautiful and mature the once-**gawky** girl had become.

【单词助记】【同义词】awkward，clumsy，gangling

pantomime [ˈpæntəmaɪm]

　　n. a way of expressing information or telling a story without words by using body

movements and facial expressions 哑剧，手势

例 In the game of charades, one player uses **pantomime** to represent a word or phrase that the other players have to try to guess.

abstain [əbˈsteɪn]

v. to refrain deliberately and often with an effort of self-denial from an action or practice 戒（尤指酒），戒除

例 He swore to **abstain** from smoking.

单词助记【同义词】forbear, renounce, avoid, shun, eschew, forgo

adamant [ˈædəmənt]

adj. not willing to change an opinion or decision：very determined 坚定的，坚强不屈的

例 We've tried to talk him into coming with us, but he's **adamant** about staying here.

单词助记【同义词】inflexible, unwavering, unswerving, uncompromising, insistent, resolute

impenetrable [ɪmˈpenɪtrəbl]

❶ *adj.* impossible to pass or see through 无法看穿的

例 **impenetrable** darkness/fog

单词助记【同义词】impassable, dense, thick

❷ *adj.* impossible to understand 不可理解的

例 His philosophical work is notoriously **impenetrable**.

malevolence [məˈlevələns]

n. the quality or state of having or showing a desire to cause harm to another person 恶意，恶毒；怨恨

例 The two old women began casting aspersions and heaping **maledictions** upon one another.

单词助记【同义词】hatred, ill-will

单词助记

List 53

lumber [ˈlʌmbə(r)]

n. wooden boards or logs that have been sawed and cut for use 木材，木料

例 He works for a **lumber** company.

impassioned [ɪmˈpæʃənd]

adj. showing or feeling very strong emotions 充满激情的，热烈的

例 Her lawyer made an **impassioned** argument in her defense.

单词助记【同义词】emotional，ardent，fervent

profane [prəˈfeɪn]

❶ *adj*. having or showing disrespect for religious things 不敬（神）的，渎神的，亵渎的

例 **profane** language

单词助记【同义词】irreverent，not sacred

❷ *adj*. relating to ordinary life：not religious or spiritual 不圣洁的，世俗的，非宗教的

例 It was hard to juggle the requirements of church and our more **profane** duties.

❸ *v*. to treat (a holy place or object) with great disrespect 不敬，亵渎，玷污

例 They have **profaned** the long upheld traditions of the church.

affinity [əˈfɪnəti]

❶ *n*. a feeling of closeness and understanding that someone has for another person because of their similar qualities，ideas，or interests 亲密关系

例 He never felt any **affinity** with the other kids in his neighborhood.

单词助记【同义词】attraction

❷ *n*. a liking for or an attraction to something 喜爱，亲切感

例 We share an **affinity** for foreign films.

sedate [siːˈdeɪt]

adj. slow and relaxed；quiet and peaceful 文静的，平静的

例 We walked the beach at a **sedate** pace.

trifling [ˈtraɪflɪŋ]

adj. having little value or importance 微不足道的，不重要的

例 Outside California these difficulties may seem fairly **trifling**.

单词助记【同义词】trivial，insignificant

temperament [ˈtempərəmənt]

n. the usual attitude，mood，or behavior of a person or animal 脾气

例 The two women were opposite in **temperament**.

单词助记【同义词】nature，character，personality

susceptible [səˈseptəbl]

adj. easily affected，influenced，or harmed by something 易受影响的，易动感情的

例 The virus can infect **susceptible** individuals.

dilatory [ˈdɪlətəri]

adj. causing a delay 拖拉的，延误的

例 The homeowner is claiming that local firefighters were **dilatory** in responding to the call.

单词助记【同义词】delaying，stalling，temporizing，procrastinating

den [den]

　　n. the home of some kinds of wild animals 兽窝，兽穴

例 The bears will spend most of the winter in their **den**.

单词助记【同义词】hole，lair，retreat

shrewd [ʃruːd]

　　adj. having or showing an ability to understand things and to make good judgments：mentally sharp or clever 机灵的，精明的

例 She's **shrewd** about her investments.

单词助记【同义词】clever，astute

dubious [ˈdjuːbjəs]

　　adj. causing doubt, uncertainty, or suspicion：likely to be bad or wrong 半信半疑的，可疑的

例 He made the highly **dubious** claim that Elvis is still alive and living in Hawaii.

单词助记【同义词】doubtful，uncertain，unsure

refrain [rɪˈfreɪn]

　　v. to stop yourself from doing something that you want to do 抑制，克制，戒除

例 I was going to make a joke but I **refrained**.

单词助记【同义词】hold back，suppress

diffidence [ˈdɪfɪdəns]

　　n. the quality or state of lacing confidence 缺乏自信

例 He had never thought of his sweetheart as of so superior a being，and he was instantly taken with a feeling of **diffidence**.

单词助记【同义词】shyness，hesitancy，reserve

tsunami [tsʊˈnɑːmɪ]

　　n. a very high，large wave in the ocean that is usually caused by an earthquake under the sea and that can cause great destruction when it reaches land 海啸

例 You see this in the faces of **tsunami** and earthquake survivors on television.

deject [dɪˈdʒekt]

　　v. to make gloomy 使沮丧，使灰心

例 Nothing **dejects** a TV pundit more than the poll that nobody cares what he thinks.

单词助记【同义词】dishearten，depress

hypnosis [hɪpˈnəʊsɪs]

　　n. a state that resembles sleep but in which you can hear and respond to questions or suggestions 催眠状态

例 He underwent **hypnosis** to treat his fear of water.

单词助记

soliloquy [səˈlɪləkwɪ]

    n. a long, usually serious speech that a character in a play makes to an audience and that reveals the character's thoughts 自言自语, 独白

    例 On the screen, a shadow flickered—a shadow with feet like boxcars and a smile like the last **soliloquy** of Hamlet. He was a tenderfoot.

felon [ˈfelən]

    n. a criminal who has committed a serious crime (called a felony) 重罪犯

    例 This is a fraudulent lawsuit brought by a convicted **felon**.

    单词助记【同义词】criminal, murderer, offender

prodigal [ˈprɒdɪɡəl]

    adj. carelessly and foolishly spending money, time, etc. 浪费的, 铺张的, 挥霍的

    例 We sipped our beers and wondered at one another, at what was left of all that and of those **prodigal** days.

    单词助记【同义词】wasteful

List 54

breach [briːtʃ]

n. a failure to do what is required by a law an agreement or a duty: failure to act in a required or promised way 破坏（规定），违反

例 Many people consider her decision to be a **breach** of trust .

单词助记 【同义词】violation

pedantic [pɪˈdæntɪk]

adj. marked by a narrow focus on or display of learning especially its trivial aspects 书生气的

例 It may seem **pedantic** to harp on what looks like mere procedure，but this is one case where the process is the forest.

disperse [dɪsˈpɜːs]

v. to go or move in different directions: to spread apart （使）散开，驱散

例 Police ordered the crowd to **disperse**.

单词助记 【同义词】scatter, go away, disband

misleading [ˌmɪsˈliːdɪŋ]

adj. designed to deceive or mislead either deliberately or inadvertently 欺骗的，误导性的

例 However，this is only one — **misleading** — side of the story.

inaugurate [ɪˈnɔːgjʊreɪt]

v. to introduce （someone，such as a newly elected official） into a job or position with a formal ceremony 为……举行就职典礼，为……举行仪式，为……举行落成（开幕）仪式

例 They **inaugurated** the new headquarters with a brief ceremony.

scrawl [skrɔːl]

v. to write or draw （something） very quickly or carelessly 潦草地写，乱涂

例 She **scrawled** her signature on the receipt.

单词助记 【同义词】scribble, doodle

单词助记

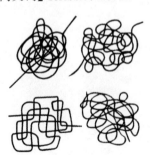

decree [dɪˈkriː]

❶ *n.* an official order given by a person with power or by a government 命令，法令

例 The President issued a **decree** making the day a national holiday.

❷ *v.* to order or decide （something） in an official way 命令，裁决；颁布……为法令

例 The City Council has **decree**d that all dogs must be kept on a leash.

beguile ［bɪˈgaɪl］

❶ *v.* to attract or interest someone 使着迷

例 I was **beguiled** by his voice.

单词助记 【同义词】deceive

❷ *v.* to trick or deceive （someone） 欺骗

例 She was cunning enough to **beguile** her classmates into doing the work for her.

lugubrious ［luːˈgjuːbrɪəs］

adj. looking or sounding sad and dismal 悲惨的

例 The boy stared fixedly at me with **lugubrious**, basset-hound eyes.

单词助记 【同义词】mournful，gloomy，glum，melancholy，woeful

devastate ［ˈdevəsteɪt］

v. to destroy much or most of （something）；to cause great damage or harm to （something） 毁坏；使荒芜

例 The disease has **devastated** the area's oak tree population.

单词助记 【同义词】lay waste，destroy，overwhelm

apathetic ［ˌæpəˈθetɪk］

adj. not having or showing much emotion or interest 缺乏兴趣的，缺乏感情的

例 Surprisingly，most Americans are **apathetic** toward this important issue.

merriment ［ˈmerɪmənt］

n. laughter and enjoyment 欢喜，嬉戏

例 Their house was always filled with **merriment**.

单词助记 【同义词】cheerfulness，happiness，fun

gouge ［gaʊdʒ］

v. to cut a deep hole in （something） 凿

例 The lamp fell and **gouged** the table.

knack ［næk］

n. an ability，talent，or special skill needed to do something 特殊能力，窍门

例 She's tried every **knack** in Cupid's book to get her guy to marry her.

单词助记 【同义词】ability，skill，talent

diverge ［daɪˈvɜːdʒ］

v. to split and move out in different directions from a single point；to be or become different 分岔，偏离

例 They were close friends in college，but after graduation，their lives **diverged**.

单词助记 【同义词】deviate，move away，wander

animosity ［ˌænɪˈmɒsɪtɪ］

n. a strong feeling of dislike or hatred 憎恨，仇恨

例 We put aside our personal **animosities** so that we could work together.

单词助记 【同义词】antipathy，hostility，friction，antagonism，acrimony，enmity

indiscriminate ［ˌɪndɪsˈkrɪmɪnɪt］

adj. affecting or harming many people or things in a careless or unfair way 不加区别的，不加鉴别的，不分好坏的

例 They participated in the **indiscriminate** slaughter of countless innocent victims.

单词助记 【同义词】widespread, not selective

kennel [ˈkenl]

　　n. a shelter for a dog or cat 狗窝,狗屋

　　例 Once you have chosen a **kennel**, make a booking for your pet.

单词助记 【同义词】lodge, keep, shelter

单词助记

speculation [ˌspekjʊˈleɪʃən]

　　n. ideas or guesses about something that is not known 思考,思索,推断,推测

　　例 He dismissed their theories as mere **speculation**.

单词助记 【同义词】conjecture

partisan [ˌpɑːtɪˈzæn]

　　❶ *adj*. devoted to a cause or party 党派性的

　　例 He is clearly too **partisan** to be a referee.

单词助记 【同义词】supporter, follower, proponent of a party

　　❷ *n*. a firm adherent to a party, faction, cause, or person; especially: one exhibiting blind, prejudiced, and unreasoning allegiance 党羽

　　例 He is a staunch **partisan** of the Republican Party.

List 55

prowess ['prauɪs]

n. distinguished bravery; great ability or skill 勇敢,勇猛;高超的技艺,非凡的才能

例 He is known for his **prowess** on the football field.

单词助记 【同义词】bravery, skill

obese [əʊ'biːs]

adj. very fat; fat in a way that is unhealthy 肥胖

例 The basset hound was so **obese** that its stomach touched the floor.

defendant [dɪ'fendənt]

n. an individual, company, or institution sued or accused in a court of law 被告

例 The jury found the **defendant** innocent.

mince [mɪns]

❶ *v*. cut up or grind (food, especially meat) into very small pieces 绞碎

例 The recipe says that you should **mince** the onions.

❷ *n*. something minced, especially mincemeat 肉末

例 beef **mince**

单词助记

malediction [ˌmælɪ'dɪkʃən]

n. curse, execration 诅咒,咒骂

例 The two old women began casting aspersions and heaping **maledictions** upon one another.

单词助记 【同义词】curse, slander

flamboyant [flæm'bɔɪənt]

adj. having a very noticeable quality that attracts a lot of attention (人或物)显眼的,浮夸的,炫耀的

例 He has a gallery of **flamboyant** gestures that makes him easy to imitate.

单词助记 【同义词】flashy, dazzling

tenable ['tenəbl]

adj. capable of being defended against attack or criticism 守得住的,(指职位等)可担任的,可维持的

例 The soldiers' encampment on the open plain was not **tenable**, so they retreated to higher ground.

decay [dɪ'keɪ]

❶ *v*. to be slowly destroyed by natural processes; to be slowly broken down by the natural processes that destroy a dead plant or body（使）腐烂

例 Tomatoes that fall off the vine will **decay** on the ground.

单词助记【同义词】spoil.

❷ *v.* to slowly lose strength, health, etc. 衰退

例 His mind/health is beginning to **decay**.

chide ［tʃaɪd］

v. to express mild disapproval of（someone）：to scold（someone）gently 责骂, 责备

例 She **chided** us for arriving late.

单词助记【同义词】scold, chastise, upbraid, berate

单词助记 chi 可以记成中文"斥"：斥责。

empathetic ［ˌempəˈθetɪk］

adj. showing an ability to understand and share the feelings of another 有同感的

例 Clinton's skills as an **empathetic** listener are remarkable.

单词助记【同义词】sympathetic, compassionate

stubborn ［ˈstʌbən］

adj. refusing to change your ideas or to stop doing something 顽固的, 顽强的

例 She's wrong, but she's too **stubborn** to admit it.

单词助记【同义词】obstinate, determined

hallowed ［ˈhæləʊd］

❶ *adj.* holy or blessed 神圣化的, 神圣的

例 The church stands on **hallowed** ground.

单词助记【同义词】holy, sacred

❷ *adj.* highly respected 受尊敬的

例 They protested that there was no place for a school of commerce in their **hallowed** halls of learning.

superb ［sjuːˈpɜː(r)b］

adj. extremely good：excellent or brilliant in a very noticeable way 卓越的, 杰出的, 极好的

例 The performance was absolutely **superb**.

benediction ［ˌbenɪˈdɪkʃən］

adj. the utterance or bestowing of a blessing, especially at the end of a religious service 祝福

例 Her arms outstretched in **benediction**.

单词助记【同义词】blessing, prayer, invocation

parochial ［pəˈrəʊkɪəl］

adj. of or relating to a church parish and the area around it; limited to only the things that affect your local area 教区的；狭隘的

例 It has never been clearer that the country's best self is a global inheritance, its worst a **parochial** self-certainty.

单词助记【同义词】narrow, narrow-minded, closed-minded

dingy ［ˈdɪndʒɪ］

adj. dark and dirty：not fresh or clean 暗淡的, 肮脏的

例 He's been staying in a **dingy** motel.

单词助记【同义词】grimy

predisposition ［ˈpriːˌdɪspəˈzɪʃən］

n. an inclination beforehand to interpret statements in a particular way 倾向

例 There is a thin dividing line between educating the public and creating a **predisposition** to panic.

单词助记 【同义词】inclination，proclivity，propensity，tendency，bent

manifest [ˈmænɪfest]

❶ *v.* able to be seen：clearly shown or visible 清楚表示，显露

例 He **manifested** a pleasing personality on stage.

❷ *adj.* easy to detect or recognize：obvious 明白的，明显的

例 His love for literature is **manifest** in his large library.

conjecture [kənˈdʒektʃə(r)]

❶ *n.* an opinion or idea formed without proof or sufficient evidence 推测，猜想

例 The biography includes **conjectures** about the writer's earliest ambitions.

单词助记 【同义词】speculation，guesswork，surmise.

❷ *v.* to form an opinion or idea without proof or sufficient evidence 推测，猜测，猜想

例 Some have **conjectured** that the distant planet could sustain life. / We only conjecture about his motives.

flourish [ˈflʌrɪʃ]

n. to be very successful：to do very well 繁荣，茂盛，兴旺

例 Regional markets have **flourished** in recent years.

单词助记 【同义词】be successful，succeed，thrive

adulation [ˌædjʊˈleɪʃən]

n. excessive or slavish admiration or flattery 繁荣，茂盛，兴旺

例 The rugby player enjoyed the **adulation** of his fans.

单词助记【同义词】idolization，adoration，admiration，veneration，awe

shard [ʃɑːd]

n. a sharp piece of something (such as glass or pottery)（玻璃、金属或其他硬物的）尖利的碎片

例 Eyewitnesses spoke of rocks and **shards** of glass flying in the air.

nebulous [ˈnebjʊləs]

adj. not clear：difficult to see，understand，describe，etc. 朦胧的，模糊的

例 These philosophical concepts can be **nebulous**.

单词助记【同义词】vague，cloudy

elegy [ˈelɪdʒɪ]

n. a sad poem or song：a poem or song that expresses sorrow for someone who is dead 哀歌，挽歌

例 "O Captain! My Captain!" is Walt Whitman's **elegy** on the death of President Lincoln.

effusive [ɪˈfjuːsɪv]

adj. expressing a lot of emotion 流露感情的，溢于言表的

例 They offered **effusive** thanks for our help.

单词助记【同义词】gushing，gushy，unrestrained，extravagant

uproarious [ʌpˈrɔːrɪəs]

adj. very noisy；extremely funny 吵闹的，引人捧腹大笑的

例 The movie follows the comic duo through a series of outrageous and **uproarious** escapades.

单词助记【同义词】noisy

cantankerous [kænˈtæŋkərəs]

adj. often angry and annoyed 脾气不好的，爱争吵的

例 A **cantankerous** old woman insisted that nothing should ever be allowed to change.

单词助记【同义词】bad-tempered，crabby，ill-tempered

tempestuous [temˈpestjʊəs]

❶ *adj.* turbulent，stormy 暴风雨的，暴风雪的

例 **tempestuous** weather

❷ *adj.* full of strong emotions (such as anger or excitement) 情绪剧烈的

例 Order was restored to the court after the judge put a stop to the defendant's **tempestuous** outburst.

peek [piːk]

❶ *v.* to look at someone or something secretly，especially from a hidden place 偷看，窥视

例 She **peeked** through a hole in the fence.

❷ *v.* to look at something briefly 看一眼，瞥

例 She **peeked** ahead to the next chapter to see what happened next.

chastise [ˈtʃæstaɪz]

v. to criticize (someone) harshly for doing something wrong 训斥，严惩

例 The waiter was **chastised** for forgetting the customer's order.

单词助记【同义词】scold, upbraid, berate, reprimand, reprove, rebuke, chide, censure, castigate

benefactor [ˈbenɪfæktə(r)]

n. someone who helps another person, group, etc., by giving money 捐助者，施主

例 With the help of a rich **benefactor** he set up a charity.

单词助记【同义词】sponsor, patron, supporter

altercation [ˌɔːltəˈkeɪʃən]

n. a noisy or angry argument 争辩，争吵

例 She got into several **altercations** with the coach this season.

单词助记【同义词】dispute, conflict

archaic [ɑːˈkeɪɪk]

adj. old and no longer used 古时的，已不通用的

例 The company needs to update its **archaic** computer systems.

单词助记【同义词】obsolete, out of date, old-fashioned, outmoded, behind the times, bygone, anachronistic, antiquated, superannuated, antediluvian

endemic [enˈdemɪk]

adj. growing or existing in a certain place or region（尤指疾病）地方性的，某地特有的

例 The fish is not an **endemic** species of the lake, and it is rapidly devouring the native trout population.

单词助记【同义词】inherent, belonging to a region

credible [ˈkredəbl]

adj. able to be believed: reasonable to trust or believe 可信的，可靠的

例 We've received **credible** information about the group's location.

单词助记【同义词】believable, convincing, plausible

composure [kəmˈpəʊʒə(r)]

n. calmness especially of mind, manner, or appearance 镇静，沉着

例 After the initial shock she regained her **composure**.

单词助记【同义词】calmness

anthology [ænˈθɒlədʒɪ]

n. a published collection of writings (such as poems or short stories) by different authors（诗、文等的）选集

例 The band will be releasing an **anthology** of their earlier albums.

jolly [ˈdʒɒlɪ]

adj. full of happiness and joy: happy and cheerful 快活的，令人高兴的

例 Our boss was a very **jolly** man, always laughing.

piety [ˈpaɪətɪ]

n. devotion to God: the quality or state of being pious 虔诚，神圣

例 He was admired for his extreme **piety**.

单词助记 【同义词】holiness

panorama [ˌpænəˈrɑːmə]

    n . a full and wide view of something 风景的全貌，概观

    例 We admired the breathtaking **panorama** from the top of the mountain.

acme [ˈækmɪ]

n. the highest point of something 顶点，最高点

例 The **acme** of their basketball season was their hard-won victory over last year's state champs.

单词助记【同义词】peak，pinnacle，zenith，crest，summit，apex

misgiving [ˌmɪsˈɡɪvɪŋ]

n. a feeling of doubt or apprehension about the outcome or consequences of something（对于未来、结果的）担心，忧虑

例 I felt some **misgiving** about his ability to do the job.

单词助记【同义词】qualm，doubt，reservation，suspicion

fatal [ˈfeɪtəl]

adj. causing death；causing ruin or failure 致命的

例 She made a **fatal** mistake.

单词助记【同义词】deadly，destructive

exhilarating [ɪɡˈzɪləreɪtɪŋ]

adj. making lively and cheerful 令人喜欢的，爽快的

例 It was **exhilarating** to be on the road again and his spirits rose.

单词助记【同义词】exciting

defiance [dɪˈfaɪəns]

n. a refusal to obey something or someone：the act of defying someone or something 蔑视，挑战

例 The troubled youth seems to have an ingrained **defiance** to authority of any sort.

单词助记【同义词】insubordination；disobedience；insolence

deplore [dɪˈplɔː(r)]

v. to hate or dislike (something) very much：to strongly disapprove of (something) 悲叹，痛惜；强烈反对

例 We deplore the **development** of nuclear weapons.

unveil [ʌnˈveɪl]

v. to show or reveal (something) to others for the first time 除去面纱使暴露，揭幕，公布

例 The developer **unveiled** plans for a new housing complex.

单词助记【同义词】display

sycophant [ˈsɪkəfænt]

n. a person who praises powerful people in order to get their approval 谄媚者，拍马屁者

例 When her career was riding high, the self-deluded actress often mistook **sycophants** for true friends.

单词助记【同义词】flatterer，brownnoser

dawdle [ˈdɔːdl]

v. to move or act too slowly 混（时间）

例 Come home immediatcly after school，and don't **dawdle**.

单词助记【同义词】loiter

leery [ˈlɪərɪ]

adj. feeling or showing a lack of trust in someone or something 狡猾的；猜疑的

例 They were **leery** of their neighbors.

单词助记【同义词】suspicious，wary，doubtful

cosmopolitan [ˌkɒzməˈpɒlɪtən]

adj. a person who has lived in and knows about many different parts of the world 世界性的

例 As someone who had lived in Paris for a year as an exchange student，she seemed very much the **cosmopolitan** to her old classmates.

单词助记【同义词】sophisticate

castigate [ˈkæstɪɡeɪt]

v. to criticize (someone) harshly 严厉责骂、批评或惩罚（某人）

例 The author **castigated** the prime minister as an ineffective leader.

单词助记【同义词】reprimand，rebuke，admonish，chastise，chide

reprimand [ˈreprɪmɑːnd]

❶ *n*. a severe or formal reproof 训斥，惩戒

例 He has been fined five thousand dollars and given a severe **reprimand**.

单词助记【同义词】scold，reproach.

❷ *v*. to speak in an angry and critical way to (someone who has done something wrong，disobeyed an order，etc.) 申斥，惩戒，谴责

例 The soldiers were severely **reprimanded**.

pinch [pɪntʃ]

n. to squeeze or press (something) together with your thumb and finger 捏，拧，掐掉

例 He **pinched** her cheeks and told her how cute she was.

单词助记【同义词】squeeze，nip，tweak

animus [ˈænɪməs]

n. hostility or ill feeling 敌意

例 Your **animus** towards him suggests that you are the wrong man for the job.

evanescence [ˌiːvəˈnesəns]

n. the process or fact of dissipating like vapor 逐渐消失，容易消失，幻灭

例 The **evanescence** of a rainbow detracts not a whit from its beauty.

harbinger [ˈhɑːbɪndʒə(r)]

❶ *n*. something that shows what is coming 预兆

例 Her father's successful job interview was seen as a **harbinger** of better times to come.

❷ *n*. a person sent ahead to provide lodgings 预言者

例 The cuckoo is a **harbinger** of spring.

remuneration [rɪˌmjuːnəˈreɪʃən]

n. an amount of money paid to someone for the work that person has done 报酬，酬劳；赔偿

例 She was given generous **remunerations** for her work.

foible [ˈfɔɪbl]

　　n. a minor fault in someone's character or behavior 小缺点,小癖好

　　例 We could tolerate my uncle's **foibles** because we loved him dearly.

单词助记【同义词】minor character flaw

conciliate [kənˈsɪlɪeɪt]

　　v. to make (someone) more friendly or less angry 安慰,取悦于

　　例 The company's attempts to **conciliate** the strikers have failed.

单词助记【同义词】appease，placate，pacify，mollify，assuage，soothe

anxiety [æŋˈzaɪətɪ]

　　n. fear or nervousness about what might happen 焦虑，不安

　　例 She suffers from chronic **anxiety**.

compact [kəmˈpækt]

　　❶ *adj*. closely or firmly packed or joined together 紧密的

　　例 The cabin was **compact** but perfectly adequate.

　　单词助记【同义词】dense，solid，small

　　❷ *v*. to press (something) so that it is harder and fills less space 使紧凑

　　例 Tractors had **compacted** the soil. / The snow had **compacted** into a hard icy layer.

prerogative [prɪˈrɒɡətɪv]

　　n. a right or privilege；especially：a special right or privilege that some people have 特权

　　例 If you'd rather sell the tickets than use them，that's your **prerogative**.

　　单词助记【同义词】privilege，right，due

eulogy [ˈjuːlədʒɪ]

　　n. a commendatory oration or writing especially in honor of one deceased 颂词；悼词

　　例 He delivered a moving **eulogy** at his father's funeral.

extroverted [ˈekstrəvɜːtɪd]

　　adj. not introspective；examining what is outside yourself；at ease in talking to others 颂词；悼词

　　例 Some young people who were easy-going and **extroverted** as children become self-conscious in early adolescence.

holistic [həʊˈlɪstɪk]

　　adj. relating to or concerned with complete systems rather than with individual parts 整体的，全盘的

　　例 We need to take a more **holistic** approach to improving our schools.

　　单词助记【同义词】whole

obsequious [əbˈsiːkwɪəs]

　　adj. too eager to help or obey someone important 谄媚的，奉承的；顺从的，死心塌地的

　　例 She's constantly followed by **obsequious** assistants who will do anything she tells them to.

　　单词助记【同义词】servile

insidious [ɪnˈsɪdɪəs]

　　adj. proceeding in a gradual，subtle way，but with harmful effects 潜伏的；暗中滋生的；有隐患的

　　例 Most people with this **insidious** disease have no idea that they are infected.

　　单词助记【同义词】stealthy，subtle，surreptitious，cunning，crafty

foreboding [ˈfɔːbəʊdɪŋ]

❶ *n*. a feeling that something bad is going to happen（对不祥之事的）预感，预知

例 It seems that her **forebodings** were justified.

单词助记【同义词】premonition，presentiment，feeling

❷ *adj*. indicative of or marked by a feeling that something bad is going to happen（对不祥之事）预感的，预知的

例 He had a **foreboding** feeling that something was wrong.

hydrate [ˈhaɪdreɪt]

❶ *n*. a substance that is formed when water combines with another substance 水合物

例 aluminium **hydrate**

❷ *v*. to add water or moisture to (something)：to supply (something) with water（使）水合

例 Drink fluids to **hydrate** the body.

nil [nɪl]

n. zero 零

例 The chances of that happening are practically/almost **nil**.

单词助记【同义词】zero

egregious [ɪˈgriːdʒəs]

adj. very bad and easily noticed 极坏的

例 The student's theme was marred by a number of **egregious** errors in spelling.

单词助记【同义词】flagrant

propensity [prəˈpensɪtɪ]

n. (to, for) a strong natural tendency to do something 倾向，爱好，嗜好，脾性

例 He had a **propensity** for crime.

单词助记【同义词】inclination，tendency

tornado [tɔːˈneɪdəʊ]

n. a violent and destructive storm in which powerful winds move around a central point 旋风，龙卷风

例 The **tornado** destroyed the whole village.

单词助记【同义词】cyclone

loathe [ləʊð]

v. to hate (someone or something) very much 憎恨，厌恶

例 They were rivals who truly **loathed** each other.

单词助记【同义词】abhor，abominate，despise

deplete [dɪˈpliːt]

v. to use most or all of (something important)：to greatly reduce the amount of (something) 使空虚，用尽

例 We completely **depleted** our life savings when we bought our new house.

haughty [ˈhɔːtɪ]

adj. having or showing the insulting attitude of people who think that they are better，smarter，or more important than other people 傲慢的，目中无人的

例 He rejected their offer with a tone of **haughty** disdain.

单词助记【同义词】supercilious，proud，arrogant

embellish [ɪmˈbelɪʃ]

v. to decorate （something） by adding special details and features：to make （something） more appealing or attractive 美化，装饰

例 He **embellished** his speech with a few quotations.

stark ［stɑːk］

❶ *adj.* having a very plain and often cold or empty appearance；unpleasant and difficult to accept or experience 僵硬的，严酷的

例 This tragedy serves as a **stark** reminder of the dangers of drunk driving.

❷ *adj.* very obvious：very plain and easily seen 明显的

例 There is a **stark** difference between them.

❸ *adv.* completely or fully 完全地

例 He was standing there **stark** naked.

单词助记【同义词】utterly，completely，entirely

nomadic ［nəʊˈmædɪk］

adj. （of groups of people） tending to travel and change settlements frequently 游牧的，流浪的

例 Some choose a **nomadic** life because they want to be more in touch with nature； others to live on the edge of society without a national insurance number or fixed address.

List 59

curative [ˈkjʊərətɪv]

adj. able to cure diseases or heal people 治病的

例 Some believe that the herb has **curative** properties.

单词助记【同义词】healing, remedial, restorative

laudatory [ˈlɔːdətərɪ]

adj. expressing or containing praise 颂扬的

例 The play received mostly **laudatory** reviews.

exuberant [ɪɡˈzjuːbərənt]

adj. very lively, happy, or energetic: filled with energy and enthusiasm 兴高采烈的, 活跃的

例 His **exuberant** personality makes him fun to be around.

单词助记【同义词】enthusiastic

swindle [ˈswɪndl]

v. to take money or property from (someone) by using lies or tricks 诈骗, 骗取

例 Hundreds of people were **swindled** out of their savings, and all they had to show for it were fake land deeds.

单词助记【同义词】cheat, con, dupe

sordid [ˈsɔːdɪd]

adj. very bad or dishonest; very dirty 肮脏的, 卑鄙的

例 He shared the **sordid** details of his past.

单词助记【同义词】filthy, corrupt

munificent [mjuːˈnɪfɪsənt]

adj. very generous (指送礼者)慷慨的,(指礼品)丰厚的

例 He is a **munificent** host who has presided over many charitable events at his mansion.

单词助记【同义词】very generous

laconic [ləˈkɒnɪk]

adj. using few words in speech or writing 简洁的, 简明的

例 We would rather have a smiling, shape-shifting Democrat we don't trust than a frowning, **laconic** Republican we trust more.

germinate [ˈdʒɜːmɪneɪt]

v. to cause (a seed) to begin to grow (使)发芽

例 The idea **germinated** and slowly grew into an obsession.

dismal [ˈdɪzməl]

adj. showing or causing unhappiness or sad feelings: not warm, cheerful, etc. 阴沉的, 凄凉的, 令人忧郁的

例 The show was a **dismal** failure.

conjure [ˈkʌndʒə(r)]

v. to make (something) appear or seem to appear by using magic 用魔术变出

例 The students **conjured** a clever scheme to raise the money they needed.

trenchant [ˈtrentʃənt]

adj. very strong, clear, and effective 锐利的，简明的

例 Even the most **trenchant** sword could not sever the bonds of loyalty between them.

单词助记 【同义词】acute, sharp, incisive

pauper [ˈpɔːpə(r)]

n. a very poor person who has no money to pay for food, clothing, etc. 穷人，贫民

例 Mozart died in 1791 and was buried in a **pauper's** grave at Vienna's St. Mark's Cemetery.

buttress [ˈbʌtrəs]

❶ *n*. a structure built against a wall in order to support or strengthen it. 扶壁，扶垛

❷ *v*. to support, strengthen, or defend (something) 支撑，加固

例 The theory has been **buttressed** by the results of the experiment.

单词助记 【同义词】strengthen, reinforce, fortify, bolster, underpin

exorbitant [ɪgˈzɔːbɪtənt]

adj. going far beyond what is fair, reasonable, or expected; too high, expensive, etc. 过度的，极高的

例 They were charged **exorbitant** rates for phone calls.

单词助记 【同义词】extravagant

controversy [ˈkɒntrəvɜːsɪ]

n. argument that involves many people who strongly disagree about something; strong disagreement about 争议，争论

例 The decision aroused much **controversy** among the students.

单词助记 【同义词】disagreement; argument; debate

flagrant [ˈfleɪgrənt]

adj. very bad; too bad to be ignored 罪恶昭彰的

例 The judge called the decision "a **flagrant** violation of international law."

单词助记 【同义词】offensive, outrageous

blasphemous [ˈblæsfəməs]

adj. impiously irreverent; profane 亵渎上帝的，亵渎宗教信仰的

例 Catholics used to believe that anyone but a priest touching a consecrated wafer was **blasphemous**.

单词助记 【同义词】sacrilegious, profane, irreverent, impious

insular [ˈɪnsjʊlə(r)]

adj. separated from other people or cultures; not knowing or interested in new or different ideas 孤立的；与世隔绝的

例 This is an **insular** community that is not receptive of new ideas, especially from outsiders.

hurricane [ˈhʌrɪkən]

n. an extremely large, powerful, and destructive storm with very strong winds 飓风

例 The economic news unleashed a **hurricane** on the trading floor.

单词助记 【同义词】storm, gale, tempest

grumpy [ˈgrʌmpɪ]

adj. easily annoyed or angered；having a bad temper or complaining often 脾气坏的；生气的

例 I was feeling **grumpy** after my long flight.

单词助记【同义词】bad-tempered，irritable

List 60

belittle [bɪˈlɪtl]

　　v. to describe (someone or something) as little or unimportant 使显得微小，轻视

　　例 Her detractors are in the habit of **belittling** her accomplishments.

　　单词助记【同义词】disparage, denigrate, deprecate, depreciate

erosion [ɪˈrəʊʒən]

　　n. the gradual destruction of something by natural forces (such as water, wind, or ice)：the process by which something is eroded or worn away 腐蚀，侵蚀，糜烂

　　例 Landscapers planted grass to stop the **erosion** of the hillside.

　　单词助记【同义词】corrosion, attrition, destruction

lofty [ˈlɒftɪ]

　　adj. rising to a great height：very tall and impressive 高耸的，极高的

　　例 She showed a **lofty** disregard for their objections.

　　单词助记【同义词】supercilious, haughty, superior

abhorrence [əbˈhɒrəns]

　　n. the act or state of disliking (someone or something) very much 憎恶

　　例 They are anxious to show their **abhorrence** of racism.

　　单词助记【同义词】refrain from, desist from, hold back from

elucidate [ɪˈluːsɪdeɪt]

　　v. to make (something that is hard to understand) clear or easy to understand 阐明，解释

　　例 When asked for details, he declined to **elucidate** further.

docile [ˈdəʊsaɪl]

　　adj. easily taught, led, or controlled 易驾驶的；驯服的

　　例 His students were **docile** and eager to learn.

　　单词助记【同义词】compliant, obedient, pliant, dutiful

botanist [ˈbɒtənɪst]

　　n. a biologist specializing in the study of plants 植物学家

　　例 A **botanist** can differentiate varieties of plants.

censure [ˈsenʃə(r)]

　　❶ *n.* official strong criticism 指责，谴责

　　例 The country faces international **censure** for its alleged involvement in the assassination.

　　单词助记【同义词】criticize, blame

　　❷ *v.* to officially criticize (someone or something) strongly and publicly 指责；非难

　　例 He was **censured** by the committee for his failure to report the problem.

myriad [ˈmɪrɪəd]

　　❶ *adj.* many 无数的

　　例 The old system's problems were **myriad**.

　　❷ *n.* a very large number of things 无数，极大数量

例 I had three weeks to make a **myriad** of arrangements.

单词助记【同义词】multitude，heap，mass

foretell [fɔːˈtel]

v. to describe (something) before it happens 预言；预示

例 We cannot **foretell** the future.

单词助记【同义词】predict

colloquial [kəˈləʊkwɪəl]

adj. used when people are speaking in an informal way 口语的，会话的

例 The new coworker's rudeness soon began—to use a **colloquial** expression—to rub me the wrong way.

hilarious [hɪˈleərɪəs]

adj. very funny 令人捧腹大笑的

例 Some people don't like his comedy，but I think he's **hilarious**.

单词助记【同义词】funny，sidesplitting，hysterical

inkling [ˈɪŋklɪŋ]

n. a slight，uncertain idea about something：a slight amount of knowledge about something 想法；暗示

例 I had no **inkling** of his real purpose until much later.

单词助记【同义词】suspicion，hint，clue

miser [ˈmaɪzə(r)]

n. a person who hates to spend money：a very stingy person 守财奴，吝啬鬼

例 The **miser** liked to sit and play with his money.

famine [ˈfæmɪn]

n. a situation in which many people do not have enough food to eat 饥荒，严重的缺乏

例 The **famine** affected half the continent.

单词助记【同义词】shortage，scarcity

gossip [ˈɡɒsɪp]

n. information about the behavior and personal lives of other people 闲谈；八卦

例 He had been spreading **gossip** about his coworkers.

单词助记【同义词】chatter

hybrid [ˈhaɪbrɪd]

❶ *n.* an animal or plant that is produced from two animals or plants of different kinds 杂交生成的生物体，混血儿

例 All these brightly coloured **hybrids** are so lovely in the garden.

❷ *n.* something that is formed by combining two or more things 混合物

例 The band plays a **hybrid** of jazz and rock.

obdurate [ˈɒbdjʊrət]

adj. refusing to do what other people want：not willing to change your opinion or the way you do something 顽固的，执拗的；麻木不仁的

例 He is known for his **obdurate** determination.

单词助记【同义词】stubborn，inflexible，intractable

stain [steɪn]

v. to leave a mark on something；to be marked or damaged by a stain 沾染，玷污；染（着）色，印上颜色

例 He **stained** the wood a dark cherry color.

fiasco [fɪˈæskəʊ]

n. a complete failure 彻底失败，惨败

例 The currency **fiasco** will accelerate these trends.

单词助记 【同义词】debacle，disaster，mess

List 61

impecunious [ˌɪmpɪˈkjuːnjəs]

adj. having little or no money 没钱的，不名一文的

例 They were so **impecunious** that they couldn't afford to give one another even token Christmas gifts.

单词助记【同义词】lacking money，penniless

surmount [səˈmaʊnt]

❶ *v.* to be placed at the top of (something) 登上，越过

例 The island is **surmounted** by a huge black castle.

❷ *v.* to deal with (a problem or a difficult situation) successfully 克服，战胜，凌驾

例 I realized I had to **surmount** the language barrier.

单词助记【同义词】overcome

exemplary [ɪɡˈzemplərɪ]

adj. extremely good and deserving to be admired and copied；serving as an example of something 杰出的；值得效仿的

例 As a hospital volunteer you have given **exemplary** service to your community.

单词助记【同义词】outstanding

allay [əˈleɪ]

v. to make (something) less severe or strong 减轻，缓和

例 The new advertising campaign is an attempt to **allay** the public's concerns about the safety of the company's products.

单词助记【同义词】reduce，diminish，decrease，lessen，assuage，alleviate，ease，relieve，soothe，soften

lexicon [ˈleksɪkən]

n. the words used in a language or by a person or group of people 词典，词汇表

例 He is an avid word enthusiast who is compiling a **lexicon** of archaic and unusual words.

单词助记【同义词】dictionary，vocabulary

mollify [ˈmɒlɪfaɪ]

v. to make (someone) less angry；to calm (someone) down 使变软，使平静，抚慰

例 The landlord fixed the heat，but the tenants still were not **mollified**.

单词助记【同义词】calm，soothe，pacify

ardor [ˈɑːdə(r)]

n. a strong feeling of energy or eagerness 热诚；激情

例 I began tracking the columnists' pronouncements with some **ardor**.

premeditated [prɪˈmedɪteɪtɪd]

adj. done or made according to a plan；planned in advance 预谋的，事先计划的

例 In a case of **premeditated** murder a life sentence is mandatory.

单词助记【同义词】planned，deliberate，intentional

exasperate [ɪɡˈzæspəreɪt]

v. to make (someone) very angry or annoyed 激怒，触怒

例 The criticism of his latest movie is sure to **exasperate** his admirers.

单词助记【同义词】irritate，annoy

apex [ˈeɪpeks]

n. the top or highest part of something, especially one forming a point 顶，顶峰

例 Tragically，she died at the **apex** of her career.

单词助记【同义词】peak，summit，pinnacle，zenith，acme

succinct [səkˈsɪŋkt]

adj. using few words to state or express an idea 简明的，简洁的

例 He gave a **succinct** overview of the expansion project.

cosmetic [kɒzˈmetɪk]

adj. used or done in order to improve a person's appearance 美容的

例 Almond oil is sometimes used in **cosmetic** products.

单词助记【同义词】enhancing，improving，highlighting

placid [ˈplæsɪd]

adj. not easily upset or excited 平静的，宁静的，温和的

例 She was a **placid** child who rarely cried.

单词助记【同义词】serene，calm

latent [ˈleɪtənt]

adj. present and capable of emerging or developing but not now visible，obvious，active，or symptomatic 潜伏的，潜在的，不易觉察的

例 He has a **latent** talent for acting that he hasn't had a chance to express yet.

单词助记【同义词】inactive

collision [kəˈlɪʒən]

n. a crash in which two or more things or people hit each other；a situation in which people or groups disagree：a clash or conflict 碰撞，冲突，抵触

例 The car was destroyed in the **collision**.

单词助记【同义词】crash；colliding

ecstatic [ɪkˈstætɪk]

adj. very happy or excited：feeling or showing ecstasy 狂喜的；入迷的

例 He was **ecstatic** when he heard that he was going to be a father.

单词助记【同义词】enraptured，elated，in raptures，euphoric，rapturous

stymie [ˈstaɪmɪ]

v. to stop (someone) from doing something or to stop (something) from happening 阻碍

例 Progress on the project has been **stymied** by lack of money.

单词助记【同义词】hinder，obstruct，impede

treason [ˈtriːzən]

n. the crime of trying to overthrow your country's government or of helping your country's enemies during war 通敌，叛国罪

例 Reading a friend's diary without permission would have to be regarded as the ultimate act of personal **treason**.

单词助记【同义词】sedition；treachery；disloyalty

quagmire [ˈkwæɡmaɪə(r)]

❶ *n*. an area of soft，wet ground 沼泽地，泥潭

例 The party was once again facing its quadrennial **quagmire**：the candidate sufficiently liberal to win the nomination would be too liberal for the general election.

❷ *n.* an awkward，complex，or hazardous situation 困难处境

例 a legal **quagmire**

smolder [ˈsməʊldə(r)]

❶ *v.* to burn slowly without flames but usually with smoke 无火焰地焖烧

例 The remains of the campfire **smoldered**.

单词助记 【同义词】burn，smoke，glow

❷ *v.* to feel a strong emotion but keep it hidden 压抑

例 Their discontent **smoldered** for years.

List 62

manuscript [ˈmænjʊskrɪpt]

    n. written by hand or typed 手稿,底稿,原稿

    例 The library owns the author's original **manuscript**.

    单词助记【同义词】document, copy, text

opulent [ˈɒpjʊlənt]

    adj. very comfortable and expensive 富裕的,富足的

    例 That **opulent** mansion is filled with priceless art and antiques.

    单词助记【同义词】wealthy, lavish

    单词助记

initiate [ɪˈnɪʃɪeɪt]

    ❶ *v*. to cause the beginning of (something): to start or begin (something) 开始,着手

    例 Doctors have **initiated** a series of tests to determine the cause of the problem.

    单词助记【同义词】admit, begin, catechize

    ❷ *v*. to teach (someone) the basic facts or ideas about something 传授;使初步了解

    例 He **initiated** her into the study of other cultures.

envy [ˈenvɪ]

    n. a feeling of discontented or resentful longing aroused by someone else's possessions, qualities, or luck 忌妒

    单词助记【同义词】jealousy, covetousness

listless [ˈlɪstlɪs]

    adj. lacking energy or spirit 倦怠的,无精打采的,冷淡的

    例 The heat made everyone tired and **listless**.

pilfer [ˈpɪlfə(r)]

    v. to steal things that are not very valuable or to steal a small amount of something 偷窃,小偷小摸

    例 She **pilfered** stamps and paper from work.

chivalrous [ˈʃɪvəlrəs]

    adj. marked by honor, generosity, and courtesy 武士精神的,侠义的

    例 However, in today's society I find that more and more often woman enjoy the idea of **chivalry** more than they enjoy the actual chivalrous gentleman.

【同义词】gallant，courtly，brave

benign [bɪˈnaɪn]

❶ *adj*. not causing harm or damage 温和的

例 This plunge came in a time of relatively **benign** economic conditions.

【同义词】harmless，mild

❷ *adj*. without cancer：not cancerous（癌症）良性的

例 We were happy to hear that the tumor was **benign**.

vehement [ˈviːɪmənt]

adj. showing strong and often angry feelings：very emotional 感情强烈的，热情的

例 The proposal has faced **vehement** opposition from many teachers.

hazardous [ˈhæzədəs]

adj. involving risk or danger 危险的

例 These are **hazardous** chemicals that can cause death if inhaled.

【同义词】dangerous，risky，unsafe

facile [ˈfæsaɪl]

adj. too simple：not showing enough thought or effort；done or achieved in a way that is too easy 易做到的；灵巧的

例 This problem needs more than just a **facile** solution.

obtrusive [əbˈtruːsɪv]

adj. tending to bother people by appearing where you are not welcome or invited 冒失的，莽撞的，强加于人的

例 The waiter was attentive without being **obtrusive**.

【同义词】protruding

cryptic [ˈkrɪptɪk]

adj. difficult to understand：having or seeming to have a hidden meaning 秘密的，隐秘的

例 Iis instructions were **cryptic**. He said only to wait until we felt certain the answer was clear.

【同义词】enigmatic，perplexing，puzzling，obscure，abstruse，arcane

eschew [ɪsˈtʃuː]

v. to avoid（something）especially because you do not think it is right，proper，etc.（尤指为道德或实际理由而）习惯性避开，回避

例 They now **eschew** the violence of their past.

【同义词】abstain，avoid

ebullient [ɪˈbʌlɪənt]

adj. lively and enthusiastic 热情奔放的；兴高采烈的

例 His natural **ebullience** began to return.

【同义词】exuberant，buoyant，merry，jaunty，lighthearted，elated

desperate [ˈdesp(ə)rət]

adj. very sad and upset because of having little or no hope：feeling or showing despair 拼死的，绝望的

例 The collapse of her business had made her **desperate**.

【同义词】frantic，anxious，worried

perspicacious [ˌpɜːspɪˈkeɪʃəs]

adj. having or showing an ability to notice and understand things that are difficult or not obvious 有洞察力的, 判断力强的, 有识别力的

例 The brilliant lawyer was known for his **perspicacious** deductions.

单词助记【同义词】discerning, insightfulm wise

surplus [ˈsɜːpləs]

❶ *n*. an amount (such as an amount of money) that is more than the amount that is needed 过多, 剩余(资源)

例 If there is any **surplus**, it will be divided equally.

❷ *adj*. left over: extra 过多的, 剩余的

例 Few people have large sums of **surplus** cash.

单词助记【同义词】excess, extra, spare

aversion [əˈvɜːʃən]

n. a strong feeling of not liking something 厌恶, 反感

例 I simply have this ingrained **aversion** to the sight of bloodshed.

migration [maɪˈɡreɪʃən]

n. the movement of persons from one country or locality to another; the periodic passage of groups of animals (especially birds or fishes) from one region to another for feeding or breeding 迁徙

例 Therefore, it must be that the pots were spread by **migration**, not trade.

List 63

banal [bə'nɑ:l]

adj. boring or ordinary：not interesting 陈旧的，平庸的

例 He made some **banal** remarks about the weather.

单词助记 【同义词】trite，hackneyed，clichéd，vapid，commonplace，threadbare，hack，humdrum

massive ['mæsɪv]

❶ *adj.* very large and heavy 粗大的，大而重的

例 The fort had **massive** walls.

单词助记 【同义词】huge，enormous，gigantic

❷ *adj.* forming or consisting of a large mass 大量的

例 You can find a **massive** amount of information on the Internet.

qualm [kwɑ:m]

n. a feeling of doubt or uncertainty about whether you are doing the right thing 不安，良心之谴责

例 He accepted their offer without a **qualm**.

frugal ['fru:gəl]

adj. careful about spending money or using things when you do not need to：using money or supplies in a very careful way 节省的，花钱少的

例 By being **frugal**, the family is able to stretch its monthly budget.

单词助记 【同义词】spending little，economical

clandestine [klæn'destɪn]

adj. done in a private place or way：done secretly 秘密的，保密的

例 I took a **clandestine** peek at the price tag on the diamond necklace.

单词助记 【同义词】secret，covert，furtive，surreptitious，stealthy

polymorphous [pɒli'mɔ:fəs]

adj. having or occurring in many different forms，styles，or stages of development 多形的，多形态的

例 a **polymorphous** rash

peripheral [pə'rɪfərəl]

adj. not relating to the main or most important part 非本质的，非主要的，次要的

例 If we focus too much on **peripheral** issues，we will lose sight of the goal.

单词助记 【同义词】outlying，marginal，fringe

pluck [plʌk]

❶ *v.* take hold of（something）and quickly remove it from its place；pick 拔；摘

例 My sister **plucked** a white hair from my head.

单词助记 【同义词】remove，pick（off），pull

❷ *n.* spirited and determined courage 勇气

例 She showed **pluck** in getting up on stage.

单词助记 【同义词】courage，bravery，nerve，backbone，spine

relish ['relɪʃ]

n. enjoyment of or delight in something；a feeling of liking something 滋味，美味；乐趣，(大量的)享受，快乐

例 He took particular **relish** in pointing out my error.

单词助记【同义词】enjoy，delight in，savor

explicit [ɪks'plɪsɪt]

adj. very clear and complete：leaving no doubt about the meaning 详述的，明确的，明晰的

例 The law is very **explicit** about how these measures should be enacted.

taciturn ['tæsɪtɜːn]

adj. tending to be quiet：not speaking frequently 沉默寡言的，不爱说话的

例 As a **taciturn** man, he almost never initiates a conversation.

单词助记【同义词】quiet

oust [aʊst]

v. to remove from or dispossess of property or position by legal action，by force，or by the compulsion of necessity 驱逐

例 Large national banks are **ousting** local banks in many communities.

单词助记【同义词】throw out，expel，get rid of

quarry ['kwɒrɪ]

❶ *n*. a heap of the game killed in a hunt 猎物，追求物

例 A person's or animal's **quarry** is the person or animal that they are hunting.

❷ *n*. an open excavation usually for obtaining building stone，slate，or limestone 采石场

例 limestone **quarry**

单词助记【同义词】digging，excavation

tentative ['tentətɪv]

adj. not done with confidence：uncertain and hesitant 试探性的，试验的，尝试性的

例 In the winter，retirees from the Midwest fill the trailer parks. They are known with **tentative** affection as snowbirds.

单词助记【同义词】hesitant，cautious，uncertain

guru ['ɡʊruː]

n. a teacher or guide that you trust 专家，老师

例 He has been a **guru** to many young writers.

单词助记【同义词】spiritual leader，sage

perplexing [pə'pleksɪŋ]

adj. lacking clarity of meaning；causing confusion or perplexity 复杂的，令人困惑的

例 It took years to understand many **perplexing** diseases.

单词助记【同义词】confusing，puzzling，confounding

sneer [snɪə(r)]

n. to smile or laugh with facial contortions that express scorn or contempt 轻蔑地笑

例 "You obviously don't know what you're talking about," she **sneered**.

placate [plə'keɪt]

v. to cause (someone) to feel less angry about something 安抚，抚慰，使平静

例 The administration **placated** protesters by agreeing to consider their demands.

单词助记【同义词】calm，pacify

miscellaneous [ˌmɪsɪˈleɪnɪəs]

　　adj. including many things of different kinds 各种各样的

　　例 The bottom of the drawer was always a **miscellaneous** accumulation of odds and ends.

　　单词助记【同义词】various，varied，assorted

incipient [ɪnˈsɪpɪənt]

　　adj. beginning to develop or exist 刚开始的，初期的

　　例 The project is still in its **incipient** stages.

　　单词助记【同义词】beginning

headstrong ['hedstrɒŋ]

adj. not willing to do what other people want；very stubborn 任性的，刚愎自用的

例 He is known for his **headstrong** behavior.

单词助记【同义词】impetuous, impulsive, reckless

abdicate ['æbdɪkeɪt]

❶ *v.* to fail to do what is required by（a duty or responsibility）放弃（职责、权利等）

例 The government **abdicated** its responsibility to provide a good education to all citizens.

单词助记【同义词】reject, renounce, give up, refuse, relinquish, repudiate, abandon

❷ *v.* to leave the position of being a king or queen 退位；逊位

例 The king **abdicated** the throne.

effervescence [ˌefə:'vesəns]

❶ *n.* bubbles that form and rise in a liquid 冒泡，泡腾

例 Bubbles are engaging because of their **effervescence**.

单词助记【同义词】ebullience, exuberance, buoyancy, sparkle, gaiety

❷ *n.* an exciting or lively quality 活泼

例 The actress's **effervescence** was charming.

brake [breɪk]

n. a device for arresting or preventing the motion of a mechanism usually by means of friction 刹车，制动

例 A seagull swooped down in front of her car, causing her to slam on the **brakes**.

alibi ['æləˌbaɪ]

n. an excuse for not being somewhere or doing something 托词，借口

例 She made up an **alibi** for why she missed the meeting.

单词助记【同义词】explanation, excuse, reason

catalog ['kætəlɒg]

n. a book containing a list of things that you can buy, use, etc., and often pictures；a group of similar or related things 目录

例 The band played many songs from their **catalog** of hits.

单词助记【同义词】collection, directory, file

opaque [əʊ'peɪk]

adj. not letting light through；not transparent 不透明的

例 Somehow listeners seem to connect with the songwriter, despite his deeply personal, often **opaque** lyrics.

acerbic [ə's3:bɪk]

adj. expressing harsh or sharp criticism in a clever way 尖酸刻薄的

例 He whispered a steady stream of **acerbic** comments as the lecturer droned on.

单词助记【同义词】harsh；sharp

condescending [ˌkɒndɪˈsendɪŋ]

adj. showing that you believe you are more intelligent or better than other people 有优越感的，显得感人一等的

例 His comments were offensive and **condescending** to us.

单词助记【同义词】patronizing, disdainful, superior

oath [əʊθ]

n. a formal and serious promise to tell the truth or to do something 誓言，誓约

例 He uttered an **oath** and walked away.

scroll [skrəʊl]

❶ *n.* a roll of parchment or paper for writing or painting on 卷纸

例 He read from the **scroll**.

❷ *v.* computer screen 滚屏

例 I **scrolled** down to find "United States of America".

catalyst [ˈkætəlɪst]

n. a substance that causes a chemical reaction to happen more quickly 催化剂

例 The bombing attack was the **catalyst** for war.

单词助记【同义词】stimulus, spur, incitement, impetus

imperious [ɪmˈpɪərɪəs]

adj. having or showing the proud and unpleasant attitude of someone who gives orders and expects other people to obey them 专横的，飞扬跋扈的

例 She is an **imperious** movie star who thinks she's some sort of goddess.

单词助记【同义词】domineering

tension [ˈtenʃən]

n. a feeling of nervousness that makes you unable to relax 紧张，紧张的状态

例 You can see she is just filled with **tension** about her job.

单词助记【同义词】strain

sluggish [ˈslʌgɪʃ]

adj. moving slowly or lazily 行动迟缓的，不机警的

例 The game picked up after a **sluggish** start.

单词助记【同义词】lethargic, inactive, slow

insane [ɪnˈseɪn]

adj. not normal or healthy in mind; very foolish or unreasonable 疯狂的

例 The murderer was found to be criminally **insane**.

单词助记【同义词】foolish, silly, stupid

insult [ɪnˈsʌlt]

❶ *v.* to treat with insolence, indignity, or contempt 侮辱，冒犯

例 I did not mean to **insult** you.

❷ *n.* a rude or offensive act or statement 侮辱，辱骂，侮辱性的言论

例 Their behaviour was an **insult** to the people they represent.

morbid [ˈmɔːbɪd]

adj. relating to unpleasant subjects (such as death)（兴趣、精神、思想等）病态的，疾病的

例 The child has a **morbid** fear of snakes.

单词助记【同义词】morose, gloomy, dark

secular [ˈsekjʊlə(r)]

adj. not spiritual: of or relating to the physical world and not the spiritual world 现世的，世俗的

例 Both **secular** and religious institutions can apply for the funds.

pebble [ˈpebl]

n. a small, round stone; especially: one that has been made smooth by the movement of water 卵石

例 As the last Ice Age came to an end, somebody picked a **pebble** out of a small river not far from Bethlehem.

List 65

frivolous [ˈfrɪvələs]

 adj. not having any serious purpose or value 轻浮的，不重要的

 例 She thinks window shopping is a **frivolous** activity.

 单词助记【同义词】flippant，glib，facetious，superficial，shallow，trivial，trifling，minor

plight [plaɪt]

 n. an unfortunate，difficult，or precarious situation 境况，困境

 例 Huckelberry decided to use the owl's **plight** as the impetus to craft a comprehensive conservation plan.

 单词助记【同义词】predicament，dilemma，quagmire

altitude [ˈæltɪtjuːd]

 n. the height of something (such as an airplane) above the level of the sea 高，高度

 例 Some visitors find it difficult to adjust to the city's high **altitude**.

 单词助记【同义词】height，elevation

fictional [ˈfɪkʃənəl]

 adj. relating to fiction；invented for the purposes of fiction：fictional texts 虚构的

 例 It is drama featuring **fictional** characters.

 单词助记【同义词】fictitious

surrogate [ˈsʌrəgeɪt]

 n. a person or thing that takes the place or performs the duties of someone or something else 替代，代理

 例 The governor and her **surrogates** asked the public to support the change.

 单词助记【同义词】substitute

clank [klæŋk]

 ❶ *v.* to make or cause (something) to make the loud，sharp sound of metal hitting against something solid 使发出叮当声

 例 The empty can **clanked** along the sidewalk.

 ❷ *n.* a sharp brief metallic ringing sound 叮当声

 例 The hammer fell with a **clank** on the floor.

perfidious [pəˈfɪdɪəs]

 adj. not able to be trusted：showing that someone cannot be trusted 不忠的，贩卖的

 例 A **perfidious** campaign worker revealed the senator's strategy to his leading rival for the nomination.

 单词助记【同义词】treacherous，disloyal

irrational [ɪˌræʃəˈnælə]

 adj. not thinking clearly：not able to use reason or good judgment 无理性的，不合理的

 例 He became **irrational** as the fever got worse.

 单词助记【同义词】illogical，unreasonable，foolish

verbose [vɜːˈbəʊs]

adj. using more words than are needed 冗长的，啰唆的

例 She has a **verbose** writing style.

单词助记 【同义词】wordy

disparage [dɪsˈpærɪdʒ]

v. to describe (someone or something) as unimportant，weak，bad，etc. 批评，轻视

例 Voters don't like political advertisements in which opponents **disparage** one another.

单词助记 【同义词】belittle，denigrate，deprecate，trivialize，make light of，undervalue，underrate

cajole [kəˈdʒəʊl]

v. to persuade someone to do something or to give you something by making promises or saying nice things (用甜言蜜语、虚假诺言等)劝诱，哄骗

例 He **cajoled** her into doing his laundry for him.

单词助记 【同义词】wheedle，coax，seduce

edify [ˈedɪfaɪ]

v. to teach (someone) in a way that improves the mind or character 开导，启发

例 These books will both entertain and **edify** readers.

单词助记 【同义词】enlighten，inform，educate

dispel [dɪsˈpel]

v. to make (something，such as a belief，feeling，or idea) go away or end 驱散，赶跑

例 This report should **dispel** any doubts you have about the plan.

单词助记 【同义词】dismiss，chase away，drive out

hazy [ˈheɪzɪ]

❶ *adj.* partly hidden，darkened，or clouded by dust，smoke，or mist 有雾的

例 The air was thin and crisp，filled with **hazy** sunshine and frost.

单词助记 【同义词】misty，foggy，cloudy

❷ *adj.* not clear in thought or meaning 模糊的

例 He gave us a **hazy** account of how he had spent the last two weeks.

inflammable [ɪnˈflæməbl]

adj. capable of being set on fire and of burning quickly 易燃的

例 Some pajamas are made of **inflammable** material，so be careful.

单词助记 【同义词】flammable，combustible，ignitable

discourse [ˈdɪskɔːs]

❶ *n.* the use of words to exchange thoughts and ideas；a long talk or piece of writing about a subject 论文；演说，讲道

例 He likes to engage in lively **discourse** with his visitors.

单词助记 【同义词】dissertation，treatise，homily

❷ *v.* to talk about something especially for a long time 讲述，著述

例 She could **discourse** for hours on/about almost any subject.

barrier [ˈbærɪə(r)]

n. something (such as a fence or natural obstacle) that prevents or blocks movement from one place to another 栅栏，关卡

例 Concrete **barriers** surround the race track to protect spectators.

194

lavish [ˈlævɪʃ]

❶ *adj.* expending or bestowing profusely 过分慷慨的，浪费的

例 He is **lavish** in cars.

（单词助记）【同义词】prodigal

❷ *adj.* expended or produced in abundance 太多的

例 This **lavish** consumption of our natural resources simply cannot continue.

（单词助记）【同义词】profuse

condone [kənˈdəʊn]

v. to regard or treat (something bad or blameworthy) as acceptable，forgivable，or harmless 宽恕，原谅，容忍

例 He is too quick to **condone** his friend's faults.

（单词助记）【同义词】overlook，excuse，disregard

heinous [ˈheɪnəs]

adj. very bad or evil：deserving of hate or contempt（道德败坏的人或行为）极邪恶的，极可耻的

例 These murders were especially **heinous**.

（单词助记）【同义词】hateful，evil

crafty [ˈkrɑːftɪ]

adj. clever in usually a deceptive or dishonest way 狡诈的

例 That **crafty** real estate broker got people to sell their property at bargain prices.

单词助记【同义词】cunning，sneaky，sly

innocent [ˈɪnəsnt]

adj. not guilty of a crime or other wrong act 清白的，无罪的，无辜的

例 He says that he is **innocent** of the crime.

单词助记【同义词】harmless

carnivorous [kɑːˈnɪvərəs]

adj. subsisting or feeding on animal tissues（动物）食肉的

例 A pitcher plant is not ordinarily a healthy place for an ant，since these plants are **carnivorous**.

单词助记【同义词】meat-eating

masquerade [ˌmæskəˈreɪd]

❶ *n.* a party at which people wear masks and often costumes 化装舞会

例 We want to join in the **masquerade**.

❷ *n.* an action or appearance that is mere disguise or show 伪装物；掩饰

例 He told a news conference that the elections would be a **masquerade**.

❸ *v.* to pretend to be someone or something else 假装，冒充

例 He was **masquerading** under a false name.

单词助记【同义词】pretend，impersonate，pose

nimble [ˈnɪmbl]

adj. quick and light in movement or action 灵活的；敏捷的

例 Possessing a **nimble** wit，he always has a cutting comeback for any intended insult thrown his way.

单词助记【同义词】agile，sprightly，lithe，limber

ample [ˈæmpl]

adj. having or providing enough or more than enough of what is needed 足够的

例 They had **ample** money for the trip.

单词助记【同义词】plentiful，abundant，copious，generous，bountiful，bounteous

vague [veɪg]

adj. not clear in meaning：stated in a way that is general and not specific 模糊的

例 The judges determined that the law was too **vague** to be fairly enforced.

etiquette [ˈetɪket]

n. the rules indicating the proper and polite way to behave 礼仪，礼节

例 Her failure to respond to the invitation was a serious breach of **etiquette**.

concoct [kənˈkɒkt]

v. create or devise（said especially of a story or plan）编造

例 He **concocted** an elaborate excuse for why he couldn't come in to work today.

单词助记【同义词】make up，fabricate，invent，formulate

revile [rɪˈvaɪl]

    v. to speak about（someone or something）in a very critical or insulting way 辱骂，斥责

    例 Many people **reviled** him for his callous behavior.

单词助记【同义词】insult，abuse，scorn

feign [feɪn]

    v. to pretend to feel or be affected by（something）假装，伪装，捏造（借口、理由等）

    例 I would never **feign** illness just to get out of a test.

单词助记【同义词】pretend，put on，fake

praiseworthy [ˈpreɪzˌwɜːðɪ]

    adj. deserving praise：worthy of praise 值得称赞的

    例 The only **praiseworthy** thing about this moral poem was that it soon got lost.

单词助记【同义词】admirable，commendable，laudable

elated [ɪˈleɪtɪd]

    adj. very happy and excited 兴高采烈的，得意洋洋的

    例 She was **elated** upon learning that she had been accepted by her first-choice college.

单词助记【同义词】thrilled，ecstatic，euphoric，joyous，gleeful，jubilant，exultant，rapturous

appease [əˈpiːz]

    v. to make（someone）pleased or less angry by giving or saying something desired 使平静

    例 They **appeased** the dictator by accepting his demands in an effort to avoid war.

单词助记【同义词】conciliate，placate，pacify，mollify，propitiate，reconcile

conserve [kənˈsɜːv]

    v. to keep（something）safe from being damaged or destroyed 保护，保藏，保存

    例 With so little rain，everyone had to **conserve** water.

inhabit [ɪnˈhæbɪt]

    v. to live in（a place）：to have a home in（a place）居住于，栖居于

    例 This part of the country is **inhabited** by native tribes.

pensive [ˈpensɪv]

    adj. quietly sad or thoughtful 沉思的

    例 The child sat by himself，looking **pensive**.

单词助记【同义词】thoughtful，meditative，contemplative

sanguine [ˈsæŋgwɪn]

    adj. confident and optimistic 充满希望的，乐观的

    例 He is **sanguine** about the company's future.

单词助记【同义词】cheerful

emancipate [ɪˈmænsɪpeɪt]

    v. to free（someone）from someone else's control or power 解除（束缚），解放（from）（尤指从法律、政治、道德等的约束中解放）

例 He felt the only way to **emancipate** himself from his parents was to move away.

单词助记【同义词】liberate

canon [ˈkænən]

n. general law，rule，principle，or criterion by which something is judged 准则

例 By the **canons** of science，the experiment was not valid.

chorus [ˈkɔːrəs]

n. a group of singers and dancers in a modern play, musical show, etc. 合唱团

例 Students played the lesser parts and sang in the **chorus**.

单词助记【同义词】refrain, chorus line, response

rigorous [ˈrɪɡərəs]

adj. very strict and demanding（性格等）严峻的

例 We subjected the data to a **rigorous** analysis.

单词助记【同义词】hard, severe, harsh

penurious [pɪˈnjʊərɪəs]

adj. very poor 吝啬的, 缺乏的

例 The **penurious** school system had to lay off several teachers.

单词助记【同义词】poor, impoverished, destitute

egotistical [ˌiɡəˈtɪstɪkl]

❶ *adj.* characteristic of those having an inflated idea of their own importance 自我本位的

例 Susan and Deborah share an intensely selfish, **egotistic** streak.

❷ *adj.* characteristic of false pride; having an exaggerated sense of self-importance 任性的

例 Perhaps today's youngsters really are more **egotistical**.

aesthetic [iːsˈθetɪk]

adj. of or relating to art or beauty 有关美的, 美学的

例 There are practical as well as **aesthetic** reasons for planting trees.

单词助记【同义词】artistic

monument [ˈmɒnjuːmənt]

n. a statue, building, or other structure erected to commemorate a famous or notable person or event 纪念碑

例 The statue serves as a **monument** to those who have served in the armed forces.

deceitful [dɪˈsiːtfʊl]

adj. not honest; making or trying to make someone believe something that is not true 欺骗性的

例 The **deceitful** salesman neglected to mention some important information about the used car.

单词助记【同义词】dishonest, mendacious, unscrupulous, fraudulent, counterfeit

calamity [kəˈlæmɪtɪ]

n. an event causing great and often sudden damage or distress; a disaster 灾难

例 He predicted **calamity** for the economy.

单词助记【同义词】disaster, catastrophe, tragedy, cataclysm, adversity

obtuse [əbˈtjuːs]

adj. stupid or unintelligent; not able to think clearly or to understand what is obvious or simple 迟钝的

例 He is too **obtuse** to take a hint.

inundate [ˈɪnʌndeɪt]

❶ *v.* to cover (something) with a flood of water 淹没;(洪水般地)涌来,充满

例 Rising rivers could **inundate** low-lying areas.

❷ *v.* to cause (someone or something) to receive or take in a large amount of things at the same time 给予或交予(太多事物)使难以应付

例 Her office was **inundated** with requests for tickets.

erudite [ˈeruːdaɪt]

adj. having or showing extensive knowledge that is learned by studying 博学的

例 The most **erudite** people in medical research attended the conference.

单词助记【同义词】learned, scholarly

vigorous [ˈvɪɡərəs]

adj. healthy and strong 有力的

例 His speech was met with **vigorous** applause.

单词助记【同义词】energetic, robust, active

sophomoric [ˌsɒfəˈmɒrɪk]

adj. having or showing a lack of emotional maturity 一知半解的

例 His behavior at the party was **sophomoric**.

单词助记【同义词】immature, foolish

impervious [ɪmˈpɜːvɪəs]

adj. not allowing something (such as water or light) to enter or pass through 不可渗透的,透不过的

例 The material for this coat is supposed to be **impervious** to rain.

doze [dəʊz]

v. to sleep lightly 打盹儿,打瞌睡

例 Some students often **doze** off in class.

单词助记【同义词】sleep lightly; nap

impromptu [ɪmˈprɒmptjuː]

adj. & adv. extemporaneous 事先无准备(的),临时(的)

例 Although five different lines had been written, the best choice turned out to be an **impromptu** from the tired actor himself.

单词助记【同义词】unrehearsed, off the cuff

kernel [ˈkɜːnl]

❶ *n.* the small, somewhat soft part inside a seed or nut 内仁,核

例 The nutshell includes the **kernel**.

❷ *n.* a central or essential part 要点,中心,核心

例 There's not a **kernel** of truth in what they say.

dogged [ˈdɒɡɪd]

adj. having or showing the attitude of a person who wants to do or get something and will not stop trying: stubborn and determined 顽强的

例 Her **dogged** efforts eventually paid off.

单词助记【同义词】tenacious, determined, resolute, resolved

poultry [ˈpəʊltrɪ]

n. domesticated birds kept for eggs or meat 家禽

例 This wine goes well with **poultry**.

bellicose [ˈbelɪkəʊs]

adj. having or showing a tendency to argue or fight 好战的；好争吵的

例 He expressed alarm about the government's increasingly **bellicose** statements.

单词助记【同义词】belligerent，aggressive，pugnacious，truculent

List 68

terse [tɜːs]

adj. brief and direct in a way that may seem rude or unfriendly（说话、文笔等）简洁的,扼要的

例 She gave me a few **terse** instructions and promptly left the room.

单词助记【同义词】concise, abrupt, pithy

industrious [ɪnˈdʌstrɪəs]

adj. working very hard; not lazy 勤劳的,勤奋的

例 He is an **industrious** worker.

单词助记【同义词】diligent, hard-working, busy

impede [ɪmˈpiːd]

v. to slow the movement, progress, or action of（someone or something）阻碍,妨碍,阻止

例 He claims that economic growth is being **impeded** by government regulations.

单词助记【同义词】obstruct, hinder, hamper

moan [məʊn]

n. a long, low sound that someone makes because of pain, unhappiness, or physical pleasure 呻吟

例 She let out a long, deep **moan**.

单词助记【同义词】complain, gripe, groan

nefarious [nɪˈfeərɪəs]

adj. evil or immoral 罪恶的,可恶的,无法无天的

例 Moreover, those starry-eyed states inclined to perceive international relations in moral terms frequently underestimate the **nefarious** machinations of their competitors on the world political stage.

conundrum [kəˈnʌndrəm]

n. a confusing or difficult problem 谜,猜不透的难题

例 It is a **conundrum** of how an ancient people were able to build such massive structures without the benefit of today's knowledge and technology.

单词助记【同义词】puzzle, problem

wince [wɪns]

n. a slight grimace or shrinking movement caused by pain or distress（因为痛苦、疼痛）龇牙咧嘴

例 He suppressed a **wince** as motion renewed the pain.

单词助记【同义词】grimace, flinch

admonish [ədˈmɒnɪʃ]

v. to speak to（someone）in a way that expresses disapproval or criticism; to tell or urge（someone）to do something 劝告,训诫

例 They were **admonished** to take advantage of the opportunity.

单词助记【同义词】reprove, warn

prologue ['prəʊlɒg]

　　n.(to) an introduction to a book，play，etc.序言，开场白；序幕，作……序幕的事件，道开场白的演员（一连串事件等的）开端

　　例 Unfortunately，the burglary，which he committed while still a teen，was but a **prologue** to a wasted life of crime.

toady ['təʊdɪ]

　　n.one who flatters in the hope of gaining favors 谄媚者，马屁精

　　例 No one liked the office **toady**，who spent most of her time complimenting the boss on what a great job he was doing.

　　单词助记【同义词】flatterer，sycophant

indignant [ɪn'dɪgnənt]

　　adj.feeling or showing anger because of something that is unfair or wrong：very angry 愤怒的，愤慨的，义愤的

　　例 She wrote an **indignant** letter to the editor.

　　单词助记【同义词】angry，offended

tawdry ['tɔːdrɪ]

　　adj.cheap and gaudy in appearance or quality 廉价而俗丽的

　　例 **tawdry** jewellery

　　单词助记【同义词】gaudy，cheap

maudlin ['mɔːdlɪn]

　　adj.showing or expressing too much emotion especially in a foolish or annoying way 易伤感的

　　例 He became **maudlin** and started crying like a child.

protract [prə'trækt]

　　v.delay；defer 延长，拖延（某事物）

　　例 The highway **project** was protracted by years of litigation.

humility [hjuː'mɪlɪtɪ]

　　n.the quality or state of not thinking you are better than other people：the quality or state of being humble 卑躬屈膝，谦逊，谦恭

　　例 He accepted the honor with **humility**.

　　单词助记【同义词】self-effacement，humbleness，modesty

pry [praɪ]

　　v.to look closely or inquisitively；also：to make a nosy or presumptuous inquiry 打听，刺探（他人的私事）

　　例 We do not want people **prying** into our affairs.

　　单词助记【同义词】interfere，meddle，snoop

retiring [rɪ'taɪərɪŋ]

　　adj.shy and fond of being on one's own 孤僻的

　　例 A banquet was held to honor the **retiring** senator.

　　单词助记【同义词】shy

parody ['pærədɪ]

　　❶ *n*.a piece of writing，music，etc.，that imitates the style of someone or something else in an amusing way 滑稽的模仿诗文，拙劣的模仿；荒谬的替代物

　　例 He has a talent for writing **parodies**.

❷ *v.* to imitate (someone or something) in an amusing way 滑稽地模仿，拙劣地模仿

例 a sketch **parodying** the views of Donald Rumsfeld

arboreal [ɑːˈbɔːrɪəl]

adj. of or relating to trees；living in or often found in trees 树木的，生活于树上的

例 **arboreal** monkeys

单词助记【同义词】of or living in trees

abyss [əˈbɪs]

n. a hole so deep or a space so great that it cannot be measured 深渊

例 Looking down at the dark ocean from the ship's rail，the cruise passenger felt as though he was staring into an **abyss**.

List 69

belie [bɪˈlaɪ]

    v. to give a false idea of (something) 给人以……假象，使被误解

    例 Their actions **belie** their claim to be innocent.

    单词助记【同义词】misrepresent

spendthrift [ˈspendθrɪft]

    adj. wasteful and improvident 挥霍的

    例 The **spendthrift** man spent all his money on the house.

    单词助记【同义词】wasteful，extravagant，improvident

implicit [ɪmˈplɪsɪt]

    adj. understood though not clearly or directly stated 不言明（含蓄）的

    例 There is a sense of moral duty **implicit** in her writings.

affront [əˈfrʌnt]

    ❶ *n.* an action or statement that insults or offends someone 侮辱，冒犯

    例 He regarded her rude behavior as a personal **affront**.

    ❷ *v.* to do or say something that shows a lack of respect for (someone or someone's feelings) 侮辱，冒犯

    例 He was **affronted** by her rude behavior.

prone [prəʊn]

    adj. having a tendency or inclination 有……倾向的

    例 He was **prone** to emotional outbursts under stress.

    单词助记【同义词】apt

paramount [ˈpærəmaʊnt]

    adj. very important；of highest rank or importance 最高的，至上的；首要的，主要的

    例 The **paramount** goal is to restore the colonial-era house with complete historical accuracy.

    单词助记【同义词】supreme

itinerary [aɪˈtɪnərəri]

    n. a planned route or journey 旅行日程

    例 Our **itinerary** included stops at several famous cathedrals.

    单词助记【同义词】travel plan，schedule，agenda

coercion [kəʊˈɜːʃən]

    n. the act，process，or power of making (someone) do something by using force or threats 强迫；胁迫

    例 They cast their votes freely and without **coercion** on election day.

    单词助记【同义词】force

parchment [ˈpɑːtʃmənt]

    n. paper made from the skin of a sheep or goat 羊皮纸，羊皮纸手稿

    例 Align the pan with a sheet of **parchment**.

rectify [ˈrektɪfaɪ]

    v. to correct (something that is wrong) 改正, 矫正

    例 The hotel management promised to **rectify** the problem.

impeach [ɪmˈpiːtʃ]

    v. to bring an accusation against 控告（某人）犯罪, 弹劾

    例 Congress will vote on whether or not to **impeach** the President.

    单词助记【同义词】accuse, indict, arraign

presumptuous [prɪˈzʌmptjuəs]

    adj. too confident especially in a way that is rude; done or made without permission, right, or good reason 自以为是的, 专横的; 冒失的

    例 The **presumptuous** doctor didn't even bother to explain to me the treatment that I would be receiving.

innate [ɪˈneɪt]

    adj. existing as part of the basic nature of something 天生的, 固有的

    例 She has an **innate** sense of rhythm.

    单词助记【同义词】inborn, natural

sparse [spɑːs]

    adj. present only in small amounts; less than necessary or normal 稀疏的, 稀少的

    例 Open land is **sparse** around here.

    单词助记【同义词】thin, spare, scant

satire [ˈsætaɪə(r)]

    n. a way of using humor to show that someone or something is foolish, weak, bad, etc.; humor that shows the weaknesses or bad qualities of a person, government, society, etc. 讽刺

    例 His movies are known for their use of **satire**.

    单词助记【同义词】mockery, irony, sarcasm

quack [kwæk]

    ❶ *n.* a pretender to medical skill 江湖医生, 庸医

    例 I went everywhere for treatment, tried all sorts of **quacks**.

    ❷ *v.* to make the characteristic cry of a duck（鸭子）发出嘎嘎声

    例 There were ducks **quacking** on the lawn.

retrospective [ˌretrəˈspektɪv]

    adj. of or relating to the past or something that happened in the past 回顾（想）的; 追溯既往的（法律, 付款等）

    例 The museum is having a **retrospective** exhibit of the artist's early works.

unyielding [ʌnˈjiːldɪŋ]

    adj. not changing or stopping; not flexible or soft 坚硬的, 不能弯曲的, 不屈的

    例 The pioneers faced the challenge of settling the frontier with **unyielding** courage.

    单词助记【同义词】firm, resolute

slander [ˈslɑːndə(r)]

    ❶ *n.* the act of making a false spoken statement that causes people to have a bad opinion of someone 诽谤, 诋毁

    例 She is being sued for **slander**.

    单词助记【同义词】defamation

    ❷ *v.* to make a false spoken statement that causes people to have a bad opinion of someone 造谣中伤

例 He accused me of **slandering** him and trying to undermine his position.

akin [əˈkɪn]

adj. similar or related 相似的

例 Foxes are closely **akin** to dogs.

单词助记【同义词】related，similar

hinge [hɪndʒ]

n. a usually metal piece that attaches a door, gate, or cover to something and allows it to open and close 合页, 折叶, 铰链

例 The wider the **hinge**, the further it folds.

单词助记 【同义词】 pivot, axis

split [splɪt]

v. to break apart or into pieces especially along a straight line; to separate or divide into parts or groups（使）裂开,（使）破裂

例 A large chunk of ice **split** off from the iceberg and crashed into the water.

单词助记 【同义词】 divide

abridge [əˈbrɪdʒ]

v. to shorten (a book, a play, etc.) by leaving out some parts 节略, 缩写（一本书等）

例 The publisher **abridged** a dictionary by omitting rare words.

单词助记 【同义词】 shorten, curtail

单词助记 中间的"bridge"就是桥, 直接把文章的两部分接在一起, 所以单词表示"缩写"的意思。

defunct [dɪˈfʌŋkt]

adj. no longer existing or being used 已故的, 不存在的, 无效的

例 She wrote for the now-**defunct** newspaper.

单词助记 【同义词】 obsolete, invalid, redundant

extricate [ˈekstrɪkeɪt]

v. to free or remove (someone or something) from something (such as a trap or a difficult situation) 使摆脱困难; 脱身

例 Several survivors were **extricated** from the wreckage.

单词助记 【同义词】 free

reprove [rɪˈpruːv]

v. to criticize or correct (someone) usually in a gentle way 指责

例 The teacher **reproved** the student for being late.

单词助记 【同义词】 censure, rebuke

bonanza [bəʊˈnænzə]

n. a situation in which people can make a lot of money or be very successful（突然的）财源, 鸿运

例 The expected sales **bonanza** hadn't materialized.

condemn [kənˈdem]

v. to say in a strong and definite way that someone or something is bad or wrong 谴责, 责备

例 We strongly **condemn** this attack against our allies.

单词助记 【同义词】 censure, denounce, revile, chastise, berate, reprimand, rebuke, reprove

aloof [əˈluːf]

adj. not involved with or friendly toward other people 冷淡的，疏远的

例 The new kid was really not so **aloof** as we thought him at first，just painfully shy.

（单词助记）【同义词】detached，indifferent，distant

topography [təˈpɒɡrəfɪ]

n. the art or science of making maps that show the height，shape，etc.，of the land in a particular area 地形学

例 A map of the **topography** of the coastline shows a significant loss of wetlands.

（单词助记）【同义词】landscape，geography，structure

intriguing [ɪnˈtriːɡɪŋ]

adj. extremely interesting 引起极大兴趣的

例 The offer is very **intriguing**.

（单词助记）【同义词】fascinating，interesting，exciting

scavenge [ˈskævɪndʒ]

v. to search through waste，junk，etc.，for something that can be saved or used（在废物中）觅食腐肉

例 The bears **scavenged** the woods for food.

exonerate [ɪɡˈzɒnəreɪt]

v. to prove that someone is not guilty of a crime or responsible for a problem，bad situation，etc. 使免罪，免除

例 The results of the DNA fingerprinting finally **exonerated** the man，but only after he had wasted 10 years of his life in prison.

ferocious [fəˈrəʊʃəs]

adj. very fierce or violent 凶猛的

例 The competition among the students was **ferocious**.

（单词助记）【同义词】fierce，vicious，violent

cupidity [kjuːˈpɪdɪtɪ]

n. a strong desire for money or possessions 贪婪，贪得

例 The evidence revealed the **cupidity** of the company's directors.

（单词助记）【同义词】greed，avarice，materialism

solicitous [səˈlɪsɪtəs]

❶ *adj*. characterized by or showing interest or concern 关切的

例 He had always been **solicitous** for the welfare of his family.

（单词助记）【同义词】concerned，caring，considerate，attentive，mindful

❷ *adj*. eager or anxious to do something 热切的，渴望的

例 I am **solicitous** of his help.

parsimony [ˈpɑːsɪmənɪ]

n. the quality of being very unwilling to spend money 异常俭省，极度节俭，吝啬，小气

例 The charity was surprised by the **parsimony** of some larger corporations.

（单词助记）【同义词】stinginess

berate [bɪˈreɪt]

v. to yell at（someone）：to criticize（someone）in a loud and angry way 严厉责备，痛斥

例 There's no need to **berate** someone for making a mistake during the first day on the job.

单词助记【同义词】scold，rebuke，reprimand，reproach，reprove，admonish，chide，criticize，upbraid

fervent ['fɜ:vənt]

adj. felt very strongly：having or showing very strong feelings 热诚的，热烈的

例 He made a **fervent** speech that called for tolerance and compassion for those who are different.

单词助记【同义词】intense，passionate

trite [traɪt]

adj. not interesting or effective because of being used too often：not fresh or original（言语、想法等）老生常谈的，陈腐的

例 The wrong sort of built environment，she argued，wrecked the social fabric of cities. This view seems almost **trite** today，but in the 1960's it was insurgent. — Robert Kuttner，New York Times Book Review，12 Mar. 2000

单词助记【同义词】hackneyed；overused

List 71

tarnish ['tɑːnɪʃ]

❶ *v.* to become or cause (metal) to become dull and not shiny (使)失去光泽,(使)变灰暗

例 Silver **tarnishes** easily.

单词助记【同义词】corroded, discolored

❷ *v.* to damage or ruin the good quality of (something, such as a person's reputation, image, etc.) 玷污,败坏(名誉等)

例 The scandal **tarnished** his reputation.

❸ *n.* a thin layer on the surface of metal which makes the metal look dull 无光泽,表面变色,锈蚀

例 The **tarnish** lay thick on the inside of the ring.

impartial [ɪmˈpɑːʃəl]

adj. treating all people and groups equally: not partial or biased 不偏不倚的,公正的,中立的

例 This is an **impartial** evaluation of the job applicant's qualifications that does not consider age, gender, or race.

单词助记【同义词】neutral, fair, unbiased

单词助记

carping ['kɑːpɪŋ]

adj. marked by or inclined to querulous and often perverse criticism 吹毛求疵的,挑毛病的

例 That peevish and **carping** old woman is not a favorite at the nursing home.

sinuous ['sɪnjuəs]

adj. having many twists and turns 弯曲的,蜿蜒的

例 She moved with **sinuous** grace.

单词助记【同义词】curving, undulating

insipid [ɪnˈsɪpɪd]

adj. not interesting or exciting: dull or boring 枯燥的;无聊的,无味的

例 The soup was rather **insipid**.

单词助记【同义词】uninteresting, bland, dull

dazzle ['dæzl]

v. to impress deeply, overpower, or confound with brilliance 炫耀,迷惑

例 George **dazzled** her with his knowledge of the world.

单词助记【同义词】 glare，brightness，reflection

neophyte [ˈniːəʊfaɪt]

n. a person who has just started learning or doing something 初学者，新手

例 **Neophytes** are assigned an experienced church member to guide them through their first year.

单词助记【同义词】 beginner，novice

petulant [ˈpetjʊlənt]

adj. having or showing the attitude of people who become angry and annoyed when they do not get what they want 暴躁的

例 He was moody and **petulant**.

单词助记【同义词】 sulky，crabby

coherent [kəʊˈhɪərənt]

adj. logical and well-organized：easy to understand 条理清楚的，连贯的；前后一致的

例 He proposed the most **coherent** plan to improve the schools.

单词助记【同义词】 logical，understandable

remorse [rɪˈmɔːs]

n. a feeling of being sorry for doing something bad or wrong in the past：a feeling of guilt 懊悔，悔恨，自责

例 I could forgive him for what he did if he showed some **remorse**.

单词助记【同义词】 regret，sorrow，repentance

elicit [ɪˈlɪsɪt]

v. to get (a response，information，etc.) from someone 引出，探出

例 She's been trying to **elicit** the support of other committee members.

单词助记【同义词】 provoke，cause，produce

overwrought [ˌəʊvəˈrɔːt]

adj. very excited or upset；extremely excited：agitated 神经紧张的，忧虑的，烦恼的

例 The witness became **overwrought** as she described the crime.

单词助记【同义词】 agitated

indefatigable [ˌɪndɪˈfætɪɡəbl]

adj. able to work or continue for a very long time without becoming tired 不倦的，不屈不挠的

例 He is an **indefatigable** laborer who can work from sunrise to sunset.

dim [dɪm]

❶ *adj*. not bright or clear：not seen clearly 暗淡的，昏暗的，不明亮的

例 I found her sitting in a **dim** / = dark/ corner of the restaurant.

单词助记【同义词】 low light，not bright

❷ *v*. to make (a light) less bright or to become less bright (使)变暗淡，(使)变模糊

例 The latest setback has **dimmed** hopes of an early settlement.

demur [dɪˈmɜː(r)]

❶ *v*. to disagree politely with another person's statement or suggestion 表示异议，反对

例 She suggested that he would win easily，but he **demurred**，saying he expected the election to be close.

❷ *n*. an act of disagreeing about something 反对,异议

例 She accepted the group's decision without **demur**.

daunt [dɔːnt]

v. to make (someone) afraid or less confident 使(某人)气馁,威吓

例 The raging inferno didn't **daunt** the firefighters for a moment.

单词助记【同义词】intimidate,discourage

divulge [daɪˈvʌldʒ]

v. to make (information) known:to give (information) to someone 吐露,泄露

例 The company will not **divulge** its sales figures.

单词助记【同义词】reveal

predominant [prɪˈdɒmɪnənt]

adj. more important,powerful,successful,or noticeable than other people or things 占主导地位的,显著的

例 Religion is the **predominant** theme of the play.

单词助记【同义词】main,chief,major

compliance [kəmˈplaɪəns]

n. the act or process of doing what you have been asked or ordered to do:the act or process of complying 服从,顺从

例 There has been a low rate of **compliance** with the new law.

单词助记【同义词】obedience

hyperbole [haɪˈpɜːbəlɪ]

n. extravagant exaggeration 夸张法

例 "Enough food to feed the world" is a common example of **hyperbole**.

单词助记【同义词】exaggeration,overstatement,overemphasis

arid [ˈærɪd]

❶ *adj.* very dry：having very little rain or water 干旱的，贫瘠的

例 an **arid** desert

❷ *adj.* lacking in interest and life 无聊的

例 It is an **arid** speech about duty and responsibility.

单词助记 单词的中间部分"ri"可以记成中文"日"。太阳大了，所以干旱。

aromatic [ˌærəʊˈmætɪk]

adj. having a noticeable and pleasant smell 芳香的

例 **Aromatic** flowers can add greatly to the ambience of a room.

单词助记【同义词】perfumed，fragrant，sweet-smelling

insolvent [ɪnˈsɒlvənt]

adj. not having enough money to pay debts 无力偿付债务的，破产的

例 Two years later，the bank was declared **insolvent**.

单词助记【同义词】bankrupt

loquacious [ləʊˈkweɪʃəs]

adj. liking to talk and talking smoothly and easily 爱说话的，多嘴的

例 He said that despite older adults being less "**loquacious**" or talkative than their younger adult counterparts，they elicit much more vocal responses when calling.

单词助记【同义词】chatty，talkative

adroit [əˈdrɔɪt]

adj. very clever or skillful 熟练的，机敏的

例 She is **adroit** at handling problems.

单词助记【同义词】adept，dexterous，deft，nimble

reproach [rɪˈprəʊtʃ]

v. an expression of rebuke or disapproval 责备（骂），指（谴）责，非难

例 Accusations and **reproaches** from both parties made it difficult to pursue discussions.

单词助记【同义词】fault，accuse，blame

prosper [ˈprɒspə(r)]

v. succeed in material terms；be financially successful 富有；繁荣

例 He hopes his business will **prosper**.

单词助记【同义词】flourish，thrive，bloom，blossom，burgeon

impoverish [ɪmˈpɒvərɪʃ]

v. to make (someone) poor 使（某人）贫穷

例 Poor farming practices **impoverished** the soil.

单词助记【同义词】deprive，ruin，bankrupt

douse [daʊs]

v. to pour a lot of liquid over；to soak in liquid 把……浸入水中，用水泼

例 The pumps were started and the crew began to **douse** the fire with water.

【同义词】drench，soak，wet

paragon [ˈpærəgən]

> *n.* a person or thing that is perfect or excellent in some way and should be considered a model or example to be copied 模范，典型
>
> 例 In Arthurian legend，Sir Galahad is depicted as the one knight who is a **paragon** of virtue.

单词助记【同义词】model of excellence，perfection

haunt [hɔːnt]

> *v.* (of a ghost) manifest itself at (a place) regularly and frequently 经常出没；常去
>
> 例 Spirits **haunted** the house.

单词助记【同义词】frequent，loiter in，linger in

porous [ˈpɔːrəs]

> *adj.* having small holes that allow air or liquid to pass through 能穿透的，能渗透的
>
> 例 The country has a **porous** border.

单词助记【同义词】absorbent，permeable，leaky

devout [dɪˈvaʊt]

> *adj.* deeply religious；devoted to a particular religion 虔诚的
>
> 例 It is his **devout** wish to help people in need.

单词助记【同义词】pious，religious，devoted，dedicated，reverent

despair [dɪˈspeə(r)]

> *n.* the feeling of no longer having any hope 绝望，失望；令人失望的人（事物）
>
> 例 I was overcome by **despair** at being unable to find them.

单词助记【同义词】misery，desolation，anguish

abstruse [æbˈstruːs]

> *adj.* hard to understand 难解的，深奥的
>
> 例 You're not the only one who finds Einstein's theory of relativity **abstruse**.

单词助记【同义词】obscure，arcane，esoteric，recondite，perplexing，cryptic，enigmatic

impair [ɪmˈpeə(r)]

> *v.* to make (something) weaker or worse 损害，削弱
>
> 例 Drinking **impairs** a person's ability to think clearly.

单词助记【同义词】damage，harm，spoil

fulminate [ˈfʌlmɪneɪt]

> ❶ *v.* to complain loudly or angrily 轰鸣；爆炸；(疾病)爆发；怒喝；闪电雷鸣
>
> 例 She was fulminating about the dangers of smoking.
>
> ❷ *n.* an often explosive salt (as mercury fulminate) containing the group 雷汞，雷酸盐

nib [nɪb]

> *n.* the pointed metal tip of a pen 笔尖
>
> 例 Make sure the **nib** has been sharpened before you try to cut anything.

单词助记【同义词】tip，point，end

slim [slɪm]

> ❶ *adj.* thin in an attractive way；small in amount，size，or degree 苗条的，修长的；微小的，渺茫的
>
> 例 She looked **slim** and fit for her age.

单词助记【同义词】small，insufficient，slender

❷ *v.* to make (something) thinner 减肥

例 She started exercising to **slim** her thighs.

belligerent [bɪˈlɪdʒərənt]

❶ *adj.* angry and aggressive：feeling or showing readiness to fight 好战的

例 The coach became quite **belligerent** and spit at an umpire after being thrown out of the game.

单词助记 【同 义 词】bellicose，aggressive，hostile，warlike，antagonistic，pugnacious，truculent，contentious，militant，combative

❷ *adj.* fighting a war：engaged in a war 卷入冲突的

例 **belligerent** nations / states

equanimity [ˌekwəˈnɪmətɪ]

n. calm emotions when dealing with problems or pressure 平和，镇静

例 His sense of humour allowed him to face adversaries with **equanimity**.

单词助记【同义词】calmness

gullible [ˈɡʌləbl]

adj. easily fooled or cheated; especially: quick to believe something that is not true 易受骗的

例 I'm not **gullible** enough to believe something that outrageous.

单词助记【同义词】naive，susceptible，innocent

allure [əˈluə(r)]

❶ *v.* to entice by charm or attraction 引诱，诱惑

例 He was so **allured** by his sister's college roommate that before long he was asking her for a date.

单词助记【同义词】entice，attract

❷ *n.* power to attract: a quality that attracts people 诱惑力，魅力

例 These rare books hold special **allure** for collectors.

gaunt [ɡɔːnt]

adj. very thin usually because of illness or suffering 憔悴的

例 He left the hospital looking tired and **gaunt**.

单词助记【同义词】thin，skinny，lean

florid [ˈflɒrɪd]

adj. very fancy or too fancy 华丽的，炫耀的

例 The President gave a **florid** speech in honor of the queen's visit.

单词助记【同义词】flowery

correlation [ˌkɒrɪˈleɪʃən]

n. the relationship between things that happen or change together 相互关系，相关（性）

例 Researchers have found a direct **correlation** between smoking and lung cancer.

单词助记【同义词】association，connection，relationship

coax [kəʊks]

v. persuade (someone) gradually or by flattery to do something 哄骗

例 He wanted to stay home，but I **coaxed** him into going out.

单词助记【同义词】persuade，wheedle，cajole，beguile，seduce

hive [haɪv]

❶ *n.* a nest for bees 蜂箱，蜂巢

例 A dark cloud of bees comes swarming out of the **hive**.

❷ *n.* a place filled with busy activity 忙碌的地方

例 The house was a **hive** of activity as we prepared for the party.

harsh [hɑːʃ]

❶ *adj.* having an unpleasant or harmful effect because of great strength or force：too intense or powerful 粗糙的；严厉的；刺眼的

例 The accident serves as a **harsh** reminder of the importance of wearing a seat belt.

单词助记【同义词】unpleasant，offensive，cruel，severe

❷ *adj.* having a coarse uneven surface that is rough or unpleasant to the touch 粗糙的

例 Yorke himself has a **harsh** face.

lithe [laɪð]

❶ *adj.* easily bent or flexed 柔软的，易弯（曲）的

例 a **lithe** young gymnast

❷ *adj.* moving in an easy and graceful way 敏捷的，轻快的

例 Tall，**lithe** and muscled，he is only 19 but is confident to the point of cockiness.

delinquent [dɪˈlɪŋkwənt]

❶ *adj.* doing things that are illegal or immoral 犯罪的

例 His **delinquent** behavior could lead to more serious problems.

单词助记【同义词】crook，criminal，felon

❷ *adj.* not paid at the required or expected time 拖欠的

例 Her credit card account was **delinquent**.

convivial [kənˈvɪvɪəl]

adj. of or relating to social events where people can eat，drink，and talk in a friendly way with others 好交际的

例 The hiking club attracts a wide range of **convivial** people who share a love of the outdoors.

单词助记【同义词】genial，affable，amiable，congenial，agreeable，cordial

setback [ˈsetbæk]

n. a problem that makes progress more difficult or success less likely 挫折

例 Despite some early **setbacks**，they eventually became a successful company.

proficient [prəˈfɪʃənt]

adj. good at doing something 精通的，熟练的

例 He has become very **proficient** at computer programming.

单词助记【同义词】skillful，adept

incorrigible [ɪnˈkɒrɪdʒəbl]

adj. not able to be corrected or changed 无法矫正的，屡教不改的，无可救药的

例 He is always the class clown and his teachers say he is **incorrigible**.

lament [ləˈment]

❶ *v.* to express sorrow，regret，or unhappiness about something（为……）哀悼，痛哭，悲伤

例 She **lamented** over the loss of her best friend.

单词助记【同义词】mourn，grieve

❷ *n.* a crying out in grief 哀悼

例 He gave his **lament** in his father's funeral.

demographics [ˌdɪməˈɡræfɪks]

n. the qualities（such as age，sex，and income）of a specific group of people 人口特征

例 The town's **demographics** suggest that the restaurant will do well there.

impudence [ˈɪmpjʊdəns]

> *n.* the quality or state of being failing to show proper respect and courtesy 粗鲁，放肆

> 例 My mother would not tolerate **impudence** from any of us.

> 单词助记【同义词】arrogance，disrespect

onerous [ˈɒnərəs]

> *adj.* difficult and unpleasant to do or deal with 困难的，沉重的，繁重的

> 例 The government imposed **onerous** taxes on imports.

> 单词助记【同义词】troublesome，oppressive

fanatic [fəˈnætɪk]

> ❶ *n.* very or overly enthusiastic or devoted 狂热者，入迷者

> 例 Both Rod and Phil are football **fanatics**.

> ❷ *adj.* marked by excessive enthusiasm and often intense uncritical devotion 狂热入迷的

> 例 a **fanatic** supporter

dogma [ˈdɒgmə]

n. (usually disapproving) a belief or set of beliefs that is accepted by the members of a group without being questioned or doubted 教条

例 These new findings challenge the current **dogma** in Evolution Theory.

单词助记【同义词】tenet, maxim, canon, creed, credo, doctrine

demolish [dɪˈmɒlɪʃ]

v. to destroy (a building，bridge，etc.)：to forcefully tear down or take apart (a structure) 拆除

例 The old factory was **demolished** to make way for a new parking lot.

单词助记【同义词】tear down，bring down，destroy，raze

libel [ˈlaɪbəl]

n. the act of publishing a false statement that causes people to have a bad opinion of someone (文字)诽谤,中伤

例 The newspaper's attorneys argued that the article was not a **libel**.

单词助记【同义词】defame，vilify，sully

voracious [vəˈreɪʃəs]

adj. having or showing a tendency to eat very large amounts of food 暴食的,贪婪的

例 It seemed like the **voracious** kitten was eating her weight in food every day.

单词助记【同义词】insatiable，avid，hungry

hull [hʌl]

n. the outer covering of a fruit or seed body, exterior 外壳,豆荚；(通常船)外体

例 Some fruits and seeds have **hulls**.

单词助记【同义词】body，exterior，underside

expunge [eksˈpʌndʒ]

v. to remove (something) completely 擦掉,除去,删去,消除

例 Time and the weather have **expunged** any evidence that a thriving community once existed here.

单词助记【同义词】erase，eliminate

repugnant [rɪˈpʌgnənt]

adj. causing a strong feeling of dislike or disgust 令人厌恶的

例 Technically speaking，it may not be a violation，but it is certainly **repugnant** to the spirit of the law.

单词助记【同义词】loathsome，hateful

illustrious [ɪˈlʌstrɪəs]

adj. admired and respected very much because a lot was achieved 著名的,杰出的

例 He has had an **illustrious** military career.

单词助记【同义词】distinguished，famous，celebrated

impious [ˈɪmpɪəs]

adj. feeling or showing a lack of respect for God；not pious 不尊敬的，无信仰的，不虔诚的

例 He was fearful of seemingly **impious**.

tremulous [ˈtremjʊləs]

adj. shaking slightly especially because of nervousness，weakness，or illness 发抖的，胆小的；不稳定的，神经过敏的

例 She opened the letter with **tremulous** hands.

单词助记【同义词】trembling，timid

wily [ˈwaɪlɪ]

adj. full of clever tricks：very clever 诡计多端的，狡猾的

例 A **wily** judge of character，she takes advantage of car buyers' insecurity to sell them a bigger machine than they really need.

单词助记【同义词】cunning

complacent [kəmˈpleɪsənt]

adj. satisfied with how things are and not wanting to change them 自满的，自鸣得意的

例 The strong economy has made people **complacent**.

单词助记【同义词】smug，conceited，gloating

starch [stɑːtʃ]

❶ *n.* an odorless tasteless white substance occurring widely in plant tissue and obtained chiefly from cereals and potatoes 淀粉

例 There is too much **starch** in your diet.

❷ *n.* stiffness of manner or character 僵硬，古板

例 The **starch** in her voice annoys the audience.

enthrall [ɪnˈθrɔːl]

v. to hold the attention of（someone）by being very exciting，interesting，or beautiful 迷惑，迷住

例 **Enthralled** by the flickering fire in the hearth，we lost all track of time.

单词助记【同义词】charm

blade [bleɪd]

n. the flat sharp part of a weapon or tool that is used for cutting 刀刃，刀片

例 Many of them will have sharp **blades**.

zealous [ˈzeləs]

adj. feeling or showing strong and energetic support for a person，cause，etc.：filled with zeal 热心的，热情的

例 The detective was **zealous** in her pursuit of the kidnappers.

cacophony [kæˈkɒfənɪ]

n. unpleasant loud sounds 刺耳的声音

例 The sounds of barking dogs and sirens added to the **cacophony** on the streets.

resolution [ˌrezəˈluːʃən]

n. the act of finding an answer or solution to a conflict，problem，etc.：the act of resolving something 坚决，坚定

例 We found a **resolution** to the dispute.

单词助记【同义词】decree，declaration，decision

vociferous [vəʊˈsɪfərəs]

adj. expressing feelings or opinions in a very loud or forceful way；expressed in a very loud or forceful way 吵吵嚷嚷的，大声叫喊的

例 He was **vociferous** in his support of the proposal.

opportune [ˈɒpətjuːn]

adj. suitable or right for a particular situation（时间）合适的，恰好的

例 There isn't a more **opportune** time to invest in the stock market.

单词助记【同义词】favorable，well-timed

grandiose [ˈɡrændɪəʊs]

　　adj. seeming to be impressive or intended to be impressive but not really possible or practical 华而不实的

　　例 The mayor made a **grandiose** plan to upgrade the entire interstate highway system in 10 years.

　　单词助记【同义词】arrogant，proud

nullify [ˈnʌlɪfaɪ]

　　v. to make (something) legally null (使)无效

　　例 The law has been **nullified** by the U.S. Supreme Court.

　　单词助记【同义词】cancel，invalidate

entourage [ˌɒntʊˈrɑːʒ]

　　n. a group of people who go with and assist an important person 随从，随行人员

　　例 For more than a year，British intelligence officers have been instigating contacts with Taliban commanders and their **entourage**.

barrage [ˈbærɑːʒ]

　　❶ *n.* a concentrated artillery bombardment over a wide area 密集火力攻击

　　例 The artillery **barrage** on the city was the heaviest since the ceasefire.

　　❷ *n.* a concentrated outpouring，as of questions or blows 一连串

　　例 She was not prepared for his **barrage** of questions.

　　单词助记【同义词】flood

torpid [ˈtɔːpɪd]

　　adj. having or showing very little energy or movement：not active 迟钝的，懒散的

　　例 My tongue and throat remained **torpid** for a time following the endoscopy.

sublime [səˈblaɪm]

　　❶ *adj.* very beautiful or good：causing strong feelings of admiration or wonder 庄严的，卓越的

　　例 He composed some of the most **sublime** symphonies in existence.

　　单词助记【同义词】beautiful，inspiring

　　❷ *adj.* complete or extreme 极端的

　　例 He displayed a **sublime** indifference to the distinction between right and wrong.

forestall [fɔːˈstɔːl]

　　v. to stop (something) from happening or to cause (something) to happen at a later time 先发制人，预先阻止

　　例 His comments were meant to **forestall** criticism of his proposal.

　　单词助记【同义词】prevent by taking action

rambunctious [ræmˈbʌŋkʃəs]

　　adj. uncontrolled in a way that is playful or full of energy 喧闹的，放纵的

　　例 That beach is often taken over by packs of **rambunctious** young people，so don't go there expecting peace and quiet.

单词助记【同义词】rowdy，high-spirited，lively

hoary [ˈhɔːrɪ]

adj. gray or white with or as if with age 灰白的；古代的，久远的

例 He bowed his **hoary** head.

单词助记【同义词】old，ancient，age-old

chauffeur [ˈʃəʊfə(r)]

n. a person whose job is to drive people around in a car 司机

例 His main job was guarding Dodi, acting as his **chauffeur**, bodyguard and dogsbody.

obnoxious [əbˈnɒkʃəs]

adj. unpleasant in a way that makes people feel offended，annoyed，or disgusted 极不愉快的，讨厌的，可憎的

例 He said some really **obnoxious** things about his ex-girlfriend at the party.

proclivity [prəˈklɪvɪtɪ]

n. (to，towards，for) a strong natural liking for something that is usually bad：a tendency to do something that is usually bad 倾向；癖性，(通常指坏的)脾气

例 Pakistan rejects these baseless and irresponsible allegations and the **proclivity** towards them.

单词助记【同义词】tendency，inclination

ornate [ɔːˈneɪt]

adj. covered with decorations：covered with fancy patterns and shapes 装饰华丽的

例 She doesn't like **ornate** jewelry.

单词助记【同义词】decorative，overelaborate，baroque

derivative [dɪˈrɪvətɪv]

❶ *n*. made up of parts from something else：not new or original 派生物，引出物

例 Tofu is one of many soybean **derivatives**.

单词助记【同义词】unoriginal，imitative，derived

❷ *adj*. something that comes from something else 模仿他人的；衍生的，派生的

例 A number of critics found the film **derivative** and predictable.

banter [ˈbæntə(r)]

❶ *v*. to speak to or address in a witty and teasing manner 玩笑；逗乐

例 The soldiers **bantered** with him as though he was a kid brother.

单词助记【同义词】repartee

❷ *n*. talk in which people make jokes about each other in a friendly way 玩笑；逗乐

例 I enjoyed hearing their good-natured **banter**.

somber [ˈsɒmbə(r)]

❶ *adj*. having a dull or dark color 阴森的，昏暗的，阴天的

例 The movie is a **somber** portrait of life on the streets.

单词助记【同义词】gloomy，depressing

❷ *adj*. very sad and serious 忧郁的

例 Pencer cried as she described the **somber** mood of her colleagues.

thrifty [ˈθrɪftɪ]

adj. managing or using money in a careful or wise way 节俭的，节约的

例 If you are **thrifty**, you can find ways to decorate your room stylishly yet inexpensively.

【单词助记】【同义词】frugal，economical，careful

irate [aɪˈreɪt]

adj. very angry 盛怒的

例 **Irate** viewers called the television network to complain about the show.

【单词助记】【同义词】angry

pedestrian [pɪˈdestrɪən]

❶ *n.* a person who is walking in a city，along a road，etc. 步行者

例 The car slid off the road and almost hit a group of **pedestrians**.

❷ *adj.* lacking inspiration or excitement；dull 缺乏想象力的；无聊的

例 He lived a **pedestrian** life，working at the paper mill and living in his trailer.

【单词助记】【同义词】tedious，monotonous，tiresome，wearisome

dilettante [ˌdɪləˈtæntɪ]

n. a person whose interest in an art or in an area of knowledge is not very deep or serious 业余爱好者；半吊子

例 You can always tell a true expert from a **dilettante**.

【单词助记】【同义词】dabbler，amateur

List 76

duplicate [ˈdjuːplɪkeɪt]

❶ *n.* something that is exactly the same as something else：an exact copy of something else 完全一样的东西,副本

例 In case you lose your keys，keep a set of **duplicates** somewhere safe.

单词助记【同义词】copy

❷ *adj.* exactly the same as something else：made as an exact copy of something else 完全一样的,复制的

例 I began receiving **duplicate** copies of the magazine every month.

❸ *v.* to make an exact copy of（something）复制,复印

例 She **duplicated** the video to give to family and friends.

mansion [ˈmænʃən]

n. a large and impressive house：the large house of a wealthy person 大厦,大楼,宅邸

例 If I ever win the lottery，I'm going to buy a **mansion** in the hills.

单词助记【同义词】hall，manor，tower

antidote [ˈæntɪdəʊt]

n. a substance that stops the harmful effects of a poison 解药

例 There is no **antidote** to this poison.

serpentine [ˈsɜːpəntaɪn]

adj. having many bends and turns 像蛇般蜷曲的,蜿蜒的

例 The country inn lies at the end of a rather **serpentine** road，but it's worth the trip.

单词助记【同义词】snake like，twisting，turning

infinitesimal [ˌɪnfɪnɪˈtesɪməl]

adj. extremely small 极微小的

例 Mineral substances present in **infinitesimal** amounts in the soil.

单词助记【同义词】tiny，minute，minuscule

spacious [ˈspeɪʃəs]

adj. having a large amount of space 宽敞的

例 Almost all of the guests were able to fit into the **spacious** living room.

raucous [ˈrɔːkəs]

adj. loud and unpleasant to listen to 粗声的,刺耳的

例 His **raucous** laughters irritated me.

choleric [ˈkɒlərɪk]

adj. made angry easily 易怒的

例 I absolutely get **choleric** when a telemarketer calls during the dinner hour.

单词助记【同义词】irascible，irritable，grumpy，cantankerous

deft [deft]

adj. skillful and clever 敏捷熟练的,灵巧的

例 The photographer is known for her **deft** use of lighting.

ponderous [ˈpɒndərəs]

adj. very boring or dull; slow or awkward because of weight and size 沉重的，笨重的

例 Read novels with an eye for what might be carved from their sometimes **ponderous** plots without losing the essence of their message and central theme.

demeanor [dɪˈmiːnə(r)]

n. a person's appearance and behavior; the way someone seems to be to other people 行为，风度

例 The director of the opera company has a haughty **demeanor** that can be irritating.

(单词助记)【同义词】manner，conduct，behavior

vain [veɪn]

adj. too proud of your own appearance，abilities，achievements，etc. 自负的

例 She is very **vain** about her appearance.

(单词助记)【同义词】conceited，proud，narcissistic

dissemble [dɪˈsembl]

v. to hide your true feelings，opinions，etc. 假装，掩饰（感情、意图等）

例 He **dissembled** happiness at the news that his old girlfriend was getting married to someone else.

(单词助记)【同义词】mislead，pretend，act

callous [ˈkæləs]

adj. not feeling or showing any concern about the problems or suffering of other people 无情的，冷漠的

例 The apparently **callous** handling of the case led to a storm of protest and headlines around the world.

(单词助记)【同义词】insensitive

narrative [ˈnærətɪv]

n. a story that is told or written 记叙文，故事

例 He is writing a detailed **narrative** of his life on the island.

(单词助记)【同义词】tale，account，description

buffoon [bəˈfuːn]

n. a stupid or foolish person who tries to be funny 愚蠢滑稽的人，逗乐小丑

例 The children at the birthday party giggled at the **buffoon's** silly tricks.

(单词助记)【同义词】clown，jester，fool，comic

slippery [ˈslɪpərɪ]

adj. difficult to stand on，move on，or hold because of being smooth，wet，icy，etc. 滑的，使人滑跤的

例 The trails were muddy and **slippery**.

tacit [ˈtæsɪt]

adj. expressed or understood without being directly stated 暗示的，不言而喻的

例 She felt that she had her parents' **tacit** approval to borrow the car.

(单词助记)【同义词】implied

sanctimonious [ˌsæŋktɪˈməʊnɪəs]

adj. pretending to be morally better than other people 假装圣洁的

例 He writes smug，**sanctimonious** rubbish.

单词助记【同义词】hypocritical，pretending be holy

weeping [ˈwiːpɪŋ]

adj. the process of shedding tears（usually accompanied by sobs or other inarticulate sounds）流泪的，哭泣的

例 I lost track after a while，happy to be home，**weeping** for my father，and thinking about what was next.

List 77

chill [tʃɪl]

❶ *v.* to make (someone or something) cold or cool 使变冷, 寒冷;

例 Let the dessert **chill** for one hour before serving it.

单词助记【同义词】sudden fear, gloom, aloofness

❷ *n.* a check to enthusiasm or warmth of feeling 沮丧, 冷淡

例 There has been a **chill** in diplomatic relations.

posterior [pɒˈstɪərɪə(r)]

adj. near or toward the back of something (such as the body) (时间上)较晚的, 后面的, 尾部的

例 The chapel's **posterior** location in the church serves to make it a quiet retreat.

malcontent [ˈmælkənˌtent]

❶ *n.* a person who is always or often unhappy or angry about something 不满者

例 He complained so much that he got a reputation for being a **malcontent**.

单词助记【同义词】mischief-maker, protester, rebel

❷ *adj.* dissatisfied with the existing state of affairs 不满的

例 Seeing other friends' husbands, she is **malcontent** with hers.

profound [prəˈfaʊnd]

adj. having or showing great knowledge or understanding; difficult to understand; requiring deep thought or wisdom 深切的, 深远的

例 Her books offer **profound** insights into the true nature of courage.

单词助记【同义词】deep

tantalizing [ˈtæntəˌlaizɪŋ]

adj. possessing a quality that arouses or stimulates desire or interest; also; mockingly or teasingly out of reach 诱人的

例 The health world is littered with **tantalizing** products and services.

单词助记【同义词】enticing, teasing, tormenting

literate [ˈlɪtərɪt]

adj. able to read and write 有读写能力的

例 She is **literate** in both English and Spanish.

单词助记【同义词】well-educated, well-read, knowledgeable

furtive [ˈfɜːtɪv]

adj. done in a quiet and secret way to avoid being noticed (指行动)偷偷摸摸的, (指人)鬼鬼祟祟的

例 We exchanged **furtive** smiles across the table.

单词助记【同义词】sneaky, secretive

caustic [ˈkɔːstɪk]

❶ *adj.* sarcastic in a scathing and bitter way 尖刻的

例 She wrote a **caustic** report about the decisions that led to the crisis.

单词助记【同义词】sarcastic, bitter, scathing, derisive, sardonic, ironic, acerbic, abrasive

❷ *adj.* able to burn or corrode organic tissue by chemical action 腐蚀性的

例 The chemical was so **caustic** that it ate through the pipes.

incite [ɪnˈsaɪt]

v. to cause (someone) to act in an angry, harmful, or violent way 刺激，激励，煽动

例 The news **incited** widespread fear and paranoia.

单词助记【同义词】stir up, cause action

dupe [djuːp]

❶ *v.* to deceive or trick (someone) into believing or doing something 欺骗或哄骗某人（做某事）

例 They **duped** her out of $300.

单词助记【同义词】cheat, con, deceive

❷ *n.* one that is easily deceived or cheated：fool 受骗的人，傻子

例 He becomes an innocent **dupe** in a political scandal.

supple [ˈsʌpl]

adj. able to bend or twist easily 柔软的；柔顺的

例 The leather is **supple** and sturdy enough to last for years.

单词助记【同义词】flexible, pliable

maverick [ˈmævərɪk]

n. a person who refuses to follow the customs or rules of a group 标新立异的人，不合常规的人

例 Let him refind his inner rebel, the famous irreverent **maverick**, let the tiger out of the cage.

单词助记【同义词】rebel, non-conformist

usurp [juːˈzɜːp]

v. to take and keep (something, such as power) in a forceful or violent way and especially without the right to do so 篡夺，霸占

例 Some people have accused city council members of trying to **usurp** the mayor's power.

amicable [ˈæmɪkəbl]

adj. showing a polite and friendly desire to avoid disagreement and argument 友好的

例 They reached an **amicable** agreement.

单词助记【同义词】friendly

malady [ˈmælədɪ]

❶ *n.* a disease or illness 疾病，不适

例 He was stricken at twenty-one with a crippling **malady**.

单词助记【同义词】illness

❷ *n.* an unwholesome or disordered condition （社会的）弊端，歪风

例 When apartheid is over the **maladies** will linger on.

peremptory [pəˈremptərɪ]

adj. having or showing the insulting attitude of people who think that they should be obeyed without question 专横的

例 The governor's **peremptory** personal assistant began telling the crowd of reporters and photographers exactly where they had to stand.

【同义词】 dictatorial，authoritative，unconditional

laggard [ˈlæɡəd]

❶ *adj*. lagging or tending to lag 缓慢的，迟缓的，落后的

例 I hate being stuck behind **laggard** motorists on the freeway.

【同义词】 slow，sluggish

❷ *n*. a person or thing that does not go or move as quickly as others 落后者

例 The company has developed a reputation as a technological **laggard** in the personal-computer arena.

fecund [ˈfiːkənd]

❶ *adj*. producing or able to produce many babies，young animals，or plants 多产的，富饶的

例 The pampas are still among the most **fecund** lands in the world.

【同义词】 fertile；productive

❷ *adj*. characterized by having produced many offspring 创造力旺盛的

例 The Franklin stove，bifocals，and the lightning rod are just a few of the inventions that we owe to the **fecund** creativity of Benjamin Franklin.

overture [ˈəʊvəˌtjʊə(r)]

❶ *n*. something that is offered or suggested with the hope that it will start a relationship，lead to an agreement，etc.（向某人做出的）提议

例 The government has made a significant peace **overture** by opening the door to negotiation.

【同义词】 proposal

❷ *n*. the first part of an event：the beginning of something 开端，序幕

例 The opera was preceded by a short **overture**.

dungeon [ˈdʌndʒən]

n. a dark underground prison in a castle 地牢

例 The king threw them in the **dungeon**.

【同义词】 dark underground cell

omnipotent [ɒmˈnɪpətənt]

　　adj. having complete or unlimited power 全能的，权力无限的

　　单词助记【同义词】almighty，all-powerful，invincible

chagrin [ˈʃægrɪn]

　　❶ *n*. a feeling of being frustrated or annoyed because of failure or disappointment （由失败等引起的）懊恼，悔恨

　　例 The fact that he'd been unable to attend the funeral was a source of **chagrin** for Ted.

　　单词助记【同义词】annoyance，sadness

　　❷ *v*. to vex or unsettle by disappointing or humiliating 使懊恼，使悔恨

　　例 He was **chagrined** when his friend poured scorn on him.

agape [əˈɡeɪp]

　　adj. having the mouth open because of wonder，surprise，or shock 瞠目结舌的，目瞪口呆的

　　例 He watched with mouth **agape**.

　　单词助记【同义词】wide open，open，ajar

waver [ˈweɪvə(r)]

　　v. to go back and forth between choices or opinions：to be uncertain about what you think about something or someone 摇摆，摇晃

　　例 They never **wavered** in their support for their leader.

　　单词助记【同义词】hesitate，vacillate

quandary [ˈkwɒndərɪ]

　　n. a situation in which you are confused about what to do 窘困，不知所措

　　例 The unexpected results of the test have created a **quandary** for researchers.

modicum [ˈmɒdɪkəm]

　　n. a small amount 少量，一点点

　　例 Only a **modicum** of skill is necessary to put the kit together.

gratuitous [ɡrəˈtjuːɪtəs]

　　adj. given unearned or without recompense 免费的

　　例 **gratuitous** treatment

　　单词助记【同义词】free

　　adj. given unearned or without recompense 无必要的

　　例 The film was criticized for its **gratuitous** violence.

　　单词助记【同义词】unwarranted

feasible [ˈfiːzəbl]

　　adj. possible to do 可行的，可能且合理的

　　例 He is looking for a **feasible** way to create new jobs.

　　单词助记【同义词】possible，viable，practicable

omniscient [ɒmˈnɪsɪənt]

adj. knowing everything：having unlimited understanding or knowledge 全知的，无所不知的

例 You consult the **omniscient** oracle of man when you crave knowledge.

单词助记【同义词】all-knowing，all-seeing

glutton [ˈɡlʌtən]

n. a person who eats too much；someone who wants a large amount of something 贪食者，贪图者

例 He's such a **glutton** that he ate the whole cake.

单词助记【同义词】gourmand，epicure

euphemism [ˈjuːfəmɪzəm]

n. a mild or pleasant word or phrase that is used instead of one that is unpleasant or offensive 委婉语；委婉说法

例 The term "early retirement" is nearly always a **euphemism** for layoffs nowadays.

creed [kriːd]

n. a statement of the basic beliefs of a religion（尤指宗教）信条，教条

例 Central to the **creed** of this organization of medical volunteers is the belief that health care is a basic human right.

单词助记【同义词】beliefs，credo，doctrine，dogma，tenet

shroud [ʃraʊd]

n. something that covers or hides something 遮蔽，遮蔽物

例 The truth of the affair will always be hidden under a **shroud** of secrecy.

jeopardize [ˈdʒepədaɪz]

v. to put（something or someone）in danger 危及，损害

例 His health has been **jeopardized** by poor nutrition.

vigilant [ˈvɪdʒɪlənt]

adj. carefully noticing problems or signs of danger 警惕的，警戒的，警觉的

例 When traveling through the city，tourists should be extra **vigilant**.

单词助记【同义词】watchful，alert，attentive

bravado [brəˈvɑːdəʊ]

n. confident or brave talk or behavior that is intended to impress other people 逞能，虚张声势

例 His stories are always told with **bravado**.

deluge [ˈdeljuːdʒ]

❶ *n.* a large amount of rain that suddenly falls in an area（大）洪水；大雨，暴雨

例 The **deluge** caused severe mud slides.

❷ *v.* to flood（a place）with water 使淹没，淹没

例 Heavy rains **deluged** the region.

engrossing [ɪnˈɡrəʊsɪŋ]

adj. taking up the attention completely 引人入胜的

例 He gave an **engrossing** lecture on Native American culture before the arrival of Europeans.

单词助记【同义词】riveting，gripping，captivating，compelling

censorious [ˈsensərɪəs]

adj. having or showing a tendency to criticize someone or something severely：very critical 苛评的，吹毛求疵的

例 The stunt earned her the scorn of her **censorious** older sister.

capacious [kəˈpeɪʃəs]

adj. able to hold or contain a lot；large in capacity 能容大量的

例 That car has a **capacious** trunk that makes it a good choice for families.

单词助记【同义词】roomy，spacious，large

surly [ˈsɜːlɪ]

　　adj. rude and unfriendly 脾气坏的，不友好的

　　例 He became **surly** and rude toward me.

　　单词助记【同义词】rude，ill-tempered

ostracize [ˈɒstrəˌsaɪz]

　　v. to not allow（someone）to be included in a group：to exclude（someone）from a group 放逐，流放，摈弃

　　例 She was **ostracized** from the scientific community for many years because of her radical political beliefs.

　　单词助记【同义词】exclude，banish

nuance [ˈnjuːɑːns]

　　n. a subtle difference in or shade of meaning，expression，or sound 细微差别

　　例 He listened to the subtle **nuances** in the song.

amorphous [əˈmɔːfəs]

　　adj. having no definite or clear shape or form 无固定形状的，模糊的

　　例 A dark，strangely **amorphous** shadow filled the room.

flaunt [flɔːnt]

　　v. to show（something）in a very open way so that other people will notice 炫耀，夸耀

　　例 She liked to **flaunt** her wealth by wearing furs and jewelry.

　　单词助记【同义词】show off，exhibit，display

assuage [əˈsweɪdʒ]

　　v. to make（something，such as an unpleasant feeling）less painful，severe，etc. 缓和；平息

　　例 He couldn't **assuage** his guilt over the divorce.

　　单词助记【同义词】relieve，ease，alleviate，soothe，mitigate，allay，palliate

prominent [ˈprɒmɪnənt]

　　❶ *adj.* important；famous 重要的；著名的

　　例 He played a **prominent** part in the campaign.

　　单词助记【同义词】eminent，distinguished，noteworthy，illustrious，celebrated，renowned

　　❷ *adj.* projecting from something 凸出的

　　例 **prominent** cheekbones

　　单词助记【同义词】protuberant，protruding，projecting

utilitarian [ˌjuːtɪlɪˈteərɪən]

　　adj. made to be useful rather than to be decorative or comfortable 有效用的，实用的

　　例 Bruce's office is **utilitarian** and unglamorous.

　　单词助记【同义词】functional，practical

flippant [ˈflɪpənt]

235

adj. lacking proper respect or seriousness 轻薄的，轻浮的

例 He made a **flippant** response to a serious question.

单词助记 【同义词】disrespectful；saucy

transcribe [trænˈskraɪb]

v. to make a written copy of（something）抄写

例 He **transcribed** all of his great-grandfather's letters.

单词助记 【同义词】write out，copy out，set down

impetuous [ɪmˈpetʃʊəs]

adj. acting or done quickly and without thought：controlled by emotion rather than thought 激烈的，急躁的，冲动的

例 He's always been an **impetuous** young man.

单词助记 【同义词】rash，impulsive

recalcitrant [rɪˈkælsɪtrənt]

adj. stubbornly refusing to obey rules or orders 倔强对抗的

例 The manager worried that the **recalcitrant** employee would try to undermine his authority.

intense [ɪnˈtens]

❶ *adj*. very great in degree：very strong 强烈的，剧烈的；极端的

例 Stevens' murder was the result of a deep-seated and **intense** hatred.

单词助记 【同义词】penetrating

❷ *adj*. done with or showing great energy, enthusiasm, or effort 热情的，热切的

例 I felt so self-conscious under Luke's mother's **intense** gaze.

commendable [kəˈmendəbl]

adj. worthy of high praise 值得称赞的

例 Such initiative is highly **commendable**.

单词助记 【同义词】admirable，praiseworthy，creditable，laudable

pompous [ˈpɒmpəs]

adj. having or showing the attitude of people who speak and behave in a very formal and serious way because they believe that they are better，smarter，or more important than other people 自高自大的，自负的

例 She found it difficult to talk about her achievements without sounding **pompous**.

meddlesome [ˈmedlsəm]

adj. interfering with the activities and concerns of other people in an unwanted or unwelcome way：inclined to meddle 爱管闲事的

例 Her neighbors saw her as a **meddlesome** nuisance.

单词助记 【同义词】interfering，intrusive，meddling

instinctive [ɪnˈstɪŋktɪv]

adj. relating to or prompted by instinct；apparently unconscious or automatic 本能的

例 Cats have an **instinctive** desire to hunt.

单词助记 【同义词】intuitive，natural，instinctual，innate，inborn，inherent

puzzlement [ˈpʌzlmənt]

n. a feeling of being confused because something is difficult to understand 迷惑

例 The cause of the accident has been a source of **puzzlement**.

单词助记 【同义词】perplexity，uncertainty，disorientation

dismantle [dɪsˈmæntl]

  v. to take (something，such as a machine or structure) apart so that it is in separate pieces 拆卸

  例 The mechanic **dismantled** the engine to repair it.

单词助记【同义词】pull pieces，pull apart，take pieces

taint [teɪnt]

  v. contaminate or pollute (something) 玷污；污染

  例 A tendency toward conceitedness **taints** that athlete's status as a role model.

单词助记【同义词】contaminate，adulterate，spoil，befoul

manifold [ˈmænɪfəʊld]

❶ *adj.* many and various 多种多样的，多方面的

例 The benefits of this approach are **manifold**.

❷ *n.* of many and various kinds 具有多种形式的东西

例 an exhaust **manifold**

sheepish [ˈʃiːpɪʃ]

adj. (of a person or expression) showing embarrassment from shame or a lack of self-confidence 难为情的

例 I asked him why. He looked a little **sheepish** when he answered.

单词助记【同义词】embarrassed，uncomfortable，hangdog，shamefaced，ashamed

brusque [bruːsk]

adj. talking or behaving in a very direct，brief，and unfriendly way（说话）粗鲁的

例 She asked for a cup of coffee and received a **brusque** reply："We don't have any."

单词助记【同义词】abrupt，curt，offhand

grimace [ɡrɪˈmeɪs]

n. an ugly，twisted expression on a person's face，typically expressing disgust，pain，or wry amusement（因为恶心，痛苦等）面部扭曲

例 The patient made a painful **grimace** as the doctor examined his wound.

单词助记【同义词】scowl，frown，sneer

trunk [trʌŋk]

n. the thick main stem of a tree 树干

例 The bark was riven off from the **trunk**.

单词助记【同义词】branch

obsessive [əbˈsesɪv]

adj. thinking about something or someone too much or in a way that is not normal：having an obsession：showing or relating to an obsession 萦绕于心的，有执着想法的

例 He is an **obsessive** workaholic who never stops thinking about his job.

单词助记【同义词】compulsive，fanatical，fixated

reminiscence [ˈremɪnɪsəns]

n. a story that someone tells about something that happened in the past 旧事，回忆

例 We wondered whether she could trust her **reminiscence** of events that happened so long ago.

penitent [ˈpenɪtənt]

❶ *adj.* feeling or showing sorrow and regret because you have done something wrong 悔罪的，悔过的

例 Robert Gates sat before them，almost **penitent** about the past.

❷ *n.* a person who is sorry for doing something wrong and asks for forgiveness：a penitent person 后悔者，忏悔者

238

例 A **penitent**'s prayer is an undeniable ambassador.

rebuff [rɪˈbʌf]

n. to reject or criticize sharply 断然拒绝，驳斥

例 Our suggestion was immediately **rebuffed**.

rotund [rəʊˈtʌnd]

adj. fat and round 近圆形的，胖得圆滚滚的，(声音)圆润的

例 The actor's distinct baritone and his clear and **rotund** elocution are especially effective in dramatic readings.

单词助记【同义词】fat

insomnia [ɪnˈsɒmnɪə]

n. the condition of not being able to sleep 失眠(症)

例 He has suffered from **insomnia** virtually his entire life.

exhaustive [ɪgˈzɔːstɪv]

adj. including all possibilities；very thorough 全面的，彻底的

例 The list was long but not **exhaustive**.

单词助记【同义词】thorough，complete，comprehensive

infectious [ɪnˈfekʃəs]

adj. capable of being passed to someone else by germs that enter the body 传染的，有传染性的

例 She has an **infectious** grin.

acquiesce [ˌækwɪˈes]

v. accept something reluctantly but without protest 不情愿地接受

例 Apparently the contractor expected me to **acquiesce** to my own fleecing.

单词助记【同义词】accept，consent to，concede，assent to，concur with，comply with

pretentious [prɪˈtenʃəs]

adj. having or showing the unpleasant quality of people who want to be regarded as more impressive，successful，or important than they really are 自命不凡的，自负的

例 It is hard to be **pretentious** or elevated in Yiddish，and easy to poke fun.

innocuous [ɪˈnɒkjʊəs]

adj. not likely to bother or offend anyone；causing no injury 无害的，无毒的

例 He told a few **innocuous** jokes.

单词助记【同义词】harmless，innocent

deadlock [ˈdedlɒk]

n. a situation in which an agreement cannot be made；a situation in which ending a disagreement is impossible because neither side will give up something that it wants 僵局

例 City councilors reached a **deadlock** over the law.

单词助记【同义词】stalemate，impasse，standoff，standstill

brawl [brɔːl]

n. to fight noisily in usually a public place 争吵，打(群)架

例 Fans were **brawling** in the streets after the game.

单词助记【同义词】fight，scuffle，tussle

palpable [ˈpælpəbl]

❶ *adj*. capable of being touched or felt 可触知的，摸得出的

239

例 a **palpable** tumour

单词助记【同义词】real；tangible

❷ *adj.* easily perceptible 明显的；明白的

例 There was a **palpable** excitement in the air as the town prepared for the festival.

单词助记【同义词】noticeable

diminish [dɪˈmɪnɪʃ]

v. to become or to cause (something) to become less in size，importance，etc.（使）减少；缩小

例 The strength of the army was greatly **diminished** by outbreaks of disease.

List 81

chasm [ˈkæzəm]

❶ *n.* a deep hole or opening in the surface of the earth 裂缝，裂口

例 The tourists luxuriated in the beauties of the **chasm**.

❷ *n.* a major division，separation，or difference between two people，groups，etc. 分歧

例 Leaders tried to bridge a **chasm** between the two religious groups.

stoic [ˈstəʊɪk]

n. a person who accepts what happens without complaining or showing emotion 坚忍主义，坚忍的人，克制情感者

例 "That would have been to dishonor him，" said Carr，a notorious **stoic** who was nearly overcome by emotion in his postgame press conference.

单词助记【同义词】expressionless

etude [eɪˈtjuːd]

n. a piece of music for the practice of a point of technique 练习曲

例 Chinese piano **etude** textbook is the important part of Chinese piano music.

compel [kəmˈpel]

v. to force（someone）to do something 强迫，迫使屈服

例 Illness **compelled** him to stay in bed.

单词助记【同义词】force，induce，require

fetid [ˈfiːtɪd]

adj. having a strong，unpleasant smell 臭的，有恶臭的

例 As temperatures climbed to 95 degrees and above，the hospital became a **fetid**，smelly hell.

单词助记【同义词】rotten，putrid，foul

doleful [ˈdəʊlfʊl]

adj. very sad 令人沮丧的，悲哀的，阴郁的

例 The girl had a **doleful** look on her face.

单词助记【同义词】mournful

exclamation [ˌekskləˈmeɪʃən]

n. a sharp or sudden cry：a word，phrase，or sound that expresses a strong emotion 呼喊，惊叫，感叹

例 Her unexpected announcement caused a few **exclamations** of surprise.

单词助记【同义词】shout，cry，yell

putrid [ˈpjuːtrɪd]

❶ *adj.* decayed with usually a very bad or disgusting smell 已腐烂的，腐败的

例 **Putrid** liquids oozed down the streets，spreading death and disease，and the air was filled with the repugnant smell of rotting fish.

单词助记【同义词】rotten，stinking

❷ *adj.* very ugly，bad，or unpleasant 卑劣的，极令人不快的

例 a **putrid** performance

garble [ˈɡɑːbl]

v. to cause（a word，name，message，etc.）to be unclear or confusing 曲解，窜改

例 The candidate complained that his views had been deliberately **garbled** by his opponent.

单词助记 【同义词】mangle，distort，jumble

pious [ˈpaɪəs]

adj. devoutly religious 虔诚的

例 I'm tired of hearing politicians making **pious** pronouncements about their devotion to the people.

单词助记 【同义词】religious，devout，spiritual

mourn [mɔːn]

v. to feel or show great sadness because someone has died 哀悼

例 She is still **mourning** her husband，who died last year.

mercurial [mɜːˈkjʊəriəl]

❶ *adj.* changing moods quickly and often；characterized by rapid and unpredictable changeableness of mood 多变的，变化莫测的

例 Few moments in English history have been more hungry for the future，its **mercurial** possibilities and its hope of richness，than the spring of 1603.

❷ *adj.* a pharmaceutical or chemical containing mercury 水银的

例 **mercurial** thermometer

occlude [əˈkluːd]

v. stop，close up，or obstruct 阻碍；堵塞

例 They were **occluding** the waterfront with a wall of buildings.

单词助记 【同义词】block（up），stop（up），obstruct

tedious [ˈtiːdɪəs]

adj. boring and too slow or long 乏味的，单调的

例 The work is **tedious**，but it needs to get done.

单词助记 【同义词】boring，dull，deadly

destitute [ˈdestɪtjuːt]

❶ *adj.* extremely poor 赤贫的，贫苦的

例 His business failures left him **destitute**.

❷ *adj.* without something that is needed or wanted 没有的，缺乏的

例 a lake **destitute** of fish / a man destitute of wisdom

messy [ˈmesɪ]

adj. not clean or tidy 肮脏的，凌乱的，杂乱的

例 Some kinds of glue are **messier** than others.

单词助记 【同义词】disordered，untidy，muddled

esoteric [ˌesəʊˈterɪk]

adj. hard to understand；limited to a small number of people 神秘的；难解的

例 Metaphysics is such an **esoteric** subject that most people are content to leave it to the philosophers.

单词助记 【同义词】obscure

impertinent [ɪmˈpɜːtɪnənt]

❶ *adj.* rude and showing a lack of respect 无礼的，粗鲁的；不恰当的

例 Would it be **impertinent** to ask where exactly you were?

单词助记 【同义词】disrespectful；rude

❷ *adj.* irrelevant 离题的，不相干的

例 The **impertinent** child had a smart answer for everything.

portent ['pɔːtent]

n. a sign or warning that something usually bad or unpleasant is going to happen （通常是坏事）预兆，征兆

例 A scout was sent to have a look at this teenage pitcher who was supposed to be the latest **portent** of the baseball world.

单词助记 【同义词】omen

dearth [dɜːθ]

n. the state or condition of not having enough of something 缺乏，稀少

例 There was a **dearth** of usable firewood at the campsite.

单词助记 【同义词】scarcity，insufficiency

List 82

nourishment ['nʌrɪʃmənt]

n. food and other things that are needed for health, growth, etc. 食物，滋养品

例 These children are suffering because they lack proper **nourishment**.

fodder ['fɒdə(r)]

n. something fed to domestic animals 饲料

例 Great white sharks, the largest predatory fish in the ocean, are supreme **fodder** for headlines.

单词助记 【同义词】food, silage, hay

proximity [prɒk'sɪmɪtɪ]

n. (to) the state of being near 接近，近似；亲近

例 The **proximity** of the curtains to the fireplace was a cause of concern for the safety inspector.

单词助记 【同义词】closeness

fickle ['fɪkl]

adj. changing often（爱情、友谊等）易变的，无常的

例 He blames poor sales on **fickle** consumers.

单词助记 【同义词】inconstant, not loyal

obstinacy ['ɒbstɪnəsɪ]

n. the quality or state of being obstinate：stubbornness 固执

例 The **obstinacy** of these people who insisted that the Earth was flat was bothering.

单词助记 【同义词】stubbornness, determination, inflexibility

transgress [trænz'gres]

❶ *v.* to go beyond limits set or prescribed by 超越，越过

例 There are legal consequences for companies that **transgress** the rules.

单词助记 【同义词】trespass

❷ *v.* to violate a command or law 做坏事，道德败坏，违反道德

例 If a politician transgresses, that is not the fault of the media.

succulent ['sʌkjʊlənt]

adj. full of juice；having thick, heavy leaves or stems that store water 多汁（液）的，肉质的，新鲜的

例 Cook pieces of **succulent** chicken with ample garlic and a little sherry.

lenient ['liːnjənt]

adj. allowing a lot of freedom and not punishing bad behavior in a strong way：not harsh, severe, or strict 宽大的，仁慈的

例 Many people felt that the punishment was too **lenient**.

单词助记 【同义词】merciful, not severe

biased ['baɪəst]

adj. having or showing a bias：having or showing an unfair tendency to believe that some people, ideas, etc., are better than others 有偏见的，有偏的

例 She is too **biased** to write about the case objectively.

单词助记 【同义词】 prejudiced，influenced

aggrandize [əˈgrændaɪz]

❶ *v.* to make great or greater 增加

例 plans to **aggrandize** the building

❷ *v.* praise highly 夸大

例 At the dinner table，my father would go on and on，showing off，**aggrandizing** himself.

eloquence [ˈeləkwəns]

n. the ability to speak or write well and in an effective way 口才；雄辩

例 She spoke with **eloquence** on the need for better schools.

单词助记 【同义词】 expressiveness，articulateness，persuasiveness

languid [ˈlæŋgwɪd]

adj. showing or having very little strength，energy，or activity 没精打采的，懒散的

例 They proceeded at a **languid** pace.

reticent [ˈretɪsənt]

adj. not willing to tell people about things 沉默不语的

例 Her husband is by nature a **reticent** person，and she resigned herself to that fact long ago.

单词助记 【同义词】 cagey，discreet，reserved

lassitude [ˈlæsɪtjuːd]

n. the condition of being tired：lack of physical or mental energy 疲乏，倦怠，懒散

例 Symptoms of the disease include paleness and **lassitude**.

savory [ˈseɪvəri]

adj. having a pleasant taste or smell 风味极佳的，可口的，味美的

例 They prepared an assortment of both sweet and **savory** foods.

单词助记 【同义词】 salty，salt，spicy

labyrinth [ˈlæbərɪnθ]

❶ *n.* a place that has many confusing paths or passages 迷宫

例 The cockpit was a **labyrinth** of instruments and controls.

单词助记 【同义词】 maze，web

❷ *n.* something extremely complex or tortuous in structure，arrangement，or character 迷，难解的事物

例 a **labyrinth** of swamps and channels

单词助记 【同义词】 intricacy，perplexity

pungent [ˈpʌndʒənt]

adj. having a strong，sharp taste or smell（味道或气味）有刺激味的，辛辣的，刺鼻的

例 The left has often complained that what it needs isn't polite speech，but voices as **pungent** as those on the right.

manipulative [məˈnɪpjʊlətɪv]

adj. skillful in influencing or controlling others to your own advantage 操纵别人的

例 We should not use dishonest tactics to destabilize competitors，or **manipulative** communications that verge on propaganda.

单词助记【同义词】scheming，calculating，controlling

cache [kæʃ]

　　n. a secure place of storage 藏物处

　　例 Police found a **cache** of stolen cars in the woods.

bald [bɔːld]

　　adj. of a person：having no hair or very little hair on the head；of a part of the body：not covered with hair 秃头的，无毛的

　　例 He covered his **bald** head with a baseball cap.

单词助记【同义词】hairless，balding

gesticulate [dʒeˈstɪkjʊleɪt]

> *v*. to move your arms and hands especially when speaking in an angry or emotional way 打手势

> 例 A man with a paper hat upon his head was **gesticulating** wildly.

genre [ˈʒɒnrə]

> *n*. a particular type or category of literature or art（文学、艺术等的）类型，体裁，风格

> 例 This book is a classic of the mystery **genre**.

> 单词助记 【同义词】category

vex [veks]

> *v*. to annoy or worry（someone）烦恼，苦恼

> 例 This problem has **vexed** researchers for years.

> 单词助记 【同义词】annoy，irritate

blithe [blaɪð]

> ❶ *adj*. showing a lack of proper thought or care：not caring or worrying 漫不经心的

> 例 He showed **blithe** disregard for the rights of others.

> 单词助记 【同义词】casual，indifferent，heedless，nonchalant

> ❷ *adj*. happy and without worry 欢乐的，愉快的

> 例 a **blithe** spirit

cramped [kræmpt]

> *adj*. constricted in size 狭窄的

> 例 There are hundreds of families living in **cramped** conditions on the floor of the airport lounge.

> 单词助记 【同义词】overcrowded，confined，restricted

disdain [dɪsˈdeɪn]

> ❶ *n*. a feeling of strong dislike or disapproval of someone or something you think does not deserve respect 鄙视，轻蔑

> 例 Laval brushed this aside with **disdain**.

> 单词助记 【同义词】despise，scorn，spurn

> ❷ *v*. to strongly dislike or disapprove of（someone or something）鄙视

> 例 They **disdained** him for being weak.

indolent [ˈɪndələnt]

> *adj*. not liking to work or be active 懒惰的，顽固性的

> 例 He is an **indolent** boy who had to be forced to help out with the chores.

flimsy [ˈflɪmzɪ]

> *adj*. easily broken，torn；not strong or solid 站不住脚的，薄的，弱的

> 例 They have only the **flimsiest** of evidence against him.

> 单词助记 【同义词】fragile，weak，delicate

bucolic [bjuːˈkɒlɪk]

adj. of or relating to the country or country life 牧民的，乡村的

例 It is a **bucolic** region where farms are still common.

单词助记【同义词】rustic，rural

induce [ɪnˈdjuːs]

v. to cause（someone or something）to do something 引诱，劝导

例 The advertisement is meant to **induce** people to eat more fruit.

antediluvian [ˌæntɪdɪˈluːvɪən]

adj. very old or old-fashioned 陈旧的；过时的

例 He has **antediluvian** notions/ideas about the role of women in the workplace.

单词助记【同义词】out of date，outdated，outmoded，old-fashioned，antiquated

curtail [kɜːˈteɪl]

v. to reduce or limit（something）截断，缩短

例 School activities are being **curtailed** due to a lack of funds.

单词助记【同义词】limit，restrain，restrict

appraise [əˈpreɪz]

v. to give your opinion about the condition，quality，or importance of（something or someone that you have studied or examined）鉴定

例 The ring must be **appraised** by a jeweler before it can be insured.

单词助记【同义词】assess，evaluate，judge

meander [mɪˈændə(r)]

❶ *v*. to wander aimlessly or casually without urgent destination 漫无目的地游荡，漫步

例 We **meandered** around the village.

单词助记【同义词】ramble，wander

❷ *v*. to wander aimlessly or casually without urgent destination（指溪流、河流等）蜿蜒而流

例 We took a gravel road that **meandered** through farmland.

garrulous [ˈɡærʊləs]

adj. tending to talk a lot；very talkative 爱说话的

例 He became more **garrulous** after drinking a couple of beers.

单词助记【同义词】chatty，talkative

indigent [ˈɪndɪdʒənt]

adj. lacking money；very poor 贫穷的，贫困的，缺少钱财的

例 Because he was **indigent**，the court appointed a lawyer to defend him.

torture [ˈtɔːtʃə(r)]

n. the act of causing severe physical pain as a form of punishment or as a way to force someone to do or say something 拷问，折磨，拷打

例 Listening to him can be **torture**.

单词助记【同义词】torment，afflict，persecute

impeccable [ɪmˈpekəbl]

adj. free from fault or error 无错误的，极好的，无瑕疵的

例 She has **impeccable** taste in music.

单词助记【同义词】perfect，flawless

cogent [ˈkəʊdʒənt]

adj. very clear and easy for the mind to accept and believe（理由，论据）有说服力的，令人信服的

例 The results of the DNA fingerprinting were the most **cogent** evidence for acquittal.

单词助记 【同义词】forceful，compelling，convincing

surfeit [ˈsɜːfɪt]

❶ *n.* an amount that is too much or more than you need 过量，过度（尤指饮食）

例 Rationing had put an end to a **surfeit** of biscuits long ago.

❷ *v.* to feed，supply，or give to surfeit 吃得过多

例 Having **surfeited** ourselves on raw oysters，we had to decline the rest of the restaurant's offerings.

❸ *v.* to indulge to satiety in a gratification 由于过量而厌腻

例 He never **surfeited** on rich wine.

fraudulent [ˈfrɔːdjʊlənt]

　　adj. done to trick someone for the purpose of getting something valuable 欺骗的，不诚实的

　　例 Corrupt leaders were chosen in a **fraudulent** election.

　　单词助记【同义词】fake，deceitful，untrue

catharsis [kəˈθɑːsɪs]

　　n. the act or process of releasing a strong emotion (such as pity or fear) especially by expressing it in an art form 宣泄，情绪的抒发

　　例 Acting is a means of **catharsis** for her.

　　单词助记【同义词】purification，cleansing

immutable [ɪˈmjuːtəbl]

　　adj. unable to be changed 不可改变的

　　例 One of the **immutable** laws of television is that low ratings inevitably lead to cancellation.

　　单词助记【同义词】unchangeable

benevolence [bɪˈnevələns]

　　n. disposition to do good；an act of kindness 仁爱心，善行

　　例 Self-effacing as well as selfless，he refused all public acknowledgement of his many **benevolences** to the community.

　　单词助记【同义词】kindness，compassion，generosity

preen [priːn]

　　❶ *v.* of a bird：to groom with the bill especially by rearranging the barbs and barbules of the feathers and by distributing oil from the uropygial gland（鸟）用嘴整理（羽毛）

　　例 The bird was **preening** its feathers.

　　❷ *v.* to dress or smooth (oneself) up 精心打扮

　　例 Bill **preened** his beard.

　　单词助记【同义词】dress up，primp

tranquility [træŋˈkwɪlətɪ]

　　n. a disposition free from stress or emotion 宁静

　　例 A psychotherapist valued for her **tranquillity** and ability to listen.

　　单词助记【同义词】serenity，calmness，quietude

annul [əˈnʌl]

　　v. to say officially that something is no longer valid；to make (something) legally void 宣告无效

　　例 Unfortunately，his arrogant attitude **annuls** the many generous favors he does for people.

　　单词助记【同义词】nullify，cancel

fatigue [fəˈtiːg]

n. the state of being very tired：extreme weariness 疲劳，劳累

例 We were overcome by **fatigue** after the long journey.

单词助记【同义词】exhaustion，weariness，extreme tiredness

gully [ˈɡʌlɪ]

n. a trench which was originally worn in the earth by running water and through which water often runs after rains 溪谷，集水沟，檐槽

例 The bodies of the three climbers were located at the bottom of a steep **gully**.

单词助记【同义词】ravine，gorge，valley

predilection [ˌpriːdɪˈlekʃən]

n. a natural liking for something：a tendency to do or to be attracted to something 偏好

单词助记【同义词】liking，preference，fondness

excerpt [ˈeksɜːpt]

❶ *n.* a small part of a longer written work 摘录，摘要

例 She read an **excerpt** from the play.

单词助记【同义词】extract，passage，quote

❷ *v.* to include（part of a longer written work）in something else 选录，摘录

例 This article was **excerpted** from the *New York Times*.

jocular [ˈdʒɒkjʊlə(r)]

adj. liking to tell jokes 爱开玩笑的，滑稽的，幽默的

例 He is a **jocular** man who could make the most serious people smile.

austere [ɔˈstɪə(r)]

adj. simple or plain：not fancy 朴素的，无装饰的

例 They choose **austere** furnishings for the office.

单词助记【同义词】strict，severe

insinuate [ɪnˈsɪnjʊeɪt]

v. to say（something，especially something bad or insulting）in an indirect way 暗示，旁敲侧击

例 Years were needed for the agent to **insinuate** himself into the terrorist organization.

scanty [ˈskæntɪ]

adj. very small in size or amount（大小或数量）不足的，勉强够的

例 The cheerleaders wore **scanty** outfits.

单词助记【同义词】meager，inadequate

amend [əˈmend]

❶ *v.* to change some of the words and often the meaning of（a law，document，etc.）修订

例 The country's constitution was **amended** to allow women to vote.

单词助记【同义词】change，alter

❷ *v.* to change and improve（something，such as a mistake or bad situation）改良

例 He tried to **amend** the situation by apologizing to me.

compliment [ˈkɒmplɪmənt]

n. a remark that says something good about someone or something 赞美

例 He told her he admired her paintings and she returned the **compliment** by saying that she was a fan of his sculptures.

单词助记【同义词】flatter，praise，admire

blaze [bleɪz]

❶ *n*. an intensely burning fire；intense direct light often accompanied by heat 火，光

例 Two people were injured in a restaurant **blaze** late last night.

单词助记【同义词】fire，inferno，conflagration

❷ *v*. to burn brightly 燃烧

例 Three people died as wreckage **blazed**，and rescuers fought to release trapped drivers.

sobriety [səʊˈbraɪətɪ]

n. the quality or state of being sober 清醒，严肃

例 They did a **sobriety** test on him.

单词助记【同义词】abstinence，temperance，moderation

apprehensive [ˌæprɪˈhensɪv]

adj. afraid that something bad or unpleasant is going to happen：feeling or showing fear or apprehension about the future 不安的，害怕的

例 He was quite **apprehensive** about the surgery.

单词助记【同义词】fearful，aware

profligate ['prɒflɪgɪt]

❶ *adj*. recklessly extravagant or wasteful in the use of resources 肆意挥霍的

例 She was very **profligate** in her spending.

单词助记【同义词】wasteful，spendthrift，improvident，prodigal

❷ *n*. a person given to wildly extravagant and usually grossly self-indulgent expenditure 放荡的人，浪子，肆意挥霍者

例 The despicable **profligate** squandered all his legacy from his ancestors.

orthodox ['ɔ:θədɒks]

adj. accepted as true or correct by most people：supporting or believing what most people think is true 规范的，公认的，普遍赞同的

例 She believes in the benefits of both **orthodox** medicine and alternative medicine.

单词助记【同义词】conventional，accepted，traditional

founder ['faʊndə(r)]

❶ *n*. a person who establishes an institution or settlement 创建者

例 He's the son of the company's **founder**.

单词助记【同义词】originator，creator，(founding) father

❷ *v*. (of a ship) fill with water and sink；(of a plan or undertaking) fail or break down 沉没；失败

例 The talks have **foundered**，largely because of the reluctance of some members of the government to do a deal with criminals.

单词助记【同义词】fail，be unsuccessful，not succeed，fall flat，fall through，collapse，backfire

fragrance ['freɪgrəns]

n. a pleasant and usually sweet smell 芳香，香味

例 He bought a flower with a lovely **fragrance**.

rancid ['rænsɪd]

adj. having a rank smell or taste 腐臭的

例 Some foods become **rancid** quickly.

单词助记【同义词】reeking，fetid，sour

congenial [kən'dʒiːnjəl]

adj. suitable or appropriate 宜人的，适宜的；意气相投的

例 The town is a **congenial** place for raising children.

单词助记【同义词】pleasant，appealing，satisfying，gratifying

squalid ['skwɒlɪd]

adj. very dirty and unpleasant；immoral or dishonest (尤指因被忽视而)污秽的，不洁的，邋遢的

例 The family lived in **squalid** conditions.

单词助记【同义词】dirty，unpleasant

forbearance [fɔː'beərəns]

n. the quality of someone who is patient and able to deal with a difficult person or situation without becoming angry 忍耐,克制;宽容

例 He showed great **forbearance** in his dealings with them.

单词勤记【同义词】patience, restraint

prosaic [prə'zeɪɪk]

adj. dull or ordinary 无聊的,乏味的

例 She believes the noises are made by ghosts, but I think there's a more **prosaic** explanation.

单词勤记【同义词】ordinary; unimaginative

comprise [kəm'praɪz]

❶ *v*. to be made up of (something): to include or consist of (something) 包含,由……组成

例 The play **comprises** three acts.

单词勤记【同义词】consist of, be made up of, be composed of, contain, encompass, include

❷ *v*. to make up or form (something) 形成,构成

例 The play is **comprised** of three acts.

affected [ə'fektɪd]

adj. not natural or genuine 做作的

例 With her pinkie extended, the four-year-old held her tiny teacup in that **affected** manner that some women have.

单词勤记【同义词】phony, pretentious

convoluted [ˌkɒnvə'l(j)uːtɪd]

adj. very complicated and difficult to understand 难懂的,复杂的

例 He gave a **convoluted** explanation that left the listeners even more confused than they were before.

单词勤记【同义词】complicated, complex, involved, elaborate, serpentine, labyrinthine, tortuous

elaborate [ɪ'læbərət]

❶ *v*. to give more details about something: to discuss something more fully 详尽说明

例 I'll be glad to **elaborate** if you want to hear more.

❷ *adj*. made or done with great care or with much detail: having many parts that are carefully arranged or planned 复杂的;精心制作的

例 I see now that her behavior was all part of an **elaborate** plot. / The dancers were wearing **elaborate** costumes.

hypocrisy [hɪ'pɒkrəsɪ]

n. a feigning to be what one is not or to believe what one does not 伪善,虚伪

例 When his private letters were made public, they revealed his **hypocrisy**.

单词勤记【同义词】insincerity, double standard, pretense

courtesy ['kɜːtɪsɪ]

n. polite behavior that shows respect for other people 礼貌,谦恭

例 She did it as a **courtesy**, not because she had to.

单词勤记【同义词】politeness, good manners, consideration

amass [ə'mæs]

v. to gather or collect（something，such as a large amount of money）especially for yourself 积累，积聚

例 They've amassed a wealth of information.

单词助记【同义词】collect

emphatic ［ɪmˈfætɪk］

adj. said or done in a forceful or definite way 强调的，着重的

例 They were emphatic about their political differences.

单词助记【同义词】forceful，categorical，vigorous

unscrupulous ［ʌnˈskruːpjʊləs］

adj. not honest or fair：doing things that are wrong, dishonest, or illegal 不择手段的，无道德原则的

例 An unscrupulous businessman manipulated them into selling their land for practically nothing.

discontent ［ˌdɪskənˈtent］

n. not pleased or satisfied 不满

例 Polls show that voters are growing increasingly discontent.

单词助记【同义词】dissatisfaction，unhappiness，displeasure

imperceptible ［ˌɪmpəˈseptəbl］

adj. impossible to see or notice 感觉不到的

例 These changes will be imperceptible to most people.

单词助记【同义词】unnoticeable，slight

corpse [kɔːps]

n. a dead body 尸体

例 The startling discovery of a **corpse** required a call to the police.

单词助记 【同义词】cadaver，dead body，stiff

subversive [səbˈvɜːsɪv]

adj. intended to weaken or destroy a political system or government 颠覆的，破坏的

例 The play was promptly banned as **subversive** and possibly treasonous.

merchandise [ˈmɜːtʃəndaɪz]

❶ *n*. goods that are bought and sold 商品，货物

例 a mail-order company that provides **merchandise** for people suffering from allergies

❷ *v*. to make the public aware of（a product being offered for sale）by using advertising and other methods 买卖，经营

例 In some markets，the product is **merchandised** as a specialty item，while in others，it's sold solely on supermarket shelves.

artifice [ˈɑːtɪfɪs]

n. dishonest or insincere behavior or speech that is meant to deceive someone 诡计，欺骗

例 The whole story was just an **artifice** to win our sympathy.

impasse [ɪmˈpɑːs]

n. a situation in which no progress seems possible 绝境，僵局

例 An arbitrator was called in to break the **impasse**.

单词助记 【同义词】blocked path；deadlock

pulverize [ˈpʌlvəraɪz]

v. to crush，beat，or grind（something）into powder or dust 将……弄碎；摧毁，粉碎

例 The mower **pulverizes** grass clippings.

单词助记 【同义词】pound，crush

knead [niːd]

v. to prepare（dough）by pressing a mixture of flour，water，etc.，with your hands 揉（面等）成团，捏制（面包、陶器等）

例 **Knead** the dough until it is smooth.

lethargic [ləˈθɑːdʒɪk]

adj. feeling a lack of energy or a lack of interest in doing things 昏睡的

例 You'll need to move your lure as slowly as possible to tempt the **lethargic** fish into feeding.

单词助记 【同义词】sluggish，weak

assail [əˈseɪl]

    v. to attack or criticize (someone or something) in a violent or angry way 攻击，猛打

    例 The movie was **assailed** by critics.

cordial [ˈkɔːdjəl]

    adj. politely pleasant and friendly 热诚的，热情友好的

    例 We received a **cordial** greeting from our hostess at the party.

    单词助记【同义词】pleasant，affable，genial

SSAT

冲刺词汇

babble [ˈbæbl]

    v. to talk rapidly in a incomprehensible manner 胡言乱语

    例 He'll **babble** on about sports all night if you let him.

    单词助记【同义词】prattle，rattle on，chatter，jabber

limerick [ˈlaɪmərɪk]

    n. a humorous, frequently bawdy, verse of three long and two short lines rhyming aabba 幽默的五行打油诗

    例 He is full of imagination and can knock off a **limerick** in a few minutes.

inscription [ɪnˈskrɪpʃən]

    n. words inscribed，as on a monument or in a book 铭文，铭刻

    例 The painting had an **inscription** that read，"To my loving wife".

    单词助记【同义词】engraving

device [dɪˈvaɪs]

    n. a thing made or adapted for a particular purpose 装置，设备

    例 The store sells TVs，VCRs，and other electronic **devices**.

demon [ˈdiːmən]

    n. an evil spirit or devil，especially one thought to possess a person or act as a tormentor in hell 恶魔

    例 He finally was able to face the **demons** from his unhappy childhood.

mimic [ˈmɪmɪk]

    v. imitate，especially in a way to make fun of someone 模仿

    例 He can **mimic** the way his father talks perfectly.

purloin [pɜːˈlɔɪn]

    v. steal（something）偷窃

    例 He managed to **purloin** a bottle of whiskey when no one was looking.

    单词助记【同义词】steal，thieve，rob

therapeutics [ˌθerəˈpjuːtɪks]

    n. relating to the healing of disease 治疗学，治疗法

    例 The **therapeutics** he applied included recipes，pills，powders and pastes.

    单词助记【同义词】healing，curative，remedial

genial [ˈdʒiːnɪəl]

    adj. friendly；cheerful 友好的，亲切的

    例 Bob was always **genial** and welcoming.

    单词助记【同义词】friendly

bind [baɪnd]

    ❶ *v.* cohere in a large mass 使结合

    例 She **bound** her hair in a ponytail.

    单词助记【同义词】unite，join，bond

    ❷ *v.* tie or fasten something tightly 捆绑；约束

例 It is the memory and threat of persecution that **binds** them together.

单词助记 【同义词】 tie (up), fasten (together), hold together

irk [ɜːk]

v. irritate; annoy 使烦恼

例 Drivers were **irked** by the higher gasoline prices.

单词助记 【同义词】 irritate, annoy, gall, pique

upbraid [ʌpˈbreɪd]

v. find fault with (someone); scold 责备,申斥,谴责

例 She **upbraided** him for not offering to help his grandfather.

单词助记 【同义词】 reprimand, rebuke, admonish, chastise

disparaging [dɪsˈpærɪdʒɪŋ]

adj. expressing the opinion that something is of little worth 蔑视的,轻视的

例 I heard her making **disparaging** remarks about her coworkers.

单词助记 【同义词】 derogatory, deprecatory, denigratory, belittling

serenity [sɪˈrenɪtɪ]

n. the state of being calm, peaceful, and untroubled 宁静,安详

例 a feeling of peace and **serenity**

prophecy [ˈprɒfɪsɪ]

n. a prediction 预言

例 She has the gift of **prophecy**.

单词助记 【同义词】 prediction, forecast, prognostication

retort [rɪˈtɔːt]

v. say something in answer to a remark or accusation, typically in a sharp, angry, or wittily incisive manner 反驳

例 She **retorted** angrily that it wasn't true.

单词助记 【同义词】 answer, reply, respond

converge [kənˈvɜːdʒ]

v. come together from different directions to meet 汇聚,汇合

例 The two roads **converge** in the center of the town.

ploy [plɔɪ]

n. a cunning plan or action designed to turn a situation into one's own advantage 策略

例 Her story about being sick is only a **ploy** to get your money.

restrained [rɪˈstreɪnd]

adj. characterized by reserve or moderation; unemotional or dispassionate 节制的,克制的

例 She was admired for her **restrained** behavior.

penury [ˈpenjʊrɪ]

n. extreme poverty 赤贫,缺乏

例 He was brought up in **penury**, without education.

单词助记 【同义词】 destitution, pennilessness, impecuniousness

muster [ˈmʌstə(r)]

    v. collect or assemble 集中，召集

    例 The soldiers **mustered** in the center of town.

query [ˈkwɪərɪ]

    n. a question, usually one addressed to an official or organization 询问，问题

    例 The librarian responded to my **query**.

    单词助记 【同义词】question，inquiry

obsess [əbˈses]

    v. preoccupy or fill the mind of continuously 使痴迷

    例 The war **obsesses** him—he talks about nothing else.

    单词助记 【同义词】preoccupy

dreary [ˈdrɪərɪ]

    adj. dull, bleak, lifeless 使人闷闷不乐的、沮丧的

    例 It was a gray, **dreary** morning.

puritanical [ˌpjʊərɪˈtænɪkəl]

    adj. practicing or affecting strict, religious or moral behavior 清教徒式的，道德极严格的

    例 He has a **puritanical** attitude towards food.

measly [ˈmiːzlɪ]

    adj. miserably small or few amounts of 少得可怜的，几乎没有的

    例 All I want is a few **measly** minutes of your time.

    单词助记 【同义词】paltry，meager，scanty

dope [dəʊp]

    ❶ *n.* a stupid person 傻瓜

    例 What a **dope** he is.

    单词助记 【同义词】fool，idiot，dunce，dolt

    ❷ *n.* an illegal drug 毒品

    例 **dope** dealers

abet [əˈbet]

    v. to encourage or assist someone to do something wrong 教唆（犯罪），怂恿

    例 She **abetted** the thief in his getaway.

    单词助记 【同义词】assist，aid，help，lend a hand to，support

asteroid [ˈæstərɔɪd]

    n. a small rocky body orbiting the sun 小行星

    例 Most **asteroids** are found between Mars and Jupiter.

diploma [dɪˈpləʊmə]

    n. a certificate awarded by an educational establishment to show that someone has successfully completed a course of study 毕业文凭

    例 He earned his high school **diploma** by attending classes at night.

carcass [ˈkɑːkəs]

❶ *n.* dead body of an animal（动物的）尸体

例 A cluster of vultures crouched on the **carcass** of a dead buffalo.

单词助记【同义词】corpse，dead body，body

❷ *n.* the decaying or worthless remains of a structure 残骸

例 the rusting **carcass** of an old truck

单词助记【同义词】debris

confess [kənˈfes]

v. admit a fault or crime 承认（错误）

例 He **confessed** after being questioned for many hours. / He willingly confessed his crime.

authoritarian [ɔːˌθɒrɪˈteərɪən]

adj. favoring or enforcing strict obedience to authority，especially of the government 权力主义的、专制的

例 They had **authoritarian** parents.

eulogistic [ˌjuːləˈdʒɪstɪk]

v. expressing praise highly... 赞颂的

例 She was extremely **eulogistic** about his work.

superimpose [ˌsjuːpərɪmˈpəʊz]

v. place or lay（one thing）over another，typically so that both are still evident 使重叠，使叠加

例 We should not try to **superimpose** our values on other cultures.

proscenium [prəˈsiːnɪəm]

n. part of the theater stage in front of the curtain 舞台，舞台前部装置（包括幕布，拱形墙等）

例 The host walked onto the **proscenium**.

flout [flaʊt]

v. openly disregard 表示轻蔑，嘲笑

例 Despite repeated warnings，they have continued to **flout** the law.

单词助记【同义词】defy，refuse to obey，disobey，break

anonymity [ˌænəˈnɪmətɪ]

n. the condition of being anonymous 无名，匿名

例 She agreed to speak to the reporter only on condition of **anonymity**.

acclamation [ˌækləˈmeɪʃən]

n. loud and enthusiastic approval 欢呼，喝彩

例 She has earned worldwide **acclamation** for her charitable works.

单词助记【同义词】praise，applause，cheers，ovation

aggressive [əˈɡresɪv]

adj. ready to confront or fight 好争斗的，富有侵略性的

例 He started to get **aggressive** and began to shout.

单词助记【同义词】hostile，belligerent，bellicose，antagonistic，truculent

List 89

twirl [twɜːl]

❶ *v*. spin quickly and lightly around, especially repeatedly 快速转动，旋转

例 The kite twisted and **twirled** in the wind.

❷ *n*. an act of spinning 快速转动，旋转

例 All around me leaves **twirl** to the ground.

单词助记【同义词】spin，whirl，turn，twist

condolence [kən'dəʊləns]

n. an act of sympathy, especially after a death 同情；吊唁

例 The governor issued a statement of **condolence** to the victims' families.

单词助记【同义词】sympathy，commiseration(s)，compassion

empathic [em'pæθik]

adj. showing the ability to share feelings with others 同情的

例 Cats, unlike dogs or even elephants, aren't associated with altruistic, **empathic** behavior.

threatening ['θretənɪŋ]

adj. having a hostile or deliberately frightening quality or manner 胁迫的

例 The police could have charged them with **threatening** behaviour.

单词助记【同义词】menacing，intimidating，bullying

recognize ['rekəgnaɪz]

v. to already be familiar with something 辨认出

例 I didn't **recognize** you at first with your new haircut.

amnesty ['æmnəstɪ]

n. an official pardon for people who have been convicted of crime 赦免

例 Illegal immigrants who came into the country before 1982 were granted/given **amnesty**.

pallid ['pælɪd]

adj. pale, usually because of malnutrition 苍白的，无生气的

例 The movie is a **pallid** version of the classic novel.

单词助记【同义词】pale，white，pasty，wan

myopic [maɪ'ɒpɪk]

❶ *adj*. lacking imagination, foresight, or intellectual insight 缺乏远见的

例 He has criticized the government's **myopic** diplomatic policies.

单词助记【同义词】unimaginative，uncreative

❷ *adj*. nearsighted 近视的

例 **myopic** vision

单词助记【同义词】nearsighted

strangle ['stræŋgl]

v. squeeze or constrict the neck of (a person or animal), especially so as to cause death 使窒息，扼死

例 He **strangled** her（to death）with a rope.

单词助记【同义词】suppress，smother，stifle

garment [ˈɡɑ:mənt]

n. an item of clothing 服装

例 expensive silk **garments**

militant [ˈmɪlɪtənt]

adj. combative and aggressive in support of a political or social cause 激进的，好战的

例 **Militant** mineworkers in the Ukraine have voted for a one-day stoppage next month.

单词助记【同义词】aggressive，violent，belligerent，bellicose

muffle [ˈmʌfl]

v. restrain or conceal（someone）with wrappings 压抑，捂住

例 Blake held his handkerchief over the mouthpiece to **muffle** his voice.

单词助记【同义词】deaden，dull，dampen，mute，soften

pecuniary [pɪˈkjuːnɪərɪ]

adj. of or relating to money 金钱的，金钱上的

例 She denies obtaining a **pecuniary** advantage by deception.

stratagem [ˈstrætədʒəm]

n. a plan or scheme，especially one used to outwit an opponent or achieve an end 计谋，花招

例 Trade discounts may be used as a competitive **stratagem** to secure customer loyalty.

单词助记【同义词】plan，scheme，tactic，maneuver，ploy

preponderant [prɪˈpɒndərənt]

adj. predominant in influence，number，or importance 占有优势的

例 A **preponderant** number of visitors are from outside the country.

单词助记【同义词】dominant，predominant，preeminent

entangle [ɪnˈtæŋɡl]

v. become twisted together with or caught in 使陷入困难或复杂环境

例 Bureaucracy can **entangle** ventures for months.

activate [ˈæktɪveɪt]

v. to make something active or operative 使活泼，激活

例 Touch the screen to **activate** the system.

单词助记【同义词】operate，switch on，turn on

relieve [rɪˈliːv]

v. make something less severe or serious 解除，减轻

例 I took a pill to **relieve** my headache.

单词助记【同义词】alleviate，mitigate，assuage

vie [vaɪ]

v. compete eagerly with someone in order to do or achieve something 争胜，竞争

例 They **vied** with each other for first place.

单词助记【同义词】compete，contend，contest，struggle

motif [məʊˈtiːf]

n. a dominant idea or central theme 争胜，竞争

例 The wallpaper has a flower **motif**.

perseverance [ˌpɜːsɪˈvɪərəns]

    n. steadfastness in doing something despite difficulties 坚持不懈,不屈不挠

    例 His **perseverance** was rewarded: after many rejections, he finally found a job.

gizmo [ˈɡɪzməʊ]

    n. a gadget 小发明

    例 He broke the **gizmo** he uses to open and close his garage door.

wispy [ˈwɪspɪ]

    adj. fine; feathery 小束状的;纤细的,微弱的

    例 She wore a dress made from some **wispy** material.

    单词助记【同义词】thin, fine, feathery

bristle [ˈbrɪsl]

    ❶ *n*. short, stiff hair 短硬毛

    例 As soon as the **bristles** on your toothbrush begin to wear, throw it out.

    ❷ *v*. to make bristly 发怒

    例 He **bristled** at the insult.

    单词助记【同义词】ruffle

dispersive [dɪsˈpəːsɪv]

    adj. disconnected or separate 分散的,弥散的

    例 The wave are of course **dispersive**.

    单词助记【同义词】rambling, digressive, meandering, wandering

bug [bʌɡ]

    ❶ *n*. a hidden microphone or other electronic eavesdropping device 窃听器

    例 The government planted/put a **bug** in her telephone/apartment.

    ❷ *n*. any insect or insectlike invertebrate 虫

    例 We noticed tiny **bugs** that were all over the walls.

    ❸ *v*. annoy 烦扰

    例 It really **bugs** me to see how he treats her.

    单词助记【同义词】irritate, vex, exasperate, irk, gall

irksome [ˈɜːksəm]

    adj. irritating; annoying 令人厌烦的

    例 **irksome** rules

    单词助记【同义词】irritating, annoying, vexing

rankle [ˈræŋkl]

    v. (of a wound or sore) continue to be painful; fester 使痛苦不已

    例 The joke about her family **rankled** her.

    单词助记【同义词】annoy, upset, anger, irritate

portfolio [ˌpɔːtˈfəʊlɪəʊ]

    ❶ *n*. a large, thin, flat, case for loose sheets such as drawings or maps 公文包

    例 He took out the **portfolio** in which were the notes he had made about it now and again.

❷ *n*. the securities held by an investor 投资组合

例 Short-term securities can also be held as part of an investment **portfolio**.

strategy [ˈstrætədʒɪ]

n. a plan of action or policy designed to achieve a major or overall aim 战略

例 They are proposing a new **strategy** for treating the disease with a combination of medications.

(单词助记)【同义词】master plan，grand design，game plan

ominous [ˈɒmɪnəs]

adj. giving the impression that something bad or unpleasant is going to happen 不吉祥的

例 There was an **ominous** silence at the other end of the phone.

(单词助记)【同义词】threatening，menacing，baleful，forbidding

domicile [ˈdɒmɪsaɪl]

n. a dwelling place 住处

例 You will need to report your change of **domicile** to your insurance company.

compliant [kəmˈplaɪənt]

adj. inclined to agree with others or obey rules 遵从的，顺从的

例 She was much naughtier than her **compliant** brother.

(单词助记)【同义词】acquiescent，amenable，biddable，tractable

appliance [əˈplaɪəns]

n. a device or piece of equipment designed to perform a task 器具，器械，装置

例 All household/domestic **appliances** are now on sale.

pivot [ˈpɪvət]

n. the central point，pin，or shaft which a mechanism turns or oscillates around 枢纽，支点

例 The pedal had sheared off at the **pivot**.

portentous [pɔːˈtentəs]

adj. a sign warning something bad is going to happen 预兆的，凶兆的

例 There was nothing **portentous** or solemn about him. He was bubbling with humour.

(单词助记)【同义词】ominous，warning，premonitory

hedge [hedʒ]

❶ *n*. a boundary formed by closely planted shrubs 树篱

例 Eventually he found a place from which he could see through a gap in the **hedge**.

❷ *v*. to enclose or protect with or as if with a hedge（包围住地）保护

例 They **hedge** against inflation by investing their money.

(单词助记)

apparatus [ˌæpəˈreɪtəs]

　　n. technical equipment （运动）器械；装置，仪器

　　例 She fell off a gymnastics **apparatus** and broke her leg.

precaution [prɪˈkɔːʃən]

　　n. a measure taken in advance to prevent something bad 预防，谨慎

　　例 When driving, she always wears her seatbelt as a **precaution**.

　　单词助记【同义词】safeguard, preventative/preventive measure, safety measure

complimentary [ˌkɒmplɪˈmentərɪ]

　　❶ *adj*. praising or approving 赞美的

　　例 She made **complimentary** remarks about his work.

　　单词助记【同义词】flattering, appreciative, congratulatory

　　❷ *adj*. supplied free of charge 免费赠送的

　　例 They handed out **complimentary** brochures.

lore [lɔː(r)]

 n. a body of transitions and knowledge on a subject or held by a particular group 学问,传统知识

 例 the **lore** of sailing

superfluity [ˌsjuːpəˈfluːətɪ]

 n. an unnecessarily or excessively large amount or number of something 过剩,多余品

 例 The city has a **superfluity** of five-star hotels.

 单词助记【同义词】surplus, excess, overabundance

radiant [ˈreɪdɪənt]

 ❶ *adj.* clearly emanating great joy, love, or health 容光焕发的

 例 She looked **radiant** at her wedding.

 单词助记【同义词】joyful, elated, thrilled

 ❷ *adj.* sending out light; shining; glowing (brightly) 辐射的

 例 The earth would be a frozen ball if it were not for the **radiant** heat of the sun.

 单词助记【同义词】shining, bright, illuminated, brilliant

warring [ˈwɔːrɪŋ]

 adj. (two or more people) conflict with each other 交战的,敌对的

 例 The **warring** factions have not yet turned in all their heavy weapons.

 单词助记【同义词】opposing, conflicting, at war

withdraw [wɪðˈdrɔː]

 ❶ *v.* remove or take away something 收回,提取

 例 He **withdrew** his hand from the doorknob.

 单词助记【同义词】remove, extract, pull out

 ❷ *v.* leave or come back from a place, especially a war zone 撤退

 例 They **withdrew** from the battlefield.

 单词助记【同义词】retract, take back, go back on

interlope [ˈɪntələʊpə]

 v. to thrust oneself into the affairs of others (为图私利)干涉他人之事

 例 They're resentful that outsiders presume to **interlope** in their affairs.

proposition [ˌprɒpəˈzɪʃən]

 n. a statement or assertion that expresses a judgement or opinion 主张,提案

 例 Her theory rejects the basic **proposition** that humans evolved from apes.

facsimile [fækˈsɪmɪlɪ]

 n. an exact copy, especially written or printed 复制品

 例 A **facsimile** of the world's first computer was exhibited in the museum.

 单词助记【同义词】copy, reproduction, duplicate, photocopy, replica

paternalistic [pəˌtɜːnəˈlɪstɪk]

adj. relating to or characterized by the restriction of freedom 家长式的

例 They resent the boss's **paternalistic** attitude.

luster [ˈlʌstə(r)]

n. a gentle sheen or soft glow; reflective 光泽，光辉

例 He polished the silverware for hours trying to restore its **luster**.

单词助记 【同义词】sheen，gloss，shine，glow

zeal [ziːl]

n. great energy or enthusiasm in pursuit of a cause or an objective 热忱，热情

例 Mr Lopez approached his task with a religious **zeal**.

单词助记 【同义词】passion，ardor，love，fervor

provident [ˈprɒvɪdənt]

adj. making or indicative of timely preparation for the future 为将来谋划的；节俭的

例 a more **provident** policy

单词助记 【同义词】prudent，farsighted，judicious

assault [əˈsɔːlt]

v. physical or military attack or raid 攻击，袭击

例 He was arrested for **assaulting** a police officer.

单词助记 【同义词】attack，hit，strike，punch，beat up

choke [tʃəʊk]

v. severe difficulty in breathing because of constricted throat or a lack of air 使窒息

例 Chew your food well so you don't **choke**.

单词助记 【同义词】suffocate，asphyxiate，smother，stifle

authority [ɔːˈθɒrəti]

n. power or right to give orders 权威，专家

例 Only department managers have the **authority** to change the schedule.

单词助记 【同义词】jurisdiction，command，control

vivify [ˈvɪvɪfaɪ]

v. enliven or animate 使生动，给予生气

例 details that **vivify** the narrative

单词助记 【同义词】disparage，denigrate，defame

sully [ˈsʌli]

v. damage the purity or integrity of; defile 玷污，破坏名声

例 The scandal **sullied** her reputation.

单词助记 【同义词】taint，defile，soil，tarnish

magnification [ˌmæɡnɪfɪˈkeɪʃən]

n. the action or process of making something larger 放大，扩大

例 Pores are visible without **magnification**.

单词助记 【同义词】enlargement，enhancement，increase

traduce [trəˈdjuːs]

v. speak badly of or tell lies about (someone) so as to damage their reputation 诋毁，中伤

例 He was **traduced** in the press.

单词助记 【同义词】defame，slander，speak ill of，misrepresent

lacerate [ˈlæsəreɪt]

    v. tear or make deep cuts in 撕伤，伤害（感情等）

    例 Her cruel remarks **lacerated** his feelings.

单词助记【同义词】gash，slash，tear，rip

deferential [ˌdefəˈrenʃəl]
　　adj. showing respect 恭敬的，惯于顺从的
　　例 He is shown much **deference** by his colleagues.
　　单词助记【同义词】respectful，humble，obsequious

unpropitious [ˈʌnprəˈpiʃəs]
　　adj. (of a circumstance) not giving or indicating a good chance of success 不吉利的
　　例 Thirteen is an **unpropitious** number.
　　单词助记【同义词】ominous，warning，premonitory

nibble [ˈnɪbl]
　　v. take small bites out of 啃，一点一点地咬
　　例 We **nibbled** cheese and crackers. / We nibbled on some cheese and crackers before dinner.

appropriate [əˈprəʊprɪət]
　　❶ *adj.* suitable and proper 恰当的，合适的
　　例 We'll need to find an **appropriate** place to store the fuel.
　　单词助记【同义词】suitable，proper，fitting
　　❷ *v.* to take exclusive possession of 挪用、盗用(资金)
　　例 The economy has been weakened by corrupt officials who have **appropriated** the country's resources for their own use.
　　单词助记【同义词】annex

adjudication [əˌdʒuːdɪˈkeɪʃən]
　　n. a formal judgement on a disputed matter（法院的）宣告、判决
　　例 The case is under **adjudication**.
　　单词助记【同义词】judgment，decision，pronouncement

broach [brəʊtʃ]
　　❶ *v.* set a sensitive or difficult subject for discussion 提出讨论
　　例 She **broached** the idea of getting another cat.
　　❷ *n.* a spit for roasting meat 尖型工具(如烤肉用的炙叉)
　　例 meat broach

harass [ˈhærəs]
　　v. subject to aggressive pressure or intimidation 骚扰
　　例 She was constantly **harassed** by the other students.
　　单词助记【同义词】persecute，intimidate，hound

dower [ˈdəʊə(r)]
　　n. a widow's share for life of her husband's estate 嫁妆
　　例 The provision of **dower** allows the wife to provide for herself and children.

propitious [prəˈpɪʃəs]
　　adj. giving or indicating a good chance of success 吉祥的，吉利的
　　例 Now is a **propitious** time to start a business.

【同义词】favorable，auspicious，promising

altruism [ˈæltrʊɪzəm]

n. the belief of showing unselfish concern for others 利他主义

例 In one final act of **altruism**，she donated almost all of her money to the hospital.

contraption [kənˈtræpʃən]

n. a machine or device that appears strange or unnecessarily complicated 新奇的装置

例 The people wondered how the **contraption** worked.

smirch [smɜːtʃ]

❶ *n.* a dirty mark or stain 污点

例 He had a **smirch** on his cheek.

❷ *v.* make（something）dirty；soil 弄脏，玷污

例 His will was a scandal，and the horror did not only **smirch** his good name，it reached to hers.

【单词助记】

endow [ɪnˈdaʊ]

v. give or bequeath an income or property 捐赠，资助

例 The money will be used to **endow** the museum and research facility.

specter [ˈspektə(r)]

n. a ghost 鬼怪，幽灵

例 "Ghost of the Future，" he exclaimed，"I fear you more than any **spectre** I have seen…"（A Christmas Carol）

【单词助记】【同义词】ghost，phantom，apparition

rancor [ˈræŋkə(r)]

n. bitterness or resentfulness 怨恨

例 She answered her accusers calmly and without **rancor**.

【单词助记】【同义词】bitterness，spite，hate，hatred

analogous [əˈnæləgəs]

adj. comparable 相似的，可比拟的

例 I could not think of a situation **analogous** to this one.

【单词助记】【同义词】comparable，parallel，similar

sashay [ˈsæʃeɪ]

v. walk in an ostentatious yet casual manner，typically with exaggerated movements of the hips and shoulders 大摇大摆地走

例 She **sashayed** into the room.

entreat [ɪnˈtriːt]

v. ask someone earnestly to do something 恳求

例 I **entreat** you to help me.

单词助记 【同义词】implore，beg，plead with

granulate [ˈɡrænjʊleɪt]

v. form something into grains or particles 使成颗粒状

例 **granulated** sugar

molest [məʊˈlest]

v. sexually assault or abuse someone 骚扰，调戏

例 He was sent to jail for **molesting** children.

单词助记 【同义词】harass，harry，hassle

List 93

abhor [əbˈhɔː(r)]

 v. to strongly dislike or hate someone；hate；loathe 憎恶，讨厌

 例 They **abhor** violence/racism.

 单词助记【同义词】detest，hate，loathe，despise

veteran [ˈvetərən]

 ❶ *n*. a person who has had long experience in a particular field 经验丰富的人

 例 He's a 10-year **veteran** with/of the team.

 单词助记【同义词】old hand，past master

 ❷ *n*. a person who has served in the military 退伍老兵

 例 They approved a ＄1.1 billion package of pay increases for the **veterans** of the Persian Gulf War.

impart [ɪmˈpɑːt]

 v. make information known；communicate 传授

 例 He has clever ways of **imparting** knowledge to his students.

verdict [ˈvɜːdɪkt]

 n. a decision on a disputed issue in a civil or criminal case or an inquest（陪审团的）裁决、裁定

 例 The jury reached a guilty **verdict**.

 单词助记【同义词】judgment，adjudication，decision

mutual [ˈmjuːtʃʊəl]

 adj. experienced or done by each of two or more parties toward the other or others 相互的

 例 **Mutual** love and respect was the key to their successful marriage.

 单词助记【同义词】reciprocal，reciprocated，returned

waive [weɪv]

 v. refrain from insisting on or using（a right or claim）放弃（权利、规则）

 例 She **waived** her right to a lawyer.

gambit [ˈgæmbɪt]

 n. opening remark，usually one with a degree of risk 策略

 例 He sees the proposal as more of a diplomatic **gambit** than a serious defense proposal.

rumination [ˌruːmɪˈneɪʃən]

 n. a deep or considered thought about something 沉思

 例 He **ruminated** over/about the implications of their decision.

hypothesis [haɪˈpɒθɪsɪs]

 n. a supposition or proposed explanation made on the basis of limited evidence as a starting point for further investigation 假说

 例 The results of the experiment did not support/confirm his **hypothesis**.

fumble [ˈfʌmbl]

❶ *v.* blunder 犯错

例 He **fumbled** his lines，not knowing what he was going to say.

单词助记【同义词】stumble，blunder，flounder

❷ *n.* to feel or grope about clumsily 笨拙地摸索

例 He was **fumbling** in the dark for the money he had dropped.

plagiarize [ˈpleɪdʒəraɪz]

v. to take someone else's idea as your own；cribbing 剽窃（著作等）

例 She **plagiarized** from an article she read on the Internet.

cede [siːd]

v. to give up power or territory 让给，割让

例 Russia **ceded** Alaska to the U.S. in 1867.

单词助记【同义词】surrender，concede，relinquish，yield

perpetuate [pəˈpetʃʊeɪt]

v. make something undesirable continue indefinitely 使永存

例 Fears about an epidemic are being **perpetuated** by the media.

obedient [əˈbiːdɪənt]

adj. complying or willing to comply with orders or request 顺从的，服从的

例 He was very respectful at home and **obedient** to his parents.

单词助记【同义词】compliant，acquiescent，tractable，amenable

diffusive [dɪˈfjʊsɪv]

adj. the spreading of something more widely 散布性的，扩散的

例 Our national life is too **diffusive** to yield the best social fruits.

ransom [ˈrænsəm]

n. a payment demanded to release a prisoner 赎金

例 The kidnappers demanded a **ransom** of one million dollars.

gyrate [ˈdʒaɪəreɪt]

v. move or cause to move in a circle or spiral 旋转，回旋

例 They **gyrated** to the music.

单词助记【同义词】rotate，revolve，wheel

abstemious [æbˈstiːmɪəs]

adj. not self-indulging（生活、吃饭、饮酒方面）有节制的

例 She is known as an **abstemious** eater and drinker.

单词助记【同义词】self-denying，temperate，abstinent

trickery [ˈtrɪkərɪ]

n. the practice of deception 欺骗，花招

例 He resorted to **trickery** to get what he wanted.

单词助记【同义词】deception，deceit，dishonesty

vapid [ˈvæpɪd]

adj. offering nothing that is stimulating or challenging 乏味的，无趣的

例 She made a **vapid** comment about the weather.

单词助记【同义词】insipid，uninspired，colorless

List 94

feminine [ˈfemɪnɪn]

adj. having qualities or appearances traditionally associated with women 有女性气质的,女子气的

例 I've always been attracted to very **feminine**, delicate women.

contract [ˈkɒntrækt]

❶ *n.* a written or spoken agreement 合约,契约

例 The **contract** requires him to finish work by the end of the year.

单词助记【同义词】agreement, commitment, arrangement, settlement

❷ *v.* to reduce to smaller size by or as if by squeezing or forcing together 使收缩

例 She **contract**ed her lips into a frown.

❸ *v.* catch or develop (a disease or infectious agent) 感染

例 Three people **contracted** a killer virus.

natal [ˈneɪtl]

adj. relating to the place or time of one's birth 出生的,先天的

例 **natal** instincts

单词助记【同义词】deadly, lethal, mortal

pedagogue [ˈpedəgɒg]

n. a teacher, especially a strict or pedantic one (尤指无聊、教条的)教师

例 De Gaulle was a born **pedagogue** who used the public platform and the television screen to great effect.

单词助记【同义词】teacher, schoolteacher, schoolmaster

inauspicious [ˌɪnɔːˈspɪʃəs]

adj. not conductive to success 不祥的

例 Despite its **inauspicious** beginnings, the company eventually became very profitable.

单词助记【同义词】unpromising, unpropitious, unfavorable

smudge [smʌdʒ]

v. cause (something) to become messily smeared by rubbing it 造成污迹

例 Don't **smudge** the picture with your dirty hands!

单词助记【同义词】streak, smear, mark, stain

coterie [ˈkəʊtərɪ]

n. a small group of people with shared interests and tastes; especially one that is exclusive of others (有共同利益的)小集团、小团体

例 His films are admired by a small **coterie** of critics.

skeptic [ˈskeptɪk]

adj. a person inclined to question or doubt all accepted opinions 怀疑者,怀疑论者

例 You can believe in ghosts if you like, but I'm still a **skeptic**.

单词助记【同义词】cynic, doubter

cataract [ˈkætərækt]

❶ *n.* a large waterfall 大瀑布

例 The rain enveloped us in a deafening **cataract**.

❷ *n.* a medical condition where the lens of the eye becomes progressively opaque 白内障

例 His grandmother developed **cataracts**.

adoral [ædˈɔrəl]

adj. relating to or denoting the side or end where the mouth is situated 口部附近的

例 The **adoral** zone and peristome agree with the details given in the family characteristics.

cyclical [ˈsɪklɪkəl]

adj. occurring in cycles 循环的，周期性的

例 the **cyclical** nature of history

corral [kɔːˈrɑːl]

n. a pen or enclosure for confining or capturing livestock 畜栏

例 They drove the ponies into a **corral**.

denigrate [ˈdenɪɡreɪt]

v. to criticize unfairly 诋毁，诽谤

例 The amendment prohibits obscene or indecent materials which **denigrate** the objects or beliefs of a particular religion.

单词助记 【同义词】disparage，belittle，deprecate，decry

puritan [ˈpjʊərɪtən]

n. a member of a group of English protestants of the late 16th and 17th centuries 清教徒

例 At least in pre-modern Europe and **Puritan** North America，witch-hunting follows certain patterns.

monition [məʊˈnɪʃən]

n. warning of impending danger 忠告，警告

例 And she gave me a meaning sign—half a wink，half a **monition**.

certify [ˈsɜːtɪfaɪ]

v. to confirm formally 证明

例 The document has been **certified** by the court.

单词助记 【同义词】verify，guarantee，attest

soloist [ˈsəʊləʊɪst]

n. a singer or other musician who performs a solo 独奏者

例 a piano **soloist**

nag [næɡ]

v. annoy or irritate (a person) with persistent fault-finding or continuous urging 唠叨，使烦恼

例 She had stopped **nagging** him about never being home.

单词助记 【同义词】harass，badger，give someone a hard time

lessen [ˈlesn]

v. diminish；reduce 减少，变少

例 Medication helps **lessen** the severity of the symptoms.

单词助记 【同义词】reduce，make less/smaller，minimize

particularize [pəˈtɪkjʊləraɪz]

　　v. mention or describe specifically；treat individually 逐一叙述，详述

　　例 My lawyer advised me to **particularize** all my complaints against my landlord.

List 95

barter [ˈbɑːtə(r)]

❶ *v.* to trade items without money 进行易货贸易

例 The farmers **bartered** for supplies with their crops. / They **barter** eggs for cheese with the neighboring farm.

单词助记【同义词】trade，swap，exchange

❷ *n.* the act or practice of carrying on trade by bartering 易货贸易；物物交换

例 The tribes use a system of **barter**.

sponsor [ˈspɒnsə(r)]

v. provide funds for (a project or activity or the person carrying it out) 赞助

例 The radio station **sponsored** the concert.

单词助记【同义词】finance，put up the money for，fund

vestment [ˈvestmənt]

❶ *n.* a garment 礼仪服装

例 The bishop was to wear a rochet，a surplice，and a cope or **vestment**.

❷ *n.* a chasuble or other robe worn by the clergy or choristers during services（牧师的）法衣

例 Behind the door hung the reverend's **vestment**，flat and black and surprisingly frail，pinned as it was，limp and small，to the wood.

diplomat [ˈdɪpləmæt]

n. an official representing a country abroad 外交官

例 The President will be meeting with foreign **diplomats**.

单词助记【同义词】ambassador，attaché，consulate

contrivance [kənˈtraɪvəns]

n. a thing that is created skillfully and inventively to serve a particular purpose 发明，发明物

例 He told the story honestly and without **contrivance**.

bestow [bɪˈstəʊ]

v. confer or present 授予，赠给

例 The university **bestowed** on/upon her an honorary degree.

muzzy [ˈmʌzɪ]

adj. unable to think clearly；confused 模糊的

例 He stopped drinking when his head started getting **muzzy**.

coincide [ˌkəʊɪnˈsaɪd]

v. occur at or during the same time 一致，符合

例 The population increase **coincided** with rapid industrial growth.

cassock [ˈkæsək]

n. a full length garment of one color worn by a certain Christian clergy（教士穿的黑色或红色的）长袍

例 He was holding apart the flaps of his **cassock** like the tails of a coat.

corresponding [ˌkɒrɪsˈpɒndɪŋ]

adj. similar in character, form, or function 相当的，对应的

例 The store earned 20 percent more this month than it did in the **corresponding** month last year.

单词助记【同义词】commensurate, parallel, correspondent, matching

decadent [ˈdekədənt]

adj. characterized by reflecting a state of moral 堕落的，颓废的

例 The book condemns some of society's wealthiest members as **decadent** fools.

单词助记【同义词】dissolute, dissipated, degenerate, corrupt

exile [ˈeksaɪl]

❶ *v.* to expel or banish (a person) from his or her country; expatriate 放逐，流放

例 The President was **exiled** by military rulers soon after the coup.

❷ *n.* the state of being barred from one's native country 放逐，流放

例 He went into **exile** to avoid capture and execution by the government.

单词助记【同义词】banishment, expulsion, expatriation

implicate [ˈɪmplɪkeɪt]

v. to show someone to be involved in a crime 牵连，涉及

例 The evidence **implicated** many government officials in the conspiracy.

单词助记【同义词】involve in, concern with, associate with

errant [ˈerənt]

❶ *adj.* straying from the expected course or standards 迷途的；行为不当的

例 Usually his cases involved **errant** husbands and wandering wives.

❷ *adj.* traveling or given to traveling 周游的

例 an **errant** knight

destitution [ˌdestɪˈtjuːʃən]

n. poverty so extreme that one lacks the means to provide for oneself 穷困，贫穷

例 The chasm between privilege and utter **destitution** made me uncomfortable.

pester [ˈpestə(r)]

v. trouble or annoy (someone) with frequent or persistent requests or interruptions 使烦恼，纠缠

例 His mother always **pesters** him (with questions) about his love life.

单词助记【同义词】badger, hound, harass, plague

junket [ˈdʒʌŋkɪt]

n. an extravagant trip or celebration, in particular one enjoyed by a government official at public expense 公费旅游

例 The senator has been criticized for expensive **junkets** to foreign countries.

cue [kjuː]

n. a thing said or done to serve as a signal 提示，信号

例 That last line is your **cue** to exit the stage.

censor [ˈsensə(r)]

n. someone who examines material that is about to be released to make sure it is appropriate（书刊、电影等的）审查员

例 Government **censors** deleted all references to the protest.

单词助记【同义词】expurgator

forbidding [fəˈbɪdɪŋ]

　　adj. threatening or unfriendly in appearance 令人生畏的

　　例 There was something a little severe and **forbidding** about her face.

List 96

abstinent [ˈæbstɪnənt]

adj. refraining from an activity or from the consumption of something 有节制的

例 He started drinking again after a long period of total/complete **abstinence** from alcohol.

glut [glʌt]

n. excessively abundant supply of something 大量

例 There's a **glut** of agricultural products in Western Europe.

brassy [ˈbrɑːsɪ]

adj. tastelessly showy or loud in appearance or manner; audacious 厚脸皮的

例 Those ladies were **brassy** and busty, with pudgy fingers and painted eyes.

单词助记【同义词】brazen, forward, bold

dull [dʌl]

adj. lacking interest or excitement 不鲜明的，枯燥无味的

例 There's never a **dull** moment in our house.

单词助记【同义词】uninteresting, boring, tedious, monotonous

sagacious [səˈgeɪʃəs]

adj. having or showing keen mental discernment and good judgment; shrewd 精明的，有判断力的

例 But he was a good businessman, and Arnold had occasionally wondered whether Freddie Keeler was a deal more **sagacious** than he appeared.

单词助记【同义词】knowledgeable, sensible, sage, judicious

abounding [əˈbaʊndɪŋ]

adj. very plentiful; abundant 充满的，富裕的

例 a stream **abounding** in/with fish

单词助记【同义词】abundant, plentiful, superabundant

constringe [kənˈstrɪndʒ]

v. shrink or contract 使收缩，使收敛

例 This kind of facial cleanser can **constringe** and clean the pores of face.

epistle [ɪˈpɪsl]

n. a letter 书信

例 He penned lengthy **epistles** to her.

plagiarism [ˈpleɪdʒərɪzəm]

n. the practice of taking someone's ideas as your own 剽窃

例 The student has been accused of **plagiarism**.

expenditure [ɪksˈpendɪtʃə(r)]

n. the action of spending funds 开销，花费

例 Your income should exceed your **expenditures**.

slaughter [ˈslɔːtə(r)]

n. the killing of animals for food 屠杀，屠宰

例 We are considered as sheep for the **slaughter**.

单词助记【同义词】massacre，murdering

circumference [sə'kʌmfərəns]

n. the perimeter of a circle 圆周，周围

例 What is the **circumference** of the Earth at the equator?

meritorious [ˌmerɪ'tɔːrɪəs]

adj. deserving award or praise 值得称赞的

例 She was given an award for **meritorious** service.

单词助记【同义词】praiseworthy，laudable，commendable

sinister ['sɪnɪstə(r)]

adj. giving the impression that something harmful or evil is happening or will happen 不吉利的，险恶的

例 There was something **sinister** about him.

单词助记【同义词】menacing，threatening，ominous，forbidding，baleful

delineate [dɪ'lɪnɪeɪt]

v. describe or portray something precisely 勾画，描述

例 The characters in the story were carefully **delineated**.

单词助记【同义词】describe，set forth/out，present

cull [kʌl]

❶ *v.* obtain from a wide variety of sources 挑出

例 They've **culled** some of the best poems from her collected works.

❷ *v.* to reduce or control the size of (as a herd) by removal (as by hunting) of especially weaker animals（为控制数量进行）选择性宰杀

例 The town issued hunting licenses in order to **cull** the deer population.

clique [kliːk]

n. an exclusive, small group of people, with shared interests or other features in common（有共同利益的）小团体，派系

例 Anna Ford recently hit out at the male **clique** which she believes holds back women in television.

单词助记【同义词】coterie，set，circle

judicious [dʒuː'dɪʃəs]

adj. having, showing, or done with good judgement 明智的

例 **Judicious** planning now can prevent problems later.

单词助记【同义词】wise，sensible，prudent

swarm [swɔːm]

n. a large or dense group of insects, especially flying ones（蜂、蚂蚁）群

例 a **swarm** of bees/mosquitoes/ants/locusts

单词助记【同义词】hive，flock，collection

n. (of insects) move in or form a **swarm** 云集

例 Spectators **swarmed** into the stadium.

单词助记【同义词】flock，crowd，throng

nemesis ['nemɪsɪs]

n. the inescapable agent of someone's or something's downfall 克星，劲敌

例 He will be playing his old **nemesis** for the championship.

单词助记【同义词】archrival，adversary，foe，opponent

List 97

bane [beɪn]

    n. the cause of great distress or annoyance 祸根

    例 The ugly school uniforms were the **bane** of the students' lives.

    单词助记【同义词】scourge，plague，curse

glee [gliː]

    n. great delight 欢乐

    例 They were dancing with/in **glee**.

    单词助记【同义词】delight

enamor [ɪ'næmə]

    v. to be filled with a feeling of love for 使倾心，使迷恋

    例 His bad temper did not **enamor** him to his employees.

adage ['ædɪdʒ]

    n. a short statement stating the truth 谚语，格言

    例 My mother always used to remind us of the（old）**adage**，"If you can't say something nice，don't say anything at all."

    单词助记【同义词】saying，maxim，axiom

zany ['zeɪnɪ]

    adj. amusingly unconventional and idiosyncratic 滑稽的

    例 He has a **zany** sense of humor.

    单词助记【同义词】eccentric，peculiar，odd

derogate ['derəʊgeɪt]

    v. detract from 减损

    例 Her parents are constantly **derogating** her achievements.

    单词助记【同义词】disparage，denigrate，belittle，deprecate

grim [grɪm]

    adj. forbidding or uninviting 严酷的，无情的

    例 The accident serves as a **grim** reminder of the dangers of drinking and driving.

    单词助记【同义词】stern，forbidding，uninviting，unsmiling

diatonic [ˌdaɪə'tɒnɪk]

    adj.（of a scale）involving only notes proper to the prevailing key without chromatic altercation 全音阶的

    例 **diatonic** harmonies/notes

stratify ['strætɪfaɪ]

    v. form or arrange into strata（使）分层，成层

    例 A gas，as explained，is of such a character that it remains fixed and will not **stratify** or condense.

exemplar [ɪg'zemplə(r)]

    n. a person or thing serving as a typical example of an excellent role model 模范，范例

例 He is an **exemplar** of this new breed of politician.

单词助记 【同义词】epitome，perfect example，paragon，ideal

bedlam [ˈbedləm]

❶ *n*. a scene of uproar and confusion 吵闹混乱的地方

例 The park had never had so many visitors at one time. It was total/complete **bedlam**.

单词助记 【同义词】uproar，pandemonium，commotion

❷ *v*. an institution of care for the mentally ill 疯人院

例 Well，go on drinking and you will end in **bedlam** instead of the workhouse.

perceptive [pəˈseptɪv]

adj. having or showing sensitive insight 洞察力强的,敏锐的

例 He is a very **perceptive** young man.

patronizing [ˈpætrənaɪzɪŋ]

adj. displaying or indicative of an offensively condescending manner 居高临下的

例 She spoke to us in a **patronizing** tone.

单词助记 【同义词】condescending，disdainful，supercilious

rescue [ˈreskjuː]

v. save（someone）from a dangerous or distressing situation 营救,救援

例 A fireman **rescued** three children from the burning building.

politic [ˈpɒlɪtɪk]

adj. seeming sensible and judicious 明智的

例 It would not be **politic** to ignore them.

pugilist [ˈpjuːdʒɪlɪst]

n. a boxer，especially a professional one 拳击运动员,拳师

例 a talented **pugilist**

slacken [ˈslækən]

❶ *v*. to make less active 变迟缓

例 She **slackened** her speed/pace after she slipped on the ice.

单词助记 【同义词】slow（down），decelerate

❷ *v*. to make slack；loosen 使松弛

例 The Conservative government will not **slacken** the pace of radical reform.

单词助记 【同义词】loosen，release，relax

barefaced [ˈbeəfeɪst]

adj. shameless，undisguised 厚颜无耻的,露骨的

例 a **barefaced** liar

corrigible [ˈkɒrɪdʒəbl]

adj. capable of being corrected 可改正的

例 You have unburdened your own soul in that matter，and if they had been **corrigible**，you would have helped a good many more.

tenacity [tɪˈnæsətɪ]

n. the quality or fact of being very determined；determination 坚韧,坚持不懈

例 When he died in prison 21 years later，he was paid honors for his courage，**tenacity**，and pride.

单词助记 【同义词】persistence，determination，perseverance

List 98

literal [ˈlɪtərəl]

adj. taking words in their most basic meaning 字面的，原义的

例 I was using the word in its **literal** sense.

单词助记【同义词】word-for-word，verbatim

jargon [ˈdʒɑːgən]

n. special words or expressions that are used by a particular profession or group and are difficult for others to understand 行话，黑话

例 The manual is full of the **jargon** and slang of self-improvement courses.

单词助记【同义词】slang，cant，idiom

galactic [gəˈlæktɪk]

❶ *adj.* immense；huge；vast 巨大的

例 the **galactic** plane

❷ *adj.* of or relating to a galaxy or galaxies 银河的

例 The change wreaked by the **galactic** showdown will take two billion years to unfold.

combatant [ˈkɒmbətənt]

adj. a person or nation engaged in fighting during a war 战斗员，格斗者

例 Britain was a main/major **combatant** in World War II.

单词助记【同义词】fighter，soldier，warrior，trooper

atonement [əˈtəʊnmənt]

n. reparation for a wrong or injury 弥补，赎罪

例 True guilt is characterized by a readiness to make **atonement** for having done wrong.

deterrent [dɪˈterənt]

n. a thing that discourages or is intended to discourage someone from doing something 起制止作用的物体等

例 They argued over whether the death penalty is an effective **deterrent** to murder.

单词助记【同义词】disincentive，discouragement，damper

Hercules [ˈhɜːkjʊlɪz]

n. a hero from Greek and Roman mythology of superhuman strength and courage 大力士（希腊神话中大力神的名字）

例 But **Hercules** was no whit disheartened，and squeezed the great snake so tightly that he soon began to hiss with pain.

potency [ˈpəʊtənsɪ]

n. the power of something to affect the mind or body 能力，力量

例 I can't deny the **potency** of his argument.

salvage [ˈsælvɪdʒ]

n. the rescue of a wrecked or disabled ship or its cargo from loss at sea 海上营救

例 The ship was beyond **salvage**.

insolence [ˈɪnsələns]

n. rude and disrespectful behavior 无礼

例 Pupils could be excluded from school for **insolence**.

单词助记【同义词】laziness, idleness, slothfulness, sloth, shiftlessness

abase [əˈbeɪs]

v. to lower; demean; degrade 使（地位、身份等）降低，屈辱

例 He wanted first to see his wife, to **abase** himself before her.

单词助记【同义词】belittle, demean, lower, degrade

diminutive [dɪˈmɪnjʊtɪv]

adj. extremely or unusually small 微小的

例 The only surprise is how he packs a heart so big in such a **diminutive** frame.

curmudgeon [kɜːˈmʌdʒən]

n. a bad tempered or surly person 坏脾气的人

例 I'm not such a **curmudgeon** and am no longer, thank God, your keeper.

单词助记【同义词】grumbler, complainer, moaner

menacing [ˈmenəsɪŋ]

adj. suggesting the presence of danger 威胁的，险恶的

例 The strong dark eyebrows give his face an oddly **menacing** look.

单词助记【同义词】threatening, ominous, intimidating

palatable [ˈpælətəbl]

adj. pleasant to the taste 可口的，美味的

例 It looked the most **palatable** of the dogs' dinners and most healthy, with a good deal of brown rice.

单词助记【同义词】pleasant, acceptable, pleasing, agreeable

embroil [ɪmˈbrɔɪl]

v. involve someone deeply in an argument 使（自己或他人）卷入纠纷

例 Any hostilities could result in retaliation and further **embroil** U.N. troops in fighting.

单词助记【同义词】involve, entangle, ensnare

thresh [θreʃ]

❶ *v*. hit (something) hard and repeatedly 重复地敲打

例 The corn was still sown, cut and **threshed** as it was a hundred years ago.

❷ *v*. separate grain from (a plant), typically with a flail or by the action of a revolving mechanism 打（麦粒）

例 The corn was still sown, cut and **threshed** as it was a hundred years ago.

idle [ˈaɪdl]

adj. not active or in use 无所事事的

例 Employees have been **idle** almost a month because of shortages.

单词助记【同义词】inactive, unused, unoccupied

impoverished [ɪmˈpɒvərɪʃt]

adj. poor 穷困的

例 That's what you need if you're an **impoverished** ex-army major trying to launch a multi-million pound airship industry.

单词助记【同义词】poor, poverty-stricken, penniless

empathy [ˈempəθɪ]

    n. the ability to understand other （感情）共鸣，感同身受

    例 Having begun my life in a children's home I have great **empathy** with the little ones.

spin [spɪn]

❶ *v.* give（a news story or other information）a particular interpretation，especially a favorable one 杜撰

例 He was surprised，and annoyed that she had **spun** a story which was too good to be condemned as a simple lie.

单词助记【同义词】weave，concoct，invent，fabricate

❷ *v.* turn or cause to turn or whirl around quickly 使旋转

例 The latest discs，used for small portable computers，**spin** 3600 times a minute.

单词助记【同义词】revolve，rotate，turn

badger [ˈbædʒə(r)]

❶ *n.* any of various burrowing，carnivorous mammals of the family Mustelidae 獾

例 **Badgers** live underground and usually come up to feed at night.

❷ *v.* ask repeatedly for something；pester 纠缠不休，烦扰

例 Richard's mother **badgered** him into taking a Spanish wife.

单词助记【同义词】pester，harass，bother

virtual [ˈvɜːtʃʊəl]

adj. almost or nearly as described，but not completely or according to strict definition 实质上的，事实上的

例 He claimed to be a **virtual** prisoner in his own home.

utensil [juːˈtensəl]

n. an implement，container，or other article，especially for household use 器具，用具，器皿

例 The best carving **utensil** is a long，sharp，flexible knife.

单词助记【同义词】implement，tool，instrument

throttle [ˈθrɒtl]

❶ *n.* a device controlling the flow of fuel or power to an engine 控制阀门

例 He gently opened the **throttle**，and the ship began to ease forward.

❷ *v.* attack or kill（someone）by choking or strangling them 勒死，使窒息

例 The attacker then tried to **throttle** her with wire.

单词助记【同义词】choke，strangle，strangulate

virtuous [ˈvɜːtʃʊəs]

adj. having or showing high moral standards 品德高尚的

例 Louis was shown as an intelligent，courageous and **virtuous** family man.

单词助记【同义词】righteous，good，pure

lava [ˈlɑːvə]

n. hot molten or semifluid rock that erupted from a volcano or fissure（火山喷发的）熔岩

例 Banana plantations and forests give way to volcanic cones and **lava** fields.

confer [kənˈfɜː(r)]

❶ *v*. to grant or bestow 授予

例 The constitution also **confers** large powers on Brazil's 25 constituent states.

❷ *v*. have discussions；exchange opinions 协商

例 He **conferred** with Hill and the others in his office.

trifle [ˈtraɪfl]

❶ *n*. a thing of little value or importance 无足轻重的东西

例 He spends all his time on crosswords and other **trifles**.

（单词助记）【同义词】trivial thing，triviality

❷ *v*. treat（someone or something）without seriousness or respect 轻视

例 You shouldn't **trifle** with their feelings.

obscene [əbˈsiːn]

adj. offensive or disgusting by accepted standards of morality and decency 淫秽的，下流的

例 A city magistrate ruled that the novel was **obscene** and copies should be destroyed.

（单词助记）【同义词】pornographic，indecent，smutty，salacious

cheeky [ˈtʃiːkɪ]

adj. not showing respect in a amusing manner；impudent；irreverent 无礼的，厚颜无耻的

例 The room lit up when he walked in with his **cheeky** smile and his cheeky ways.

（单词助记）【同义词】impudent，irreverent，insolent，impertinent

appendix [əˈpendɪks]

❶ *n*. tube-shaped sac attached to and opening into the lower end of the large intestine 阑尾

例 He then missed the beginning of the season that year after having an **appendix** operation.

❷ *n*. a section or table of additional matter at the end of a book or document 附录

例 An **appendix** to a book is extra information that is placed after the end of the main text.

dominant [ˈdɒmɪnənt]

adj. most important，powerful，or influential 占优势的，支配的

例 The second change was that rock and pop music became the **dominant** form of popular music.

（单词助记）【同义词】main，principal，prime，premier，chief

veracity [vəˈræsətɪ]

n. conformity to facts；accuracy 诚实

例 We have total confidence in the **veracity** of our research.

（单词助记）【同义词】ruthfulness，truth，accuracy，correctness

sneak [sniːk]

❶ *v*. move or go in a furtive or stealthy manner 潜行

例 Sometimes he would **sneak** out of his house late at night to be with me.

（单词助记）【同义词】creep，slink，steal，slip

❷ *v*. do or obtain（something）in a stealthy or furtive way 偷偷携带，夹带

例 She **sneaked** some cigars through customs.

（单词助记）【同义词】smuggle，bring/take surreptitiously

equivocal [ɪˈkwɪvəkəl]

adj. ambiguous 模棱两可的，模糊的

例 He was tortured by an awareness of the **equivocal** nature of his position.

单词助记 【同义词】ambiguous，indefinite，noncommittal

cribbing [ˈkrɪbɪŋ]

n. plagiarism 剽窃，抄袭

例 **Cribbing** in an exam is not allowed.

muddle [ˈmʌdl]

v. bring into a disordered or confusing state 糊涂，混乱

例 We are beginning to **muddle** the extended royal family and the monarchy.

单词助记 【同义词】confuse，mix up，jumble（up）

attribute [əˈtrɪbjuːt]

❶ *v.* regard something being caused by 归于

例 Women tend to **attribute** their success to external causes such as luck.

单词助记 【同义词】ascribe

❷ *n.* an inherent characteristic 属性，特征

例 Cruelty is a normal **attribute** of human behaviour.

单词助记 【同义词】characteristic

sweltering [ˈsweltərɪŋ]

adj. uncomfortably hot uncomfortably hot 闷热的

例 The weather through late June and July was mostly **sweltering**，and nobody had much energy for games.

单词助记 【同义词】hot，stifling，humid，sultry

dispassionate [dɪsˈpæʃənət]

    adj. not influenced by strong emotion，allowing one to be impartial and rational 公正的

    例 We，as prosecutors，try to be **dispassionate** about the cases we bring.

    单词助记【同义词】objective，detached，neutral，disinterested，impartial

prelude [ˈpreljuːd]

    n. an action or event serving as an introduction to something more important 序曲，序幕

    例 The conference，which closed yesterday，was a **prelude** to a Communist Party Central Committee meeting.

    单词助记【同义词】preliminary，overture，opening，preparation

finesse [fɪˈnes]

    ❶ *n.* refinement or delicacy of workmanship，structure，or texture 灵巧

    例 The whole ballet is made with great **finesse**.

    ❷ *n.* skillful handling of a situation 技巧，手腕

    例 Perhaps your social skills lack **finesse**.

satiate [ˈseɪʃɪeɪt]

    v. satisfy (a desire or an appetite) to the full 使充分满足，使厌腻

    例 The dinner was enough to **satiate** the gourmets.

canvass [ˈkænvəs]

    v. to solicit votes（政治）游说

    例 I'm **canvassing** for the Conservative Party.

dissertation [ˌdɪsəˈteɪʃən]

    n. a long essay on a certain subject 学位论文，专题论文

    例 He is currently writing a **dissertation** on the Somali civil war.

slavish [ˈsleɪvɪʃ]

    adj. relating to or characteristic of a slave，typically by behaving in a servile or submissive way 奴隶的，奴性的

    例 She herself insists she is no **slavish** follower of fashion.

    单词助记【同义词】servile，subservient，fawning，obsequious

overindulgence [ˈəʊvəɪnˈdʌldʒəns]

    n. having too much of something enjoyable 过分放纵

    例 Better the sugar hit than the **overindulgence** of alcohol，which，the Colonel had pointed out，was slowly killing him.

embellishment [ɪmˈbelɪʃmənt]

    n. a decorative detail added to something to make it more attractive 装饰

    例 Their wonderful stories did not need **embellishment** with ridiculous rumour or vile gossip.

bond [bɒnd]

❶ *n*. physical restraints 羁绊，桎梏

例 The experience created a very special **bond** between us.

单词助记【同义词】chains, fetters, shackles, manacles

❷ *v*. establish relationship with someone else 结合

例 We were strangers at first，but we **bonded**（with each other）quickly.

单词助记【同义词】join, fasten, fix, affix, attach

❸ *n*. agreement with a legal force 契约，票据

例 When a government or company issues a **bond**，it borrows money from investors.

单词助记【同义词】promise, pledge, vow, oath

❹ *v*. join or be joined securely to something else 使结合

例 What had **bonded** them instantly and so completely was their similar background.

unparalleled [ʌnˈpærəleld]

adj. having no parallel or equal；exceptional 无比的，空前的

例 The country is facing a crisis **unparalleled** since the Second World War.

单词助记【同义词】exceptional, unique, singular, rare

onslaught [ˈɒnslɔːt]

n. a fierce or destructive attack 猛攻

例 The rebels responded to a military **onslaught** against them by launching a major assault on an army camp.

单词助记【同义词】assault, attack, offensive

predestinate [priˈdestɪnet]

adj. predetermined to be a certain way 预先确定的，注定的

例 It seemed **predestined** since the beginning of the world.

culinary [ˈkʌlɪnərɪ]

adj. of or for cooking 厨房的，烹饪的

例 She was keen to acquire more advanced **culinary** skills.

torment [ˈtɔːmənt]

❶ *v*. cause to experience severe mental or physical suffering（肉体上或精神上）折磨

例 My older brother and sister used to **torment** me by singing it to me.

单词助记【同义词】torture, afflict, rack

❷ *n*. severe physical or mental suffering（肉体或精神上的）折磨

例 After years of **torment**，she left her husband.

单词助记【同义词】ordeal, affliction, scourge

lustrous [ˈlʌstrəs]

adj. having luster；shiny；large 有光泽的

例 Her once **lustrous** hair was dirty and infested by lice.

单词助记【同义词】shiny, shining, satiny

minute [ˈmɪnɪt]

adj. extremely small 微小的

例 The party was planned in the **minutest** detail.

单词助记【同义词】tiny, minuscule, microscopic

relinquish [rɪˈlɪŋkwɪʃ]

v. voluntarily cease to keep or claim；give up 交出，放弃

例 Ministers of any government have no intention of **relinquishing** control over local government spending.

【同义词】renounce，give up/away，hand over

meddle [ˈmedl]

 v. interfere or mess with 干涉

例 Already some people are asking whether scientists have any right to **meddle** in such matters.

【同义词】interfere in/with，butt in/into

optimize [ˈɒptɪmaɪz]

 v. make the best or most effective use of 使最优

例 Doctors are concentrating on understanding the disease better，and on **optimizing** the treatment.

sequence [ˈsiːkwəns]

n. a particular order in which related events, movements, or things follow each other 顺序

例 Sometimes they formed a **sequence**, sometimes they seemed to have no apparent connection.

单词助记【同义词】succession, order, course, series

sooty [ˈsʊtɪ]

adj. covered with or colored like soot 煤烟熏黑的，乌黑的

例 Their uniforms are torn and **sooty**.

abhorrent [əbˈhɒrənt]

adj. inspiring hate and loathing 令人讨厌的

例 There are many people who still find the act of abortion **abhorrent**.

单词助记【同义词】detestable, hateful, loathsome

assemble [əˈsembl]

v. to put together 装配，组合

例 She had been trying to **assemble** the bomb when it went off in her arms.

swivel [ˈswɪvəl]

n. a coupling between two parts enabling one to revolve without turning the other 旋转

例 He tried the aerial at every angle its **swivel** allowed.

单词助记【同义词】turn, rotate, revolve

ruse [ruːz]

n. an action intended to deceive someone; a trick 诡计，计策

例 It is now clear that this was a **ruse** to divide them.

单词助记【同义词】ploy, stratagem, tactic, scheme

necessitous [nɪˈsesɪtəs]

adj. (of a person) lacking the basic necessities; needy 贫苦的，贫穷的

例 The bishop planned to visit **necessitous** areas of the city.

单词助记【同义词】needy, poor, short of money, disadvantaged

apparel [əˈpærəl]

n. clothing 衣服，服装

例 Women's **apparel** is offered in petite, regular, and tall models.

episode [ˈepɪsəʊd]

n. an event or group of events occurring as part of a larger sequence 插曲，片段

例 This **episode** is bound to be a deep embarrassment for Washington.

epilogue [ˈepɪlɒg]

n. the end of a book or play that serves as a conclusion 结语，收场白

例 The narrative is structured in nine sections, and framed by a prologue and **epilogue**.

encroach [ɪnˈkrəʊtʃ]

❶ *v.* to enter by gradual steps or by stealth into the possessions or rights of another 侵犯；侵占

例 If you are in love，anyone **encroaching** on your territory will prompt insecurity.

单词助记【同义词】intrude on，trespass on，impinge on

❷ *v.* to advance beyond the usual or proper limits 蚕食；侵蚀

例 The movie industry had chosen to ignore the **encroaching** competition of television.

voyage [ˈvɒɪɪdʒ]

n. a long journey by sea or in space 航行，航海，航天

例 He aims to follow Columbus's **voyage** to the West Indies.

单词助记【同义词】journey，trip，expedition

analysis [əˈnæləsɪs]

n. detailed examination 分析；诊断

例 We did an **analysis** of the way that government money has been spent in the past.

hem [hem]

n. the edge of a piece of cloth or clothing that has been turned under and sewn 褶边，边沿

例 She quickly grabbed the **hem** of her dress to protect her modesty.

anonym [ˈænənɪm]

n. a fake name 无名氏，匿名者

例 It is a conversation between an ancient and a modern person，a monk and a contemporary artist，a believer and an atheist，an **anonym** and a signer.

单词助记【同义词】pseudonym

debase [dɪˈbeɪs]

v. reduce something in quality or value 降低（质量、地位、价值等）

例 The man have **debased** the meaning of the word "love".

单词助记【同义词】depreciate

ditty [ˈdɪtɪ]

n. a short，simple song 小曲，歌谣

例 One senior fireman was singing an old music-hall **ditty** over and over again as he worked at the pump.

incendiary [ɪnˈsendɪərɪ]

❶ *n.* a person who commits arson 纵火犯

例 Investigators questioned everyone on the plane to identify the **incendiary**.

❷ *n.* a person who excites factions，quarrels，or sedition 煽动者

例 The article written by the **incendiaries** has in some degree instigated the racial rioting

countenance [ˈkaʊntɪnəns]

❶ *n.* a person's face or facial expression 面容

例 Before receiving him，Henry had so possessed himself that no one could guess from his **countenance** with what sentiments he remembered the young king.

单词助记【同义词】face，features，physiognomy，profile

❷ *n.* support 容许，接受

例 She was giving her specific **countenance** to the occasion.

cluster [ˈklʌstə(r)]

n. group of similar things（果实、花等的）串，簇

例 The flowers grow in little white **clusters** and are just opening.

List 102

covertly [ˈkʌvətlɪ]

adj. without being openly acknowledged 神秘地

例 They have been supplying **covert** military aid to the rebels.

collateral [kəˈlætərəl]

adj. additional but subordinate；secondary 间接相关的；次要的

例 Brothers，cousins，uncles，and nephews are **collateral** kinsmen.

spat [spæt]

❶ *n.* a petty quarrel 口角，小争吵

例 Last month there was a rare diplomatic **spat** between southeast Asian nations over plans to exploit the Mekong for energy.

❷ *n.* a short cloth gaiter covering the instep and ankle 鞋套

例 a pair of **spats**

scull [skʌl]

n. each of a pair of small oars used by a single rower 桨

例 One day when the river burst its banks he ignored the school's evacuation plan，borrowed a **scull** and rowed away across the flooded fields.

progeny [ˈprɒdʒənɪ]

n. the descendant(s) of a person，animal，or plant 子孙，后代

例 In peacetime，the dead king's **progeny** succeed him — male and female without discrimination.

单词勋记【同义词】offspring，young，babies

smother [ˈsmʌðə(r)]

v. kill（someone）by covering their nose and mouth so that they suffocate 使窒息，透不过气

例 A father was secretly filmed as he tried to **smother** his six-week-old son in hospital.

单词勋记【同义词】suffocate，asphyxiate

statue [ˈstætjuː]

n. a carved or cast figure of a person or animal，especially one that is life-size or larger 雕像，塑像

例 The only question that is how many will be converted into a golden **statue** at the ceremony next month.

单词勋记【同义词】sculpture，figure，effigy

asphyxiate [æsˈfɪksɪeɪt]

v. to kill someone by depriving them of air 使窒息

例 Three people were **asphyxiated** in the crush for last week's train.

单词勋记【同义词】choke（to death），suffocate，smother，stifle

interloper [ˈɪntələʊpə(r)]

    n. a person who becomes involved in a place or situation where they are not wanted or are considered to not belong 干涉他人事务者

    例 She had no wish to share her father with any outsider and regarded us as **interlopers**.

    单词助记【同义词】intruder，encroacher，trespasser，invader

approving [əˈpruːvɪŋ]

    adj. showing or feeling approval of someone or something 认可的，满意的

    例 His mother leaned forward and gave him an **approving** look.

immodest [ɪˈmɒdɪst]

    adj. lacking humility or decency 不谦虚的，自负的

    例 He could become ungraciously **immodest** about his own capacities.

    单词助记【同义词】indecorous，improper，indecent

piracy [ˈpaɪərəsɪ]

    ❶ *n.* the practice of attacking and robbing ships at sea 海上掠夺

    例 The price of Somali **piracy** is rising fast.

    ❷ *n.* the unauthorized use of another's production，invention，or conception especially in infringement of a copyright 盗版

    例 Internet providers will issue warnings to users accused of online **piracy**.

augment [ɔːɡˈment]

    v. to make something greater by adding to it 扩大，增强

    例 While searching for a way to **augment** the family income，she began making dolls.

    单词助记【同义词】increase，add to，supplement

unduplicated [ʌnˈdjʊpləˌketɪd]

    adj. not capable of being duplicated 无法复制的

    例 These collections in major part are **unduplicated** anywhere else and totally irreplaceable.

remiss [rɪˈmɪs]

    adj. lacking care or attention to duty；negligent 玩忽职守的，马虎的

    例 She had been so **remiss**，so timid in her guilt，but now she would make up for it.

omen [ˈəʊmən]

    n. an event regarded as a portent of good or evil 预兆

    例 Her appearance at this moment is an **omen** of disaster.

    单词助记【同义词】portent，sign，signal，token

placidity [pləˈsɪdətɪ]

    n. calm，little emotion 平静

    例 They are nice **placid** animals and very good mothers.

exaggeration [ɪɡˌzædʒəˈreɪʃn]

    n. a statement that represents something as better or worse than it really is 夸张，夸大

    例 Francie's is small，but mirrors cunningly **exaggerate** the space she has.

dire [ˈdaɪə(r)]

    adj. extremely serious or urgent 可怕的，恐怖的

例 A government split would have **dire** consequences for domestic peace.
单词助记【同义词】urgent，desperate，pressing

bother [ˈbɒðə(r)]

v. take the trouble to do something 烦扰，打扰

例 Lots of people don't **bother** to go through a marriage ceremony these days.

单词助记【同义词】disturb，trouble，inconvenience

authentic [ɔːˈθentɪk]

adj. genuine 真实的

例 They crave genuine relationships and **authentic** friendships.

单词助记 【同义词】genuine，real，bona fide，true，veritable

antiquated [ˈæntɪkweɪtɪd]

adj. old-fashioned，outdated 陈旧的，古老的

例 Many factories are so **antiquated** they are not worth saving.

单词助记 【同义词】outdated，out of date，outmoded

alias [ˈeɪlɪæs]

n. used to indicate that a named person is more well known under 别名，化名

例 He adopted three **aliases** and was given passports and driving licenses in his new identities.

单词助记 【同义词】another name

offspring [ˈɒfˈsprɪŋ]

n. a person's child or children 子孙，后代

例 The safari staff hope that the happy couple will produce an **offspring**.

单词助记 【同义词】children，sons and daughters，progeny

presage [ˈpresɪdʒ]

v. a sign or warning that something bad will happen 预言

例 In medicine it is used to describe the symptoms which **presage** the onset of an epileptic fit.

单词助记 【同义词】portend，augur，foreshadow

dissociate [dɪˈsəʊʃɪeɪt]

v. disconnect or separate 分开，断绝（关系）

例 It is getting harder for the president to **dissociate** himself from the scandal.

单词助记 【同义词】separate，detach，disconnect，sever

stifle [ˈstaɪfl]

v. make (someone) unable to breathe properly；suffocate 使窒息

例 Critics have accused the U.S. of trying to **stifle** debate.

单词助记 【同义词】suffocate，choke，asphyxiate

superpose [ˌsupəˈpoz]

v. place (something) on or above something else 放在上面，重叠

例 A triangle **superposed** on an inverted triangle forms a six-pointed star.

swipe [swaɪp]

❶ *v.* hit or try to hit with a swinging blow 重击，挥击

例 She **swiped** at Rusty as though he was a fly.

单词助记 【同义词】stroke，strike，hit

❷ *v.* steal 扒窃

例 They **swiped** some candy from the store.

单词助记 【同义词】pilfer，purloin，snatch

enliven [ɪnˈlaɪvən]

v. to make something more interesting 使活泼或愉快

例 Even the most boring meeting was **enlivened** by Dan's presence.

whim [wɪm]

n. a sudden desire or change of mind 突发奇想，异想天开

例 Lately，the president has been sacking and picking new ministers at **whim**.

单词助记 【同义词】impulse，urge，notion

contemplation [ˌkɒntemˈpleɪʃən]

n. an act of considering with attention 沉思

例 Good human lives have been devoted to religious **contemplation**，scholarship or justice.

单词助记 【同义词】thought，reflection，meditation，consideration

palliate [ˈpælɪeɪt]

v. make a disease or its symptoms less severe or unpleasant with out getting rid of the cause 减轻，缓和

例 Don't try to **palliate** your constant lying by claiming that everybody lies

单词助记 【同义词】alleviate，ease，relieve

conciliatory [kənˈsɪlɪeɪtərɪ]

adj. intended to placate or pacify；make less severe 安抚的；调和的

例 The President's speech was hailed as a **conciliatory** gesture toward business.

单词助记 【同义词】propitiatory，placatory，appeasing，pacifying

jaunt [dʒɔːnt]

n. a short excursion or journey for pleasure 短途旅行

例 The dolphin had made this little **jaunt** merely for the fun of it.

单词助记 【同义词】trip，pleasure trip，outing

pit [pɪt]

n. a large hole in the ground 坑，矿坑

例 In many more former **pit** towns，the funeral was simply ignored by locals.

pilferage [ˈpɪlfrɪdʒ]

n. petty theft 偷窃（小东西）

例 It is even more distressed to discover that the **pilferage** had been going on for some time.

combative [ˈkɒmbətɪv]

adj. ready or eager to fight；pugnacious 好斗的，好争论的

例 He conducted the meeting in his usual **combative** style，refusing to admit any mistakes.

单词助记 【同义词】pugnacious，aggressive，antagonistic，quarrelsome

herculean [ˌhɜːkjʊˈliːən]

adj. requiring great strength or effort 力大无比的

例 His shoulders were **Herculean** with long arms that terminated in huge hands with delicately strong fingers.

单词助记【同义词】arduous，grueling，laborious，back-breaking，onerous

widget [ˈwɪdʒɪt]

    n. a small device or mechanical device 小器具，装饰品

    例 The secret is a little **widget** in the can.

List 104

bigot [ˈbɪgət]

n. a person who is intolerant towards those holding other beliefs 抱偏见的人，心胸狭窄的人

例 In terms of voter turnout, it appears that the apathy of the nation's youth was as big a problem as old **bigots**.

parity [ˈpærɪtɪ]

n. state or condition of being equal 同等，对等

例 Women have yet to achieve wage or occupational **parity** in many fields.

单词助记【同义词】equality, equivalence, uniformity

retrospect [ˈretrəspekt]

n. a survey or review of a past course of events or period of time 回顾，回想

例 Her fight with the unions was not as predictable as it seemed in **retrospect**.

suffocate [ˈsʌfəkeɪt]

v. die or cause to die from lack of air or inability to breathe 使窒息，呼吸困难

例 The atmosphere of the room **suffocated** her.

单词助记【同义词】smother, asphyxiate, stifle

demote [ˌdiːˈməʊt]

v. to give someone a lower rank 使降级，使降职

例 If they prove ineffective they should be **demoted** or asked to retire.

单词助记【同义词】downgrade, relegate, declass

delusion [dɪˈluːʒən]

n. an idiosyncratic belief or impression that is firmly maintained despite being contradicted by what is generally accepted as reality or rational argument 迷惑，错觉

例 I was under the **delusion** that he intended to marry me.

quiescence [kwaɪˈesns]

adj. state or period of inactivity or dormancy 静态

例 She could feel their power, even as they lay there **quiescent**.

accumulate [əˈkjuːmjʊleɪt]

v. gather together or gather an increasingly large amount of 堆积，积累

例 Lead can **accumulate** in the body until toxic levels are reached.

单词助记【同义词】gather, collect, assemble

polite [pəˈlaɪt]

adj. having or showing behavior that is respectful and considerate of other people 有礼貌的

例 Everyone around him was trying to be **polite**, but you could tell they were all bored.

单词助记【同义词】well mannered, civil, courteous, mannerly

deception [dɪˈsepʃən]

n. the action of deceiving someone 欺骗，诡计

例 He admitted conspiring to obtain property by **deception**.

单词助记【同义词】trick，deceit，sham，fraud

score [skɔː(r)]

❶ *n*. the number of points, goals, runs, etc. 分数

例 They beat the Giants by a **score** of 7 to 3.

❷ *n*. a group or set of twenty or about twenty 二十

❸ *n*. a written representation of a musical composition showing all the vocal and instrumental parts arranged one below the other 乐谱

例 The dance is accompanied by an original **score** by Henry Torgue.

glorification [ˌɡlɔːrɪfɪˈkeɪʃən]

n. describing or representing something as admirable 荣耀，赞颂

例 Gradually it developed a distrust of wealth and a **glorification** of poverty.

attire [əˈtaɪə(r)]

n. clothes, usually formal 服装，衣着

例 Working women there are famous for their conservative office **attire**.

gadget [ˈɡædʒɪt]

n. a small mechanical or electronic device or tool 小机械，小器具

例 What kitchen **gadget** would you recommend?

successor [səkˈsesə(r)]

n. a person or thing that succeeds another 继任者，继承人

例 He set out several principles that he hopes will guide his **successors**.

单词助记【同义词】heir，inheritor

placatory [pləˈkeɪtərɪ]

adj. intended to make someone less angry or hostile 安抚的，抚慰的

例 When next he spoke he was more **placatory**.

capsize [ˈkæpsaɪz]

n. overturn in the water 弄翻，倾覆

例 The sea got very rough and the boat **capsized**.

单词助记【同义词】overturn，turn over，turn upside down

fleck [flek]

n. a very small patch of color or light 斑点，小点

例 He went to the men's room to wash **flecks** of blood from his shirt.

单词助记【同义词】spot，mark，dot，speck

speck [spek]

n. a tiny spot 斑点，污点

例 Billy leaned forward and brushed a **speck** of dust off his shoes.

单词助记【同义词】dot，pinprick，spot，fleck

poverty [ˈpɒvətɪ]

n. the state of being extremely poor 贫困，贫穷

例 According to World Bank figures, 41 per cent of Brazilians live in absolute **poverty**.

List 105

ignominious [ˌɪɡnəʊˈmɪnɪəs]

adj. deserving or causing public disgrace or shame 卑鄙的，可耻的

例 Many thought that he was doomed to **ignominious** failure.

单词助记【同义词】humiliating，undignified，embarrassing，mortifying

cryptonym [ˈkrɪptənɪm]

n. a secret name 假名

例 Although he did not identify the officer，whose **cryptonym** is on the list，intelligence officials confirm that he was talking about a legendary spy.

pseudonym [ˈsjuːdənɪm]

n. a fake pen name 假名，化名

例 Both plays were published under the **pseudonym** of Philip Dayre.

单词助记【同义词】anonym

grant [ɡrɑːnt]

❶ *v*. agree to give or allow something requested 授予

例 It was a Labour government which **granted** independence to India and Pakistan.

单词助记【同义词】give，award，bestow on

❷ *v*. to be willing to concede 承认

例 The magistrates **granted** that the charity was justified in bringing the action.

soothe [suːð]

v. gently calm (a person or their feelings) 安慰，抚慰

例 He would take her in his arms and **soothe** her.

单词助记【同义词】calm (down)，pacify，comfort

security [sɪˈkjʊərɪtɪ]

❶ *n*. the state of being free from danger or threat 安全

例 They are now under a great deal of pressure to tighten their airport **security**.

单词助记【同义词】safety，freedom from danger，protection

❷ *n*. a certificate attesting credit，the ownership of stocks or bonds，or the right to ownership connected with tradable derivatives 有价证券

例 National banks can package their own mortgages and underwrite them as **securities**.

indigence [ˈɪndɪdʒəns]

n. the state of extreme poverty 贫乏

例 There are various state and federal programs to help relieve **indigence**.

redundancy [rɪˈdʌndənsɪ]

n. the state of being not or no longer needed or useful 过多，过剩

例 The ministry has said it hopes to avoid compulsory **redundancies**.

stake [steɪk]

n. a strong wooden or metal post with a point at one end，driven into the ground to support a tree，form part of a fence，act as a boundary mark，etc 桩，柱

例 A **stake** is pushed into the ground to support a young tree.

intrigue [ˈɪntriːg]

　　v. to spark curiosity or interest 激起……的好奇心

例 The moon moves into your personality chart to give you a special something that **intrigues** people.

单词助记【同义词】interest，be of interest to，fascinate

gown [gaʊn]

　　n. a long dress 长袍，女礼服

例 She and two friends once paraded in wedding **gowns** daubed with red paint to highlight domestic violence.

insinuation [ɪnˌsɪnjʊˈeɪʃən]

　　n. an unpleasant hint or suggestion of something bad 暗示，含蓄的批评

例 She cursed him as much for losing his temper in her house as for his **insinuation**.

单词助记【同义词】implication，inference，suggestion

sin [sɪn]

　　n. an immoral act considered to be a transgression against divine law 罪孽

例 The Vatican's teaching on abortion is clear：it is a **sin**.

单词助记【同义词】immoral act，wrong，wrongdoing

defiant [dɪˈfaɪənt]

　　adj. showing open resistance 公然违抗的，藐视的

例 Despite the risk of suspension，he remained **defiant**.

单词助记【同义词】intransigent，resistant，obstinate

resuscitation [rɪˌsʌsɪˈteɪʃən]

　　n. the action or process of reviving someone from unconsciousness or apparent death 复活，复苏

例 A policeman and then a paramedic tried to **resuscitate** her.

frock [frɒk]

❶ *n*. a woman's dress 连衣裙

例 Can there be anything more ageing than a clumsily cut shift dress and boxy **frock** coat?

❷ *n*. a coarse outer garment with large sleeves，worn by monks 僧袍

例 a monk **frock**

asperse [əˈspɜːs]

　　v. attack or criticize the reputation or integrity of 损害（名誉），中伤

例 How dare you **asperse** the character of our dedicated pastor！

annotation [ˌænəʊˈteɪʃən]

　　n. a note of explanation or comment added to a text or diagram 注解，注释

例 He supplied **annotations** to nearly 15,000 musical works.

单词助记【同义词】note，notation，comment

sect [sekt]

　　n. a group of people with somewhat different religious beliefs 宗派，教派

例 Would you rather belong to a **sect** or a church?

单词助记【同义词】cult，religious group，denomination

amorous [ˈæmərəs]

　　　adj. having to do or relating with love 爱的

　　例 In fact，it is a female letting a male know on no uncertain terms she is not interested in his **amorous** advances.

　单词助记【同义词】romantic，lustful，sexual，erotic

impoverishment [ɪmˈpɒvərɪʃmənt]

n. the process of becoming poor 穷困

例 National isolation can only cause economic and cultural **impoverishment**.

clan [klæn]

❶ *n*. a group of close-knit & interrelated families 宗族，氏族

例 Any advice the son gets from his father needs to be understood in light of the father's desire to remain chief of the **clan**.

单词助记【同义词】group of families，sept

❷ *n*. a group united by a common interest or common characteristics 团体

例 The dispute almost triggered a clash between rival mafia **clans**, it is alleged.

mighty [ˈmaɪtɪ]

adj. possessing great power and strength 强有力的，强大的

例 They think themselves too high and **mighty** to listen to common sense.

单词助记【同义词】powerful，forceful，violent

distress [dɪˈstres]

n. extreme anxiety，sorrow，or pain 痛苦，苦恼

例 Jealousy causes **distress** and painful emotions.

单词助记【同义词】anguish，suffering，pain

alleviate [əˈliːvɪeɪt]

v. to improve & make a problem better 减轻，缓解

例 He couldn't prevent her pain，only **alleviate** it.

单词助记【同义词】reduce，ease，relieve

revivify [rɪˈvɪvɪfaɪ]

v. give new life or vigor to 使再生，使振奋精神

例 Our perception of the world is tired and jaded：a poet seeks to **revivify** that perception by making us look at it in some new way.

单词助记【同义词】give new life or vigor to

annoy [əˈnɔɪ]

v. to irritate，make someone angry 打扰、干扰

例 It **annoyed** me that I didn't have time to do more reading.

单词助记【同义词】irritate，vex，make angry/cross

ecumenical [ˌiːkjuːˈmenɪkəl]

❶ *adj*. worldwide or general in extent，influence，or application 普遍的

例 Even if the students whose grades are **ecumenical** may become whiz kid by mending habit of study.

❷ *adj*. promoting or tending toward worldwide Christian unity or cooperation（基督教各教派）大公的

例 Church relations were tentative and the **ecumenical** movement was still in its early stages.

paltry ['pɔːltrɪ]

adj. small or meager 微小的，不重要的

例 Military figures say these sums are **paltry**.

单词助记【同义词】small，meager，trifling，insignificant

ease [iːz]

v. to mitigate，lighten，or lessen 减轻，舒缓

例 I gave him some brandy to **ease** the pain.

gangly ['gæŋlɪ]

adj. awkwardly tall and spindly；lank and loosely built 瘦高且难看的

例 He was very tall and **gangly** and looked different.

单词助记【同义词】lanky，rangy，tall，thin，skinny

meditation [ˌmedɪ'teɪʃən]

n. a written or spoked discourse expressing considered thoughts on a subject 沉思，冥想

例 Many busy executives have begun to practice yoga and **meditation**.

单词助记【同义词】contemplation，thought，thinking

encumber [ɪn'kʌmbə(r)]

v. restrict or burden 妨碍，拖累

例 Lead weights and air cylinders **encumbered** the divers as they walked to the shore.

单词助记【同义词】hamper，hinder，obstruct，impede

solemn ['sɒləm]

adj. formal and dignified 严肃的，庄重的

例 His **solemn** little face broke into smiles.

单词助记【同义词】dignified，ceremonious，ceremonial

stipulation [ˌstɪpjʊ'leɪʃən]

n. a condition or requirement that is specified or demanded as part of an agreement 条文

例 We agreed to the deal with the **stipulation** that she pay the expenses herself.

单词助记【同义词】condition，precondition，proviso，provision

equipoise ['ekwɪpɔɪz]

n. balance of forces or interests 平衡，均衡

例 When participating in any dangerous sport，one should maintain an **equipoise** between fearless boldness and commonsense caution

drab [dræb]

adj. lacking brightness or interest；drearily dull 土褐色的，乏味的

例 The rest of the day's activities often seemed **drab** or depressing.

单词助记【同义词】dull，boring，tedious，monotonous

parallel ['pærəlel]

adj. side by side and having the same distance continuously between them 与……平行

例 Parthing Lane's just above the High Street and **parallel** with it.

flattering ['flætərɪŋ]

adj. full of praise and confidence 谄媚的，讨好的

例 There were pleasant and **flattering** obituaries about him.

单词助记【同义词】complimentary，praising，favorable，commending

scheme [skiːm]

　　n. a large-scale systematic plan or arrangement 阴谋，诡计

　　例 Tourists can be vulnerable to scams and con **schemes** of all kinds.

单词助记【同义词】plan，project，plan of action，program，strategy

List 107

dispatch [dɪsˈpætʃ]

❶ *v.* send off to a location or for a purpose 派发，派遣

例 The Italian government was preparing to **dispatch** 4,000 soldiers to search the island.

单词助记【同义词】dispose

❷ *v.* deal with (a task, problem, or opponent) quickly and efficiently 快速完成，迅速解决

例 They **dispatched** the opposition.

单词助记【同义词】deal with, finish, conclude, settle

homage [ˈhɒmɪdʒ]

n. special honor or respect shown publicly 尊敬

例 The ritual gave the dead monarch's subjects a last chance to render **homage**, or to see for themselves that he was truly dead.

equidistant [ˌiːkwɪˈdɪstənt]

adj. at equal distances 等距的

例 Points on a circle are **equidistant** from its center.

acoustic [əˈkuːstɪk]

adj. relating to sound or hearing 声学的，听觉的

例 She loves listening to **acoustic** folk music.

lull [lʌl]

❶ *v.* to quiet down, let up, or subside 使放松

例 **Lulled** by almost uninterrupted economic growth, too many European firms assumed that this would last for ever.

❷ *v.* calm or send to sleep 使休息或睡觉

例 With the shutters half-closed and the calm airy height of the room to **lull** me, I soon fell into a doze.

jocund [ˈdʒɑkənd]

adj. cheerful and lighthearted 兴奋的，欢快的

例 Her **jocund** character made her the most popular girl in the county.

单词助记【同义词】jolly, merry, bright, glad

garnish [ˈgɑːnɪʃ]

v. decorate or embellish something (especially food) 装饰

例 She had finished the vegetables and was **garnishing** the roast.

单词助记【同义词】decorate, adorn, ornament, trim

unprecedented [ʌnˈpresɪdəntɪd]

adj. never done or known before 前所未有的，无前例的

例 She went to Japan, as part of a team investigating the effects of the **unprecedented** birth-rate on society.

单词助记【同义词】unheard of, unknown, new, novel

warrant ['wɒrənt]

n. a document issued by a legal or government official to carry out an action relating to the administration of justice 保证，担保

例 Police confirmed that they had issued a **warrant** for his arrest.

单词助记 【同义词】authorization，order，license

rescind [rɪ'sɪnd]

v. revoke，cancel，or repeal a law，order，or agreement 废除，取消

例 The Navy barred its personnel from his church，but he challenged the decree in federal court as a constitutional violation of freedom of religion. Eventually，the Navy **rescinded** its ban.

单词助记 【同义词】revoke，repeal，cancel

quintessence [kwɪn'tesns]

❶ *n.* the most perfect，typical example of a quality or class 精华

例 It's the **quintessence** of a free society not to be intimidated into silence.

❷ *n.* the most typical example or representative 典范

例 He was the **quintessence** of all that Eva most deeply loathed.

statute ['stætʃuːt]

n. a written law passed by a legislative body 法令，法规

例 The new **statute** covers the care for，bringing up and protection of children.

单词助记 【同义词】law，regulation，enactment，act，bill，decree

complaisant [kəm'pleɪzənt]

adj. willing to please others 殷勤的，讨好的

例 She was an old - fashioned wife，entirely **complaisant** to her husband's will.

单词助记 【同义词】willing，acquiescent，agreeable，amenable

elude [ɪ'luːd]

v. evade or escape from in a cunning way 规避，躲避

例 He **eluded** capture many times.

单词助记 【同义词】evade，avoid，get away from，dodge

veracious [və'reɪʃəs]

adj. speaking or representing the truth 诚实的

例 Her mother was a strictly **veracious** reporter.

单词助记 【同义词】unvarnished，unembellished

besmirch [bɪ'smɜːtʃ]

v. damage the reputation of someone or something 玷污，糟蹋（名誉）

例 People were trying to **besmirch** his reputation.

单词助记 【同义词】sully，tarnish，blacken

sleazy ['sliːzɪ]

adj. squalid and seedy 肮脏的，污秽的

例 Tom has lived in a **sleazy** hotel since he ran away from home.

单词助记 【同义词】squalid，seedy，seamy，sordid，insalubrious

petition [pə'tɪʃən]

n. a formal written request，usually one signed by many people 请愿，祈求

例 They collected 2 000 signatures on a **petition** demanding that women be allowed to join the club.

单词助记 【同义词】supplication，plea，prayer

hospitable [ˈhɒspɪtəbl]

      adj. welcoming；friendly 好客的，殷勤的

      例 The people of that country are very **hospitable**.

单词助记【同义词】welcoming，friendly，congenial，genial